TRAFFIC ACCIDENT INVESTIGATORS' HANDBOOK

TRAFFIC ACCIDENT INVESTIGATORS' HANDBOOK

By

R. W. RIVERS

Inspector • Traffic Branch
Royal Canadian Mounted Police
Province of British Columbia
Canada

With a Foreword by

G. W. Mortimer

Chairman
British Columbia Police Commission
British Columbia, Canada

CHARLES C THOMAS • PUBLISHER
Springfield • Illinois • U.S.A.

Published and Distributed Throughout the World by
CHARLES C THOMAS · PUBLISHER
Bannerstone House
301-327 East Lawrence Avenue, Springfield, Illinois, U.S.A.

© *1980, by* CHARLES C THOMAS · PUBLISHER
ISBN 0-398-03917-8
Library of Congress Catalog Card Number: 79-9765

*With THOMAS BOOKS careful attention is given to all details of
manufacturing and design. It is the Publisher's desire to present books that are
satisfactory as to their physical qualities and artistic possibilities and
appropriate for their particular use. THOMAS BOOKS will be true to those
laws of quality that assure a good name and good will.*

Library of Congress Cataloging in Publication Data

Rivers, Robert W
    Traffic accident investigators' handbook.

    Bibliography: p. 306
    Includes index.
    1. Traffic accident investigation—Handbooks, manuals,
etc. I. Title.
HV8079.55.R58   363.2'33   79-9765
ISBN 0-398-03917-8

Printed in the United States of America

C-1

to my wife Astrid

FOREWORD

THE ROLE OF THE POLICE in today's world continues to become more and more challenging and complex. The public demands that the police offer a wide range of services in a professional manner twenty-four hours a day, every day of the year.

Traffic law enforcement is one area where a professional police approach is demanded not only by the public, but by the courts as well. There are few aspects of law enforcement that require more expertise than traffic accident investigation. The complexities involved dictate the need for a professional approach to establishing whether a traffic violation has been committed and what evidence must be collected to support court action. At the same time, it takes a background of education, training, expertise and experience for the police to determine in a professional way whether the causes of an accident are related to highway engineering, vehicle design or driver qualifications and training.

During his twenty-five years' service in the Royal Canadian Mounted Police, Inspector Bob Rivers has been employed on general police duties, highway patrol, traffic accident investigation, training and development, and research and planning. During these years, he has responded to the demands for professionalism by attending the Northwestern University Traffic Institute where he completed their *On-Scene Traffic Accident Investigation* and *Technical Accident Investigation* courses, as well as their *Police Management* course. Drawing on his background of education, training and experience, he devoted four years of his own time to research and write this Handbook.

In this text, Bob Rivers has attempted, in concisely written and illustrative detail, to cover those situations that daily confront the traffic accident investigator. In an easily understandable manner, he has set out the many circumstances encountered in traffic accident investigation, together with the recommended procedure to complete a thorough investigation.

I know this *Traffic Accident Investigators' Handbook* will contribute considerably to the reader's understanding of the principles and procedures involved in traffic accident investigation and, consequently, to a higher degree of professionalism in the traffic law enforcement field.

G. W. MORTIMER

PREFACE

THIS *Traffic Accident Investigators' Handbook* has been prepared to meet the needs of various individuals involved in traffic accident investigation, particularly police officers, insurance adjusters or investigators, private investigators, and instructors and students involved in cadet or advanced traffic accident investigation training programs.

The text covers in written and illustrative detail those situations that confront an investigator: e.g., action to be taken upon receiving the accident call; what to look for at the scene; evidence that must be gathered; and how to interpret or evaluate evidence under actual field and follow-up investigations.

The training of a traffic accident investigator should not be considered complete with the termination of a course or the reading of a manual. All training and studying must be associated with practical experience which allows the student to put into practice those things he has learned.

This handbook is not intended to be the last word on the subject of traffic accident investigation. By itself, it will not make an expert of the reader. It does, however, bring to the reader's attention the major and essential ingredients of the total traffic accident investigation process. There are many other texts the reader should consult in order to increase his knowledge of the total traffic accident problem, particularly in the areas of physics, psychology and vehicle mechanics. It is hoped that this handbook will provide the beginning of a course of enquiry that, through application and further research and study, will enable the reader to acquire proficiency in traffic accident investigation.

One aim of this handbook is to introduce the metric measurement system into traffic accident investigation. It must be realized, however, that the older imperial or United States measurement system will be around for a considerable time yet. In light of this, this text has been prepared in such a way that mathematical references and examples are worked out in both systems of measurement.

Many published books and papers have been studied in the research and preparation of this handbook. A Bibliography lists several of these works.

The contents of this text are not intended to supercede established policies or legislation that are or may be in effect in any jurisdiction. The views

ix

expressed herein are not necessarily those of the Royal Canadian Mounted Police.

I wish to acknowledge my gratitude to the following persons: Jack Lisman, for reviewing areas of the manuscript involving physics, vehicle mechanics and dynamics; Steve D. Green, for reviewing the various formulae and calculations; J. D. A. LeComte, Traffic Accident Analyst, for reviewing the chapter on field measurements and scale diagrams; and J. R. E. D'Aoust, Traffic Accident Analyst, for reviewing the entire manuscript, all of whom offered many helpful and detailed suggestions regarding the preparation of this manuscript.

CONTENTS

TRAFFIC ACCIDENT INVESTIGATORS' HANDBOOK

Chapter 1

INTRODUCTION TO TRAFFIC ACCIDENT INVESTIGATION

TRAFFIC ACCIDENT

1.001   The U.S. National Safety Council defines an accident as "That occurrence in a sequence of events which usually produces unintended injury, death or property damage."[1] This definition applies to all types of accidents including *traffic accidents.*

1.002   For the purposes of this handbook, the term *traffic accident* is synonymous with the term *traffic collision.*

1.003   A *traffic unit* is a road vehicle or a pedestrian.[2]

1.004   An accident investigator's first duty upon arrival at an accident scene is to protect or ensure the protection of the lives and safety of victims and their property, as well as the protection of others at or travelling by the scene. Once he has attended to this task, he should obtain information that is immediately required and then restore the normal flow of traffic.

1.005   An investigation should reveal facts that will:

   a. Determine the cause or reason for the accident
   b. Determine whether or not there has been a violation of law, and if so, secure evidence that will support a prosecution or other police action
   c. Determine necessity for highway maintenance or improvement or for traffic engineering
   d. Support traffic safety and accident prevention programs
   e. Determine need for traffic accident investigation or training programs
   f. Support those involved in an accident in exercising legitimate claims under civil proceedings

SERIES OF EVENTS

1.006   Every traffic accident involves two sets of events:

   1. *Pre-scene series of events.* These are the events that lead up to the driver's point of possible perception of a hazard.
   2. *On-scene series of events.* These are the events that occur within the on-scene area including the point of possible perception.

There are separate series of events for each traffic unit involved in an accident. Each series must be investigated separately.

3

PRE—SCENE SERIES OF EVENTS

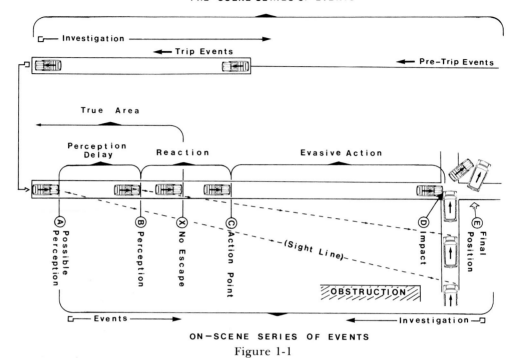

Figure 1-1

1.007 The pre-scene series of events may be divided into two areas, namely (1) pre-trip events, and (2) trip events.

  1. *Pre-trip events* are those events that occur *before* and include situations that exist before the trip is started. They may be considered as backgrounds of the driver and vehicle. Examples of pre-trip events or situations are:

> *Driver*
>   a. Driving experience
>   b. Driver training
>   c. Intelligence
>   d. Alertness
>   e. Reaction
>   f. Habits
>   g. General health condition, including age, illnesses and permanent or temporary injury or disability
>   h. Fatigue
>   i. A happening that caused emotional upset, stress, depression or preoccupation
>   j. Attendance at a party
>   k. Limited sleep or no sleep
>   l. Consumption of alcohol or drugs

Vehicle
  a. Defective headlights, steering, brakes, windshield wipers, tires, etc.
  b. Overloaded

2. *Trip events* are those events that occur after or situations that arise after the trip starts and lead up to the point of possible perception. Trip events include such events or situations as:

Driver
  a. Stopping for a meal or coffee
  b. Fatigue, illness or depression
  c. Consumption of alcohol or drugs
  d. Erratic or other unsafe driving (possibly observed by other motorists, pedestrians, businessmen or other witnesses)

Vehicle
  a. Tire blowout
  b. Brake, headlight or steering failure
  c. Other mechanical failure
  d. View obstructions, e.g., dirty windshield, defective windshield or load transfer
  e. Load falling off vehicle

1.008   On-scene series of events include the following points.

Point of Possible Perception

The point of possible perception is the place and time at which a *normal* person could perceive a hazard. It precedes actual perception and is the beginning of perception delay.[3]

Perception Delay

Perception delay is the time from the point of possible perception to actual perception.[4] Inattention or distractions may cause perception delay. In many instances, actual perception immediately follows the point of possible perception, and there is no actual perception delay. When there is a known perception delay, it may be considered to be 0.75 seconds for investigation purposes. The distance travelled during perception delay is *perception distance*.

The point of possible perception and the point of actual perception may be influenced by many driver and environmental factors, some of which are:

Driver
  a. Experience
  b. Intelligence
  c. Judgement
  d. Alertness

 e. Natural senses (age must be considered)
 f. Knowledge of area
 g. Distractions

Environmental
 a. Weather and light conditions
 b. Load on vehicle and protrusions
 c. Location of traffic-control devices
 d. View obstructions

Point of Perception

The point of perception or *actual perception* is the point where a situation such as a hazard is comprehended or perceived as a hazard.

Reaction

Reaction is a person's voluntary or involuntary response to a hazard or other situation that has been perceived.[5] *Reaction time* is the length of time from when a person perceives a given situation as being a hazard to when he reacts to his perception. When a person's reaction time is unknown, a reaction time of 0.75 seconds may be used for investigation purposes.

Reaction distance is the distance travelled during reaction time. To calculate reaction distance, use Formula 1-1:

<table>
<tr><td align="center">United States</td><td align="center">Metric</td></tr>
<tr><td align="center">$D = S \times 1.47 \times t$</td><td align="center">$D = S \times .278 \times t$</td></tr>
</table>

where D = distance
    S = speed
    t = time in seconds

The numbers 1.47 and .278 are constants in converting speeds in mph to ft/sec and km/h to m/s.

Example
 A vehicle was travelling at 50 mph (80 km/h). The driver, whose reaction time was .70 second, perceived a hazard and then reacted. The distance the vehicle travelled during the driver's reaction time was:

<table>
<tr><td>$D = 50 \times 1.47 \times .70$</td><td>$D = 80 \times .278 \times .70$</td></tr>
<tr><td>$D = 51.45$</td><td>$D = 15.568$</td></tr>
<tr><td>$D = 51$ ft</td><td>$D = 16$ m</td></tr>
</table>

Action Point

The action point follows reaction and is the place where a person puts into action his decision based on his perception of a hazard, such as braking or steering. The action point will be influenced by the driver's:

 a. Operating skills and habits
 b. Ability to control the vehicle

TABLE 1-1-A

REACTION DISTANCE IN FEET

Reaction Time in Seconds	Speed (mph)										
	5	6	7	8	9	10	11	12	13	14	15
0.2	1.470	1.764	2.058	2.352	2.646	2.940	3.234	3.528	3.822	4.116	4.410
0.3	2.205	2.646	3.087	3.528	3.969	4.410	4.851	5.292	5.733	6.174	6.615
0.4	2.940	3.528	4.116	4.704	5.292	5.880	6.468	7.056	7.644	8.232	8.820
0.5	3.675	4.410	5.145	5.880	6.615	7.350	8.085	8.820	9.555	10.290	11.025
0.6	4.410	5.292	6.174	7.056	7.938	8.820	9.702	10.584	11.466	12.348	13.230
0.7	5.145	6.174	7.203	8.232	9.261	10.290	11.319	12.348	13.377	14.406	15.435
0.8	5.880	7.056	8.232	9.408	10.584	11.760	12.936	14.112	15.288	16.464	17.640
0.9	6.615	7.938	9.261	10.584	11.907	13.230	14.553	15.876	17.199	18.522	19.845
1.0	7.350	8.820	10.290	11.760	13.230	14.700	16.170	17.640	19.110	20.580	22.050
1.1	8.085	9.702	11.319	12.936	14.553	16.170	17.787	19.404	21.021	22.638	24.255
1.2	8.820	10.584	12.348	14.112	15.876	17.640	19.404	21.168	22.932	24.696	26.460
1.3	9.555	11.466	13.377	15.288	17.199	19.110	21.021	22.932	24.843	26.754	28.665
1.4	10.290	12.348	14.406	16.464	18.522	20.580	22.638	24.696	26.754	28.812	30.870
1.5	11.025	13.230	15.435	17.640	19.845	22.050	24.255	26.460	28.665	30.870	33.075
1.6	11.760	14.112	16.464	18.816	21.168	23.520	25.872	28.224	30.576	32.928	35.280
1.7	12.495	14.994	17.493	19.992	22.491	24.990	27.489	29.988	32.487	34.986	37.485
1.8	13.230	15.876	18.522	21.168	23.814	26.460	29.106	31.752	34.398	37.044	39.690
1.9	13.965	16.758	19.551	22.344	25.137	27.930	30.723	33.516	36.309	39.102	41.895
2.0	14.700	17.640	20.580	23.520	26.460	29.400	32.340	35.280	38.220	41.160	44.100

TABLE 1-1-A (Continued)
REACTION DISTANCE IN FEET

Reaction Time in Seconds	Speed (mph)										
	16	17	18	19	20	21	22	23	24	25	26
0.2	4.704	4.998	5.292	5.586	5.880	6.174	6.468	6.762	7.056	7.350	7.644
0.3	7.056	7.497	7.938	8.379	8.820	9.261	9.702	10.143	10.584	11.025	11.466
0.4	9.408	9.996	10.584	11.172	11.760	12.348	12.936	13.524	14.112	14.700	15.288
0.5	11.760	12.495	13.230	13.965	14.700	15.435	16.170	16.905	17.640	18.375	19.110
0.6	14.112	14.994	15.876	16.758	17.640	18.522	19.404	20.286	21.168	22.050	22.932
0.7	16.464	17.493	18.522	19.551	20.580	21.609	22.638	23.667	24.696	25.725	26.754
0.8	18.816	19.992	21.168	22.344	23.520	24.696	25.872	27.048	28.224	29.400	30.576
0.9	21.168	22.491	23.814	25.137	26.460	27.783	29.106	30.429	31.752	33.075	34.398
1.0	23.520	24.990	26.460	27.930	29.400	30.870	32.340	33.810	35.280	36.750	38.220
1.1	25.872	27.489	29.106	30.723	32.340	33.957	35.574	37.191	38.808	40.425	42.042
1.2	28.224	29.988	31.752	33.516	35.280	37.044	38.808	40.572	42.336	44.100	45.864
1.3	30.576	32.487	34.398	36.309	38.220	40.131	42.042	43.953	45.864	47.775	49.686
1.4	32.928	34.986	37.044	39.102	41.160	43.218	45.276	47.334	49.392	51.450	53.508
1.5	35.280	37.485	39.690	41.895	44.100	46.305	48.510	50.715	52.920	55.125	57.330
1.6	37.632	39.984	42.336	44.688	47.040	49.392	51.744	54.096	56.448	58.800	61.152
1.7	39.984	42.483	44.982	47.481	49.980	52.479	54.978	57.477	59.976	62.475	64.974
1.8	42.336	44.982	47.628	50.274	52.920	55.566	58.212	60.858	63.504	66.150	68.796
1.9	44.688	47.481	50.274	53.067	55.860	58.653	61.446	64.239	67.032	69.825	72.618
2.0	47.040	49.980	52.920	55.860	58.800	61.740	64.680	67.620	70.560	73.500	76.440

Reaction Time in Seconds	Speed (mph)										
	27	28	29	30	31	32	33	34	35	36	37
0.2	7.938	8.232	8.526	8.820	9.114	9.408	9.702	9.996	10.290	10.584	10.878
0.3	11.907	12.348	12.789	13.230	13.671	14.112	14.553	14.994	15.435	15.876	16.317
0.4	15.876	16.464	17.052	17.640	18.228	18.816	19.404	19.992	20.580	21.168	21.756
0.5	19.845	20.580	21.315	22.050	22.785	23.520	24.255	24.990	25.725	26.460	27.195
0.6	23.814	24.696	25.578	26.460	27.342	28.224	29.106	29.988	30.870	31.752	32.634
0.7	27.783	28.812	29.841	30.870	31.899	32.928	33.957	34.986	36.015	37.044	38.073
0.8	31.752	32.928	34.104	35.280	36.456	37.632	38.808	39.984	41.160	42.336	43.512
0.9	35.721	37.044	38.367	39.690	41.013	42.336	43.659	44.982	46.305	47.628	48.951
1.0	39.690	41.160	42.630	44.100	45.570	47.040	48.510	49.980	51.450	52.920	54.390
1.1	43.659	45.276	46.893	48.510	50.127	51.744	53.361	54.978	56.595	58.212	59.829
1.2	47.628	49.392	51.156	52.920	54.684	56.448	58.212	59.976	61.740	63.504	65.268
1.3	51.597	53.508	55.419	57.330	59.241	61.152	63.063	64.974	66.885	68.796	70.707
1.4	55.566	57.624	59.682	61.740	63.798	65.856	67.914	69.972	72.030	74.088	76.146
1.5	59.535	61.740	63.945	66.150	68.355	70.560	72.765	74.970	77.175	79.380	81.585
1.6	63.504	65.856	68.208	70.560	72.912	75.264	77.616	79.968	82.320	84.672	87.024
1.7	67.473	69.972	72.471	74.970	77.469	79.968	82.467	84.966	87.465	89.964	92.463
1.8	71.442	74.088	76.734	79.380	82.026	84.672	87.318	89.964	92.610	95.256	97.902
1.9	75.411	78.204	80.997	83.790	86.583	89.376	92.169	94.962	97.755	100.548	103.341
2.0	79.380	82.320	85.260	88.200	91.140	94.080	97.020	99.960	102.900	105.840	108.780

TABLE 1-I-A (*Continued*)

REACTION DISTANCE IN FEET

Reaction Time in Seconds	Speed (mph)										
	38	39	40	41	42	43	44	45	46	47	48
0.2	11.172	11.466	11.760	12.054	12.348	12.642	12.936	13.230	13.524	13.818	14.112
0.3	16.758	17.199	17.640	18.081	18.522	18.963	19.404	19.845	20.286	20.727	21.168
0.4	22.344	22.932	23.520	24.108	24.696	25.284	25.872	26.460	27.048	27.636	28.224
0.5	27.930	28.665	29.400	30.135	30.870	31.605	32.340	33.075	33.810	34.545	35.280
0.6	33.516	34.398	35.280	36.162	37.044	37.926	38.808	39.690	40.572	41.454	42.336
0.7	39.102	40.131	41.160	42.189	43.218	44.247	45.276	46.305	47.334	48.363	49.392
0.8	44.688	45.864	47.040	48.216	49.392	50.568	51.744	52.920	54.096	55.272	56.448
0.9	50.274	51.597	52.920	54.243	55.566	56.889	58.212	59.535	60.858	62.181	63.504
1.0	55.860	57.330	58.800	60.270	61.740	63.210	64.680	66.150	67.620	69.090	70.560
1.1	61.446	63.063	64.680	66.297	67.914	69.531	71.148	72.765	74.382	75.999	77.616
1.2	67.032	68.796	70.560	72.324	74.088	75.852	77.616	79.380	81.144	82.908	84.672
1.3	72.618	74.529	76.440	78.351	80.262	82.173	84.084	85.995	87.906	89.817	91.728
1.4	78.204	80.262	82.320	84.378	86.436	88.494	90.552	92.610	94.668	96.726	98.784
1.5	83.790	85.995	88.200	90.405	92.610	94.815	97.020	99.225	101.430	103.635	105.840
1.6	89.376	91.728	94.080	96.432	98.784	101.136	103.488	105.840	108.192	110.544	112.896
1.7	94.962	97.461	99.960	102.459	104.958	107.457	109.956	112.455	114.954	117.453	119.952
1.8	100.548	103.194	105.840	108.486	111.132	113.778	116.424	119.070	121.716	124.362	127.008
1.9	106.134	108.927	111.720	114.513	117.306	120.099	122.892	125.684	128.478	131.271	134.064
2.0	111.720	114.660	117.600	120.540	123.480	126.420	129.360	132.300	135.240	138.180	141.120

Speed (mph)

Reaction Time in Seconds	49	50	51	52	53	54	55	56	57	58	59
0.2	14.406	14.700	14.994	15.288	15.582	15.876	16.170	16.464	16.758	17.052	17.346
0.3	21.609	22.050	22.491	22.932	23.373	23.814	24.255	24.696	25.137	25.578	26.019
0.4	28.812	29.400	29.988	30.576	31.164	31.752	32.340	32.928	33.516	34.104	34.692
0.5	36.015	36.750	37.485	38.220	38.955	39.690	40.425	41.160	41.895	42.630	43.365
0.6	43.218	44.100	44.982	45.864	46.746	47.628	48.510	49.392	50.274	51.156	52.038
0.7	50.421	51.450	52.479	53.508	54.537	55.566	56.595	57.624	58.653	59.682	60.711
0.8	57.624	58.800	59.976	61.152	62.328	63.504	64.680	65.856	67.032	68.208	69.384
0.9	64.827	66.150	67.473	68.796	70.119	71.442	72.765	74.088	75.411	76.734	78.057
1.0	72.030	73.500	74.970	76.440	77.910	79.380	80.850	82.320	83.790	85.260	86.730
1.1	79.233	80.850	82.467	84.084	85.701	87.318	88.935	90.552	92.169	93.786	95.403
1.2	86.436	88.200	89.964	91.728	93.492	95.256	97.020	98.784	100.548	102.312	104.076
1.3	93.639	95.550	97.461	99.372	101.283	103.194	105.105	107.016	108.927	110.838	112.749
1.4	100.842	102.900	104.958	107.016	109.074	111.132	113.190	115.248	117.306	119.364	121.422
1.5	108.045	110.250	112.455	114.660	116.865	119.070	121.275	123.480	125.685	127.890	130.095
1.6	115.248	117.600	119.952	122.304	124.656	127.008	129.360	131.712	134.064	136.416	138.768
1.7	122.451	124.950	127.449	129.948	132.447	134.946	137.445	139.944	142.443	144.942	147.441
1.8	129.654	132.300	134.946	137.592	140.238	142.884	145.530	148.176	150.822	153.468	156.114
1.9	136.857	139.650	142.443	145.236	148.029	150.822	153.615	156.408	159.201	161.994	164.787
2.0	144.060	147.000	149.940	152.880	155.820	158.760	161.700	164.640	167.580	170.520	173.460

TABLE 1-1-A (Continued)
REACTION DISTANCE IN FEET

Reaction Time in Seconds	Speed (mph) 60	61	62	63	64	65	66	67	68	69	70
0.2	17.640	17.934	18.228	18.522	18.816	19.110	19.404	19.698	19.992	20.286	20.580
0.3	26.460	26.901	27.342	27.783	28.224	28.665	29.106	29.547	29.988	30.429	30.870
0.4	35.280	35.868	36.456	37.044	37.632	38.220	38.808	39.396	39.984	40.572	41.160
0.5	44.100	44.835	45.570	46.305	47.040	47.775	48.510	49.245	49.980	50.715	51.450
0.6	52.920	53.802	54.684	55.566	56.448	57.330	58.212	59.094	59.976	60.858	61.740
0.7	61.740	62.769	63.798	64.827	65.856	66.885	67.914	68.943	69.972	71.001	72.030
0.8	70.560	71.736	72.912	74.088	75.264	76.440	77.616	78.792	79.968	81.144	82.320
0.9	79.380	80.703	82.026	83.349	84.672	85.995	87.318	88.641	89.964	91.287	92.610
1.0	88.200	89.670	91.140	92.610	94.080	95.550	97.020	98.490	99.960	101.430	102.900
1.1	97.020	98.637	100.254	101.871	103.488	105.105	106.722	108.339	109.956	111.573	113.190
1.2	105.840	107.604	109.368	111.132	112.896	114.660	116.424	118.188	119.952	121.716	123.480
1.3	114.660	116.571	118.482	120.393	122.304	124.215	126.126	128.037	129.948	131.859	133.770
1.4	123.480	125.538	127.596	129.654	131.712	133.770	135.828	137.886	139.944	142.002	144.060
1.5	132.300	134.505	136.710	138.915	141.120	143.325	145.530	147.735	149.940	152.145	154.350
1.6	141.120	143.472	145.824	148.176	150.528	152.880	155.232	157.584	159.936	162.288	164.640
1.7	149.940	152.439	154.938	157.437	159.936	162.435	164.934	167.433	169.932	172.431	174.930
1.8	158.760	161.406	164.052	166.698	169.344	171.990	174.636	177.282	179.928	182.574	185.220
1.9	167.580	170.373	173.166	175.959	178.752	181.545	184.338	187.131	189.924	192.717	195.510
2.0	176.400	179.340	182.280	185.220	188.160	191.100	194.040	196.980	199.920	202.860	205.800

Speed (mph)

Reaction Time in Seconds	71	72	73	74	75	76	77	78	79	80	81
0.2	20.874	21.168	21.462	21.756	22.050	22.344	22.638	22.932	23.226	23.520	23.814
0.3	31.311	31.752	32.193	32.634	33.075	33.516	33.957	34.398	34.839	35.280	35.721
0.4	41.748	42.336	42.924	43.512	44.100	44.688	45.276	45.864	46.452	47.040	47.628
0.5	52.185	52.920	53.655	54.390	55.125	55.860	56.595	57.330	58.065	58.800	59.535
0.6	62.622	63.504	64.386	65.268	66.150	67.032	67.914	68.796	69.678	70.560	71.442
0.7	73.059	74.088	75.117	76.146	77.175	78.204	79.233	80.262	81.291	82.320	83.349
0.8	83.496	84.672	85.848	87.024	88.200	89.376	90.552	91.728	92.904	94.080	95.256
0.9	93.933	95.256	96.579	97.902	99.225	100.548	101.871	103.194	104.517	105.840	107.163
1.0	104.370	105.840	107.310	108.780	110.250	111.720	113.190	114.660	116.130	117.600	119.070
1.1	114.807	116.424	118.041	119.658	121.275	122.892	124.509	126.126	127.743	129.360	130.977
1.2	125.244	127.008	128.772	130.536	132.300	134.064	135.828	137.592	139.356	141.120	142.884
1.3	135.681	137.592	139.503	141.414	143.325	145.236	147.147	149.058	150.969	152.880	154.791
1.4	146.118	148.176	150.234	152.292	154.350	156.408	158.466	160.524	162.582	164.640	166.698
1.5	156.555	158.760	160.965	163.170	165.375	167.580	169.785	171.990	174.195	176.400	178.605
1.6	166.992	169.344	171.696	174.048	176.400	178.752	181.104	183.456	185.808	188.160	190.512
1.7	177.429	179.928	182.427	184.926	187.425	189.924	192.423	194.922	197.421	199.920	202.419
1.8	187.866	190.512	193.158	195.804	198.450	201.096	203.742	206.388	209.034	211.680	214.326
1.9	198.303	201.096	203.889	206.682	209.475	212.268	215.061	217.854	220.647	223.440	226.233
2.0	208.740	211.680	214.620	217.560	220.500	223.440	226.380	229.320	232.260	235.200	238.140

TABLE 1-I-A (Continued)
REACTION DISTANCE IN FEET

Reaction Time in Seconds	Speed (mph)										
	82	83	84	85	86	87	88	89	90	91	92
0.2	24.108	24.402	24.696	24.990	25.284	25.578	25.872	26.166	26.460	26.754	27.048
0.3	36.162	36.603	37.044	37.485	37.926	38.367	38.808	39.249	39.690	40.131	40.572
0.4	48.216	48.804	49.392	49.980	50.568	51.156	51.744	52.332	52.920	53.508	54.096
0.5	60.270	61.005	61.740	62.475	63.210	63.945	64.680	65.415	66.150	66.885	67.620
0.6	72.324	73.206	74.088	74.970	75.852	76.734	77.616	78.498	79.380	80.262	81.144
0.7	84.378	85.407	86.436	87.465	88.494	89.523	90.552	91.581	92.610	93.639	94.668
0.8	96.432	97.608	98.784	99.960	101.136	102.312	103.488	104.664	105.840	107.016	108.192
0.9	108.486	109.809	111.132	112.455	113.778	115.101	116.424	117.747	119.070	120.393	121.716
1.0	120.540	122.010	123.480	124.950	126.420	127.890	129.360	130.830	132.300	133.770	135.240
1.1	132.594	134.211	135.828	137.445	139.062	140.679	142.296	143.913	145.530	147.147	148.764
1.2	144.648	146.412	148.176	149.940	151.704	153.468	155.232	156.996	158.760	160.524	162.288
1.3	156.702	158.613	160.524	162.435	164.346	166.257	168.168	170.079	171.990	173.901	175.812
1.4	168.756	170.814	172.872	174.930	176.988	179.046	181.104	183.162	185.220	187.278	189.336
1.5	180.810	183.015	185.220	187.425	189.630	191.835	194.040	196.245	198.450	200.655	202.860
1.6	192.864	195.216	197.568	199.920	202.272	204.624	206.976	209.328	211.680	214.032	216.384
1.7	204.918	207.417	209.916	212.415	214.914	217.413	219.912	222.411	224.910	227.409	229.908
1.8	216.972	219.618	222.264	224.910	227.556	230.202	232.848	235.494	238.140	240.786	243.432
1.9	229.026	231.819	234.612	237.405	240.198	242.991	245.784	248.577	251.370	254.163	256.956
2.0	241.080	244.020	246.960	249.900	252.840	255.780	258.720	261.660	264.600	267.540	270.480

Speed (mph)

Reaction Time in Seconds	93	94	95	96	97	98	99	100	101	102	103
0.2	27.342	27.636	27.930	28.224	28.518	28.812	29.106	29.400	29.694	29.988	30.282
0.3	41.013	41.454	41.895	42.336	42.777	43.218	43.659	44.100	44.541	44.982	45.423
0.4	54.684	55.272	55.860	56.448	57.036	57.624	58.212	58.800	59.388	59.976	60.564
0.5	68.355	69.090	69.825	70.560	71.295	72.030	72.765	73.500	74.235	74.970	75.705
0.6	82.026	82.908	83.790	84.672	85.554	86.436	87.318	88.200	89.082	89.964	90.846
0.7	95.697	96.726	97.755	98.784	99.813	100.842	101.871	102.900	103.929	104.958	105.987
0.8	109.368	110.544	111.720	112.896	114.072	115.248	116.424	117.600	118.776	119.952	121.128
0.9	123.039	124.362	125.685	127.008	128.331	129.654	130.977	132.300	133.623	134.946	136.269
1.0	136.710	138.180	139.650	141.120	142.590	144.060	145.530	147.000	148.470	149.940	151.410
1.1	150.381	151.998	153.615	155.232	156.849	158.466	160.083	161.700	163.317	164.934	166.551
1.2	164.052	165.816	167.580	169.344	171.108	172.872	174.636	176.400	178.164	179.928	181.692
1.3	177.723	179.634	181.545	183.456	185.367	187.278	189.189	191.100	193.011	194.922	196.833
1.4	191.394	193.452	195.510	197.568	199.626	201.684	203.742	205.800	207.858	209.916	211.974
1.5	205.065	207.270	209.475	211.680	213.885	216.090	218.295	220.500	222.705	224.910	227.115
1.6	218.736	221.088	223.440	225.792	228.144	230.496	232.848	235.200	237.552	239.904	242.256
1.7	232.407	234.906	237.405	239.904	242.403	244.902	247.401	249.900	252.399	254.898	257.397
1.8	246.078	248.724	251.370	254.016	256.662	259.308	261.954	264.600	267.246	269.892	272.538
1.9	259.749	262.542	265.335	268.128	270.921	273.714	276.507	279.300	282.093	284.886	287.679
2.0	273.420	276.360	279.300	282.240	285.180	288.120	291.060	294.000	296.940	299.880	302.820

TABLE 1-1-A (Continued)
REACTION DISTANCE IN FEET

Reaction Time in Seconds	Speed (mph)										
	104	105	106	107	108	109	110	111	112	113	114
0.2	30.576	30.870	31.164	31.458	31.752	32.046	32.340	32.634	32.928	33.222	33.516
0.3	45.864	46.305	46.746	47.187	47.628	48.069	48.510	48.951	49.392	49.833	50.274
0.4	61.152	61.740	62.328	62.916	63.504	64.092	64.680	65.268	65.856	66.444	67.032
0.5	76.440	77.175	77.910	78.645	79.380	80.115	80.850	81.585	82.320	83.055	83.790
0.6	91.728	92.610	93.492	94.374	95.256	96.138	97.020	97.902	98.784	99.666	100.548
0.7	107.016	108.045	109.074	110.103	111.132	112.161	113.190	114.219	115.248	116.277	117.306
0.8	122.304	123.480	124.656	125.832	127.008	128.184	129.360	130.536	131.712	132.888	134.064
0.9	137.592	138.915	140.238	141.561	142.884	144.207	145.530	146.853	148.176	149.499	150.822
1.0	152.880	154.350	155.820	157.290	158.760	160.230	161.700	163.170	164.640	166.110	167.580
1.1	168.168	169.785	171.402	173.019	174.636	176.253	177.870	179.487	181.104	182.721	184.338
1.2	183.456	185.220	186.984	188.748	190.512	192.276	194.040	195.804	197.568	199.332	201.096
1.3	198.744	200.655	202.566	204.477	206.388	208.299	210.210	212.121	214.032	215.943	217.854
1.4	214.032	216.090	218.148	220.206	222.264	224.322	226.380	228.438	230.496	232.554	234.612
1.5	229.320	231.525	233.730	235.935	238.140	240.345	242.550	244.755	246.960	249.165	251.370
1.6	244.608	246.960	249.312	251.664	254.016	256.368	258.720	261.072	263.424	265.776	268.128
1.7	259.896	262.395	264.894	267.393	269.892	272.391	274.890	277.389	279.888	282.387	284.886
1.8	275.184	277.830	280.476	283.122	285.768	288.414	291.060	293.706	296.352	298.998	301.644
1.9	290.472	293.265	296.058	298.851	301.644	304.437	307.230	310.023	312.816	315.609	318.402
2.0	305.760	308.700	311.640	314.580	317.520	320.460	323.400	326.340	329.280	332.220	335.160

Reaction Time in Seconds	Speed (mph)					
	115	116	117	118	119	120
0.2	33.810	34.104	34.398	34.692	34.986	35.280
0.3	50.715	51.156	51.597	52.038	52.479	52.920
0.4	67.620	68.208	68.796	69.384	69.972	70.560
0.5	84.525	85.260	85.995	86.730	87.465	88.200
0.6	101.430	102.312	103.194	104.076	104.958	105.840
0.7	118.335	119.364	120.393	121.422	122.451	123.480
0.8	135.240	136.416	137.592	138.768	139.944	141.120
0.9	152.145	153.468	154.791	156.114	157.437	158.760
1.0	169.050	170.520	171.990	173.460	174.930	176.400
1.1	185.955	187.572	189.189	190.806	192.423	194.040
1.2	202.860	204.624	206.388	208.152	209.916	211.680
1.3	219.765	221.676	223.587	225.498	227.409	229.320
1.4	236.670	238.728	240.786	242.844	244.902	246.960
1.5	253.575	255.780	257.985	260.190	262.395	264.600
1.6	270.480	272.832	275.184	277.536	279.888	282.240
1.7	287.385	289.884	292.383	294.882	297.381	299.880
1.8	304.290	306.936	309.582	312.228	314.874	317.520
1.9	321.195	323.988	326.781	329.574	332.367	335.160
2.0	338.100	341.040	343.980	346.920	349.860	352.800

Traffic Accident Investigators' Handbook

TABLE 1-I-B
REACTION DISTANCE IN METERS

Reaction Time in Seconds	Speed (km/h)									
	10	11	12	13	14	15	16	17	18	19
0.2	.556	.612	.667	.723	.778	.834	.890	.945	1.001	1.056
0.3	.834	.917	1.001	1.084	1.168	1.251	1.334	1.418	1.501	1.585
0.4	1.112	1.223	1.334	1.446	1.557	1.668	1.779	1.890	2.002	2.113
0.5	1.390	1.529	1.668	1.807	1.946	2.085	2.224	2.363	2.502	2.641
0.6	1.668	1.835	2.002	2.168	2.335	2.502	2.669	2.836	3.002	3.169
0.7	1.946	2.141	2.335	2.530	2.724	2.919	3.114	3.308	3.503	3.697
0.8	2.224	2.446	2.669	2.891	3.114	3.336	3.558	3.781	4.003	4.226
0.9	2.502	2.752	3.002	3.253	3.503	3.753	4.003	4.253	4.504	4.754
1.0	2.780	3.058	3.336	3.614	3.892	4.170	4.448	4.726	5.004	5.282
1.1	3.058	3.364	3.670	3.975	4.281	4.587	4.893	5.199	5.504	5.810
1.2	3.336	3.670	4.003	4.337	4.670	5.004	5.338	5.671	6.005	6.338
1.3	3.614	3.975	4.337	4.698	5.060	5.421	5.782	6.114	6.505	6.867
1.4	3.892	4.281	4.670	5.060	5.449	5.838	6.227	6.616	7.006	7.395
1.5	4.170	4.587	5.004	5.421	5.838	6.255	6.672	7.089	7.506	7.923
1.6	4.448	4.893	5.338	5.782	6.227	6.672	7.117	7.562	8.006	8.451
1.7	4.726	5.199	5.671	6.144	6.616	7.089	7.562	8.034	8.507	8.974
1.8	5.004	5.504	6.005	6.505	7.006	7.506	8.006	8.507	9.007	9.508
1.9	5.282	5.810	6.338	6.867	7.395	7.923	8.451	8.979	9.508	10.036
2.0	5.560	6.116	6.672	7.228	7.784	8.340	8.896	9.452	10.008	10.564

Reaction Time in Seconds	Speed (km/h)									
	20	21	22	23	24	25	26	27	28	29
0.2	1.112	1.168	1.223	1.279	1.334	1.390	1.446	1.501	1.557	1.612
0.3	1.668	1.751	1.835	1.918	2.002	2.085	2.168	2.252	2.335	2.419
0.4	2.224	2.335	2.446	2.558	2.669	2.780	2.891	3.002	3.114	3.225
0.5	2.780	2.919	3.058	3.197	3.336	3.475	3.614	3.753	3.892	4.031
0.6	3.336	3.503	3.670	3.836	4.003	4.170	4.337	4.504	4.670	4.837
0.7	3.892	4.087	4.281	4.476	4.670	4.865	5.060	5.254	5.449	5.643
0.8	4.448	4.670	4.893	5.115	5.338	5.560	5.782	6.005	6.227	6.450
0.9	5.004	5.254	5.504	5.755	6.005	6.255	6.505	6.755	7.006	7.256
1.0	5.560	5.838	6.116	6.394	6.672	6.950	7.228	7.506	7.784	8.062
1.1	6.116	6.422	6.728	7.033	7.339	7.645	7.951	8.257	8.562	8.868
1.2	6.672	7.006	7.339	7.673	8.006	8.340	8.674	9.007	9.341	9.674
1.3	7.228	7.589	7.951	8.312	8.674	9.035	9.396	9.758	10.119	10.481
1.4	7.784	8.173	8.562	8.952	9.341	9.730	10.119	10.508	10.898	11.287
1.5	8.340	8.757	9.174	9.591	10.008	10.425	10.824	11.259	11.676	12.093
1.6	8.896	9.341	9.786	10.230	10.675	11.120	11.565	12.010	12.454	12.899
1.7	9.452	9.925	10.397	10.870	11.342	11.815	12.288	12.760	13.233	13.705
1.8	10.008	10.508	11.009	11.509	12.010	12.510	13.010	13.511	14.011	14.512
1.9	10.564	11.092	11.620	12.149	12.677	13.205	13.733	14.261	14.790	15.318
2.0	11.120	11.676	12.232	12.788	13.344	13.900	14.456	15.012	15.568	16.124

TABLE 1-I-B *(Continued)*

REACTION DISTANCE IN METERS

Reaction Time in Seconds	Speed (km/h)									
	30	31	32	33	34	35	36	37	38	39
0.2	1.668	1.724	1.779	1.835	1.890	1.946	2.002	2.057	2.113	2.168
0.3	2.502	2.585	2.669	2.752	2.836	2.919	3.002	3.086	3.169	3.253
0.4	3.336	3.447	3.558	3.670	3.781	3.892	4.003	4.114	4.226	4.337
0.5	4.170	4.309	4.448	4.587	4.726	4.865	5.004	5.143	5.282	5.421
0.6	5.004	5.171	5.338	5.504	5.671	5.838	6.005	6.172	6.338	6.505
0.7	5.838	6.033	6.227	6.422	6.616	6.811	7.006	7.200	7.395	7.589
0.8	6.672	6.894	7.117	7.339	7.562	7.784	8.006	8.229	8.451	8.674
0.9	7.506	7.756	8.006	8.257	8.507	8.757	9.007	10.257	9.508	9.758
1.0	8.340	8.618	8.896	9.174	9.452	9.730	10.008	10.286	10.564	10.842
1.1	9.174	9.480	9.786	10.091	10.397	10.703	11.009	11.315	11.620	11.926
1.2	10.008	10.342	10.675	11.009	11.342	11.676	12.010	12.343	12.677	13.010
1.3	10.842	11.203	11.565	11.926	12.288	12.649	13.010	13.372	13.733	14.095
1.4	11.676	12.065	12.454	12.844	13.233	13.622	14.011	14.400	14.790	15.179
1.5	12.510	12.927	13.344	13.761	14.178	14.595	15.012	15.429	15.846	16.263
1.6	13.344	13.789	14.234	14.678	15.123	15.568	16.013	16.458	16.902	17.347
1.7	14.178	14.651	15.123	15.596	16.068	16.541	17.014	17.486	17.959	18.431
1.8	15.012	15.512	16.013	16.513	17.014	17.514	18.014	18.515	19.015	19.516
1.9	15.846	16.374	16.902	17.431	17.959	18.487	19.015	19.543	20.072	20.600
2.0	16.680	17.236	17.792	18.348	18.904	19.460	20.016	20.572	21.128	21.684

Reaction Time in Seconds	Speed (km/h)									
	40	41	42	43	44	45	46	47	48	49
0.2	2.224	2.280	2.335	2.391	2.446	2.502	2.558	2.613	2.669	2.724
0.3	3.336	3.419	3.503	3.586	3.670	3.753	3.836	3.920	4.003	4.087
0.4	4.448	4.559	4.670	4.782	4.893	5.004	5.115	5.226	5.338	5.449
0.5	5.560	5.699	5.838	5.977	6.116	6.255	6.394	6.533	6.672	6.811
0.6	6.672	6.839	7.006	7.172	7.339	7.506	7.673	7.840	8.006	8.173
0.7	7.784	7.974	8.173	8.368	8.562	8.757	8.952	9.146	9.341	9.535
0.8	8.896	9.118	9.341	9.563	9.786	10.008	10.230	10.453	10.675	10.898
0.9	10.008	10.258	10.508	10.759	11.009	11.259	11.509	11.759	12.010	12.260
1.0	11.120	11.398	11.676	11.954	12.232	12.510	12.788	13.066	13.344	13.622
1.1	12.232	12.538	12.844	13.149	13.455	13.761	14.067	14.373	14.678	14.984
1.2	13.344	13.678	14.011	14.345	14.678	15.120	15.346	15.679	16.013	16.346
1.3	14.456	14.817	15.789	15.540	15.902	16.263	16.624	16.986	17.347	17.709
1.4	15.568	15.957	16.346	16.736	17.125	17.514	17.903	18.292	18.682	19.071
1.5	16.680	17.097	17.514	17.931	18.348	18.765	19.182	19.599	20.016	20.433
1.6	17.792	18.237	18.682	19.126	19.571	20.016	20.461	20.906	21.350	21.795
1.7	18.904	19.377	19.849	20.322	20.794	21.267	21.740	22.212	22.685	23.157
1.8	20.016	20.516	21.017	21.517	22.018	22.518	23.018	23.519	24.019	24.520
1.9	21.128	21.656	22.184	22.713	23.241	23.769	24.297	24.825	25.354	25.882
2.0	22.240	22.796	23.352	23.908	24.464	25.020	25.576	26.132	26.688	27.244

Traffic Accident Investigators' Handbook

TABLE 1-I-B *(Continued)*
REACTION DISTANCE IN METERS

Reaction Time in Seconds	Speed (km/h)									
	50	51	52	53	54	55	56	57	58	59
0.2	2.780	2.836	2.891	2.947	3.002	3.058	3.114	3.169	3.225	3.280
0.3	4.170	4.253	4.337	4.420	4.504	4.587	4.670	4.754	4.837	4.921
0.4	5.560	5.671	5.782	5.894	6.005	6.116	6.227	6.338	6.450	6.561
0.5	6.950	7.089	7.228	7.367	7.506	7.645	7.784	7.923	8.062	8.201
0.6	8.340	8.507	8.674	8.840	9.007	9.174	9.341	9.508	9.674	9.841
0.7	9.730	9.925	10.119	10.314	10.508	10.703	10.898	11.092	11.287	11.481
0.8	11.120	11.342	11.565	11.787	12.010	12.232	12.454	12.677	12.899	13.122
0.9	12.510	12.760	13.010	13.261	13.511	13.761	14.011	14.261	14.512	14.762
1.0	13.900	14.178	14.456	14.734	15.012	15.290	15.568	15.846	16.124	16.402
1.1	15.290	15.596	15.902	16.207	16.513	16.819	17.125	17.431	17.736	18.042
1.2	16.680	17.014	17.347	17.681	18.014	18.348	18.682	19.015	19.349	19.682
1.3	18.070	18.431	18.793	19.154	19.516	19.877	20.238	20.600	20.961	21.323
1.4	19.460	19.849	20.238	20.628	21.017	21.406	21.795	22.184	22.574	22.963
1.5	20.850	21.267	21.684	22.101	22.518	22.935	23.352	23.769	24.186	24.603
1.6	22.240	22.685	23.130	23.574	24.019	24.464	24.909	25.354	25.798	26.243
1.7	23.630	24.103	24.575	25.048	25.520	25.993	26.466	26.938	27.411	27.883
1.8	25.020	25.520	26.021	26.521	27.022	27.522	28.022	28.523	29.023	29.524
1.9	26.410	26.938	27.466	27.995	28.523	29.051	29.579	30.107	30.636	31.164
2.0	27.800	28.356	28.912	29.468	30.024	30.580	31.136	31.692	32.248	32.804

Reaction Time in Seconds	Speed (km/h)									
	60	61	62	63	64	65	66	67	68	69
0.2	3.336	3.392	3.447	3.503	3.558	3.614	3.670	3.735	3.781	3.836
0.3	5.004	5.087	5.171	5.254	5.338	5.421	5.504	5.588	5.671	5.755
0.4	6.672	6.783	6.894	7.006	7.117	7.228	7.339	7.450	7.562	7.673
0.5	8.340	8.479	8.618	8.757	8.896	9.035	9.174	9.313	9.452	9.591
0.6	10.008	10.175	10.342	10.508	10.675	10.842	11.009	11.176	11.342	11.509
0.7	11.676	11.871	12.065	12.260	12.454	12.649	12.844	13.038	13.233	13.427
0.8	13.344	13.566	13.889	14.011	14.234	14.456	14.678	14.901	15.123	15.346
0.9	15.012	15.262	15.512	15.763	16.013	16.263	16.513	16.763	17.014	17.264
1.0	16.680	16.958	17.236	17.514	17.792	18.070	18.348	18.626	18.904	19.182
1.1	18.348	18.654	18.960	19.265	19.571	19.877	20.182	20.489	20.794	21.100
1.2	20.016	20.350	20.683	21.017	21.350	21.684	22.018	22.351	22.685	23.018
1.3	21.684	22.045	22.407	22.768	23.130	23.491	23.852	24.214	24.575	24.937
1.4	23.352	23.741	24.130	24.520	24.909	25.298	25.687	26.076	26.466	26.855
1.5	25.020	25.437	25.854	26.271	26.688	27.105	27.522	27.939	28.356	28.773
1.6	26.688	27.133	27.578	28.022	28.467	28.912	29.357	29.802	30.246	30.691
1.7	28.356	28.829	29.301	29.774	30.246	30.719	31.192	31.664	32.137	32.609
1.8	30.024	30.524	31.025	31.525	32.026	32.526	33.026	33.527	34.027	34.528
1.9	31.692	32.220	32.748	33.277	33.805	34.333	34.861	35.389	35.918	36.446
2.0	33.360	33.916	34.472	35.028	35.584	36.140	36.696	37.252	37.808	38.364

TABLE 1-I-B *(Continued)*
REACTION DISTANCE IN METERS

Reaction Time in Seconds	Speed (km/h)									
	70	71	72	73	74	75	76	77	78	79
0.2	3.892	3.948	4.003	4.059	4.114	4.170	4.226	4.281	4.337	4.392
0.3	5.838	5.921	6.005	6.088	6.172	6.255	6.338	6.422	6.505	6.589
0.4	7.784	7.895	8.006	8.118	8.229	8.340	8.451	8.562	8.674	8.785
0.5	9.730	9.869	10.008	10.147	10.286	10.425	10.564	10.703	10.842	10.981
0.6	11.676	11.843	12.010	12.176	12.343	12.510	12.677	12.844	13.010	13.177
0.7	13.622	13.817	14.011	14.206	14.400	14.595	14.790	14.984	15.179	15.373
0.8	15.568	15.790	16.013	16.235	16.458	16.680	16.902	17.125	17.347	17.570
0.9	17.514	17.764	18.014	18.265	18.515	18.765	19.015	19.265	19.516	19.766
1.0	19.460	19.738	20.016	20.294	20.572	20.850	21.128	21.406	21.684	21.962
1.1	21.406	21.712	22.018	22.323	22.629	22.935	23.241	23.547	23.852	24.158
1.2	23.352	23.686	24.019	24.353	24.686	25.020	25.354	25.687	26.021	26.354
1.3	25.298	25.659	26.021	26.382	26.744	27.105	27.466	27.828	28.189	28.551
1.4	27.244	27.633	28.022	28.412	28.801	29.190	29.579	29.968	30.358	30.747
1.5	29.190	29.607	30.024	30.441	30.858	31.275	31.692	32.109	32.526	32.943
1.6	31.136	31.581	32.026	32.470	32.915	33.360	33.805	34.250	34.694	35.139
1.7	33.082	33.555	34.027	34.500	34.972	35.445	35.918	36.390	36.863	37.335
1.8	35.028	35.528	36.029	36.529	37.030	37.530	38.030	38.531	39.031	39.532
1.9	36.947	37.502	38.030	38.559	39.087	39.615	40.143	40.671	41.200	41.728
2.0	38.920	39.476	40.032	40.588	41.144	41.700	42.256	42.812	43.368	43.924

Reaction Time in Seconds	Speed (km/h)									
	80	81	82	83	84	85	86	87	88	89
0.2	4.448	4.504	4.559	4.615	4.670	4.726	4.782	4.837	4.893	4.948
0.3	6.672	6.755	6.839	6.922	7.006	7.089	7.172	7.256	7.339	7.423
0.4	8.896	9.007	9.118	9.230	9.341	9.452	9.563	9.674	9.786	9.897
0.5	11.120	11.259	11.398	11.537	11.676	11.815	11.954	12.093	12.232	12.371
0.6	13.344	13.511	13.678	13.849	14.011	14.178	14.345	14.512	14.678	14.845
0.7	15.568	15.763	15.957	16.152	16.346	16.541	16.736	16.930	17.125	17.319
0.8	17.792	18.014	18.237	18.459	18.682	18.904	19.126	19.349	19.571	19.794
0.9	20.016	20.266	20.516	20.767	21.017	21.267	21.517	21.767	22.018	22.268
1.0	22.240	22.518	22.796	23.074	23.352	23.630	23.908	24.186	24.464	24.742
1.1	24.464	24.770	25.076	25.381	25.687	25.993	26.299	26.605	26.910	27.216
1.2	26.688	27.022	27.355	27.689	28.022	28.356	28.690	29.023	29.357	29.690
1.3	28.912	29.273	29.635	29.996	30.358	30.719	31.080	31.442	31.803	32.165
1.4	31.136	31.525	31.914	32.304	32.693	33.082	33.471	33.860	34.250	34.639
1.5	33.360	33.777	34.194	34.611	35.028	35.445	35.862	36.279	36.696	37.113
1.6	35.584	36.029	36.474	36.918	37.363	37.808	38.253	38.698	39.142	39.587
1.7	37.808	38.281	38.753	39.226	39.698	40.171	40.644	41.116	41.589	42.061
1.8	40.032	40.532	41.033	41.533	42.034	42.534	43.034	43.535	44.035	44.536
1.9	42.256	42.784	43.312	43.841	44.369	44.897	45.425	45.953	46.482	47.010
2.0	44.480	45.036	45.592	46.148	46.704	47.260	47.816	48.372	48.928	49.484

TABLE 1-I-B *(Continued)*
REACTION DISTANCE IN METERS

Reaction Time in Seconds	Speed (km/h)									
	90	91	92	93	94	95	96	97	98	99
0.2	5.004	5.060	5.115	5.171	5.226	5.282	5.338	5.393	5.449	5.504
0.3	7.506	7.589	7.673	7.756	7.840	7.923	8.006	8.090	8.173	8.257
0.4	10.008	10.119	10.230	10.342	10.453	10.564	10.675	10.786	10.898	11.009
0.5	12.510	12.649	12.788	12.927	13.066	13.205	13.344	13.483	13.622	13.761
0.6	15.012	15.179	15.346	15.512	15.679	15.846	16.013	16.180	16.346	16.513
0.7	17.514	17.709	17.903	18.098	18.292	18.487	18.682	18.876	19.071	19.265
0.8	20.016	20.238	20.461	20.683	20.906	21.128	21.350	21.573	21.795	22.018
0.9	22.518	22.768	23.018	23.269	23.519	23.769	24.019	24.269	24.520	24.770
1.0	25.020	25.298	25.576	25.854	26.132	26.410	26.688	26.966	27.244	27.522
1.1	27.522	27.828	28.134	28.439	28.745	29.051	29.357	29.663	29.968	30.274
1.2	30.024	30.358	30.691	31.025	31.358	31.692	32.026	32.359	32.693	33.026
1.3	32.526	32.887	33.249	33.610	33.972	34.333	34.694	35.056	35.417	35.779
1.4	35.028	35.417	35.806	36.196	36.585	36.974	37.363	37.752	38.142	38.531
1.5	37.530	37.947	38.364	38.781	39.198	39.615	40.032	40.449	40.866	41.283
1.6	40.032	40.477	40.922	41.366	41.811	42.256	42.701	43.146	43.590	44.035
1.7	42.534	43.007	43.479	43.952	44.424	44.897	45.370	45.842	46.315	46.787
1.8	45.036	45.536	46.037	46.537	47.038	47.538	48.038	48.539	49.039	49.540
1.9	47.538	48.066	48.594	49.123	49.651	50.179	50.707	51.235	51.764	52.292
2.0	50.040	50.596	51.152	51.708	52.264	52.820	53.376	53.932	54.488	55.044

Reaction Time in Seconds	Speed (km/h)									
	100	101	102	103	104	105	106	107	108	109
0.2	5.560	5.616	5.671	5.727	5.782	5.838	5.894	5.949	6.005	6.060
0.3	8.340	8.423	8.507	8.590	8.674	8.757	8.840	8.924	9.007	9.091
0.4	11.120	11.231	11.342	11.454	11.562	11.676	11.787	11.898	12.010	12.121
0.5	13.900	14.039	14.178	14.317	14.456	14.595	14.734	14.873	15.012	15.151
0.6	16.680	16.847	17.014	17.180	17.347	17.514	17.681	17.848	18.014	18.181
0.7	19.460	19.655	19.849	20.044	20.238	20.433	20.628	20.822	21.017	21.211
0.8	22.240	22.462	22.685	22.907	23.130	23.352	23.574	23.797	24.019	24.242
0.9	25.020	25.270	25.520	25.771	26.021	26.271	26.521	26.771	27.022	27.272
1.0	27.800	28.078	28.356	28.634	28.912	29.190	29.468	29.746	30.024	30.302
1.1	20.580	20.886	31.192	31.497	31.803	32.109	32.415	32.721	33.026	33.332
1.2	33.360	33.694	34.027	34.361	34.694	35.028	35.362	25.695	36.029	36.362
1.3	36.140	36.501	36.863	37.224	37.586	37.947	38.308	38.670	39.031	39.393
1.4	38.920	29.309	39.698	40.088	40.477	40.866	41.255	41.644	42.034	42.423
1.5	41.700	42.117	42.534	42.951	43.368	43.785	44.202	44.619	45.036	45.453
1.6	44.480	44.925	45.370	45.814	46.259	46.704	47.149	47.594	48.038	48.483
1.7	47.260	47.733	48.205	48.678	49.150	49.623	50.096	50.568	51.041	51.513
1.8	50.040	50.540	51.041	51.541	52.042	52.542	53.042	53.543	54.043	54.544
1.9	52.820	53.348	53.876	54.405	54.933	55.461	55.989	56.517	57.046	57.574
2.0	55.600	56.156	56.712	57.268	57.824	58.380	58.936	59.492	60.048	60.604

TABLE 1-I-B *(Continued)*
REACTION DISTANCE IN METERS

Reaction Time in Seconds	Speed (km/h)									
	110	111	112	113	114	115	116	117	118	119
0.2	6.116	6.172	6.227	6.283	6.338	6.394	6.450	6.505	6.561	6.616
0.3	9.174	9.257	9.341	9.424	9.508	9.591	9.674	9.758	9.841	9.925
0.4	12.232	12.343	12.454	12.566	12.677	12.788	12.899	13.010	13.122	13.233
0.5	15.290	15.429	15.568	15.707	15.846	15.985	16.124	16.263	16.402	16.541
0.6	18.348	18.515	18.687	18.848	19.015	19.182	19.349	19.516	19.682	19.849
0.7	21.406	21.601	21.795	21.990	22.184	22.379	22.574	22.768	22.963	23.157
0.8	24.464	24.686	24.909	25.131	25.354	25.576	25.798	26.021	26.243	26.466
0.9	27.522	27.772	28.022	28.273	28.523	28.772	29.023	29.273	29.524	29.774
1.0	30.580	30.858	31.136	31.414	31.692	31.970	32.248	32.526	32.804	33.082
1.1	33.638	33.944	34.250	34.555	34.861	35.167	35.473	35.779	36.084	36.390
1.2	36.696	37.030	37.363	37.697	38.030	38.364	38.698	39.031	39.365	39.698
1.3	39.754	40.115	40.477	40.838	41.200	41.561	41.922	42.284	42.645	43.007
1.4	42.812	43.201	43.590	43.980	44.369	44.758	45.147	45.536	45.926	46.315
1.5	45.870	46.287	46.704	47.121	47.538	47.955	48.372	48.789	49.206	49.623
1.6	48.928	49.373	49.818	50.262	50.707	51.152	51.597	52.042	52.486	52.931
1.7	51.986	52.459	52.931	53.404	53.876	54.349	54.822	55.294	55.767	56.239
1.8	55.044	55.544	56.045	56.545	57.046	57.546	58.046	58.547	59.047	59.548
1.9	58.102	58.630	59.158	59.687	60.215	60.743	61.271	61.799	62.328	62.856
2.0	61.160	61.716	62.272	62.828	63.384	63.940	64.496	65.052	65.608	66.164

Reaction Time in Seconds	Speed (km/h)									
	120	121	122	123	124	125	126	127	128	129
0.2	6.672	6.728	6.783	6.839	6.894	6.950	7.006	7.061	7.117	7.172
0.3	10.008	10.091	10.175	10.258	10.342	10.425	10.508	10.592	10.675	10.759
0.4	13.344	13.455	13.566	13.678	13.789	13.900	14.011	14.122	14.234	14.345
0.5	16.680	16.819	16.958	17.097	17.236	17.375	17.514	17.653	17.792	17.931
0.6	20.016	20.183	20.350	20.516	20.683	20.850	21.017	21.184	21.350	21.517
0.7	23.352	23.547	23.741	23.936	24.130	24.325	24.520	24.714	24.909	25.103
0.8	26.688	26.910	27.133	27.355	27.578	27.800	28.022	28.245	28.467	28.690
0.9	30.024	30.274	30.524	30.775	31.025	31.275	31.525	31.775	32.026	32.276
1.0	33.360	33.638	33.916	34.194	34.472	34.750	35.028	35.306	35.584	35.862
1.1	36.696	37.002	37.308	37.613	37.919	38.225	38.531	38.837	39.142	39.448
1.2	40.032	40.366	40.699	41.033	41.366	41.700	42.034	42.367	42.701	43.034
1.3	43.368	43.729	44.091	44.452	44.814	45.175	45.536	45.898	46.259	46.621
1.4	46.704	47.093	47.482	47.872	48.261	48.650	49.039	49.428	49.818	50.207
1.5	50.040	50.457	50.874	51.291	51.708	52.125	52.542	52.959	53.376	53.793
1.6	43.376	53.821	54.266	54.710	55.155	55.600	56.045	56.490	56.934	57.379
1.7	56.712	57.185	57.657	58.130	58.602	59.075	59.548	60.020	60.493	60.965
1.8	60.048	60.548	61.049	61.549	62.050	62.550	63.050	63.551	64.051	64.552
1.9	63.384	63.912	64.440	64.969	65.497	66.025	66.553	67.081	67.610	68.138
2.0	66.720	67.276	67.832	68.388	68.944	69.500	70.056	70.612	71.168	71.724

Traffic Accident Investigators' Handbook

TABLE 1-I-B *(Continued)*
REACTION DISTANCE IN METERS

Reaction Time in Seconds	Speed (km/h)									
	130	131	132	133	134	135	136	137	138	139
0.2	7.228	7.284	7.339	7.395	7.450	7.506	7.562	7.617	7.673	7.728
0.3	10.842	10.925	11.009	11.092	11.176	11.259	11.342	11.426	11.509	11.593
0.4	14.456	14.567	14.678	14.790	14.901	15.012	15.123	15.234	15.346	15.457
0.5	18.070	18.209	18.348	18.487	18.626	18.765	18.904	19.043	19.182	19.321
0.6	21.684	21.851	22.018	22.184	22.351	22.518	22.685	22.852	23.018	23.185
0.7	25.298	25.493	25.687	25.882	26.076	26.271	26.466	26.660	26.855	27.049
0.8	28.912	29.134	29.357	29.579	29.802	30.024	30.246	30.469	30.691	30.914
0.9	32.526	32.776	33.026	33.277	33.527	33.777	34.027	34.277	34.528	34.778
1.0	36.140	36.418	26.696	36.974	37.252	37.430	37.808	38.086	38.364	38.642
1.1	39.754	40.060	40.366	40.671	40.977	41.283	41.589	41.895	42.200	42.506
1.2	43.368	43.702	44.035	44.369	44.702	45.036	45.370	45.703	46.037	46.370
1.3	46.982	47.343	47.705	48.066	48.428	48.789	49.150	49.512	49.873	50.235
1.4	50.596	50.985	51.374	51.764	52.153	52.542	52.931	53.320	53.710	54.099
1.5	54.210	54.627	55.044	55.461	55.878	56.295	56.712	57.129	57.546	57.963
1.6	57.824	58.269	58.714	59.158	59.603	60.048	60.493	60.938	61.382	61.827
1.7	61.438	61.911	62.383	62.856	63.328	63.801	64.274	64.746	65.219	65.691
1.8	65.052	65.552	66.053	66.553	67.054	67.554	68.054	68.555	69.055	69.556
1.9	68.666	69.194	69.722	70.251	70.779	71.307	71.835	72.363	72.892	73.420
2.0	72.280	72.836	73.392	73.948	74.504	75.060	75.616	76.172	76.728	77.284

Reaction Time in Seconds	Speed (km/h)									
	140	141	142	143	144	145	146	147	148	149	150
0.2	7.784	7.840	7.895	7.951	8.006	8.062	8.118	8.173	8.229	8.284	8.340
0.3	11.676	11.759	11.843	11.926	12.010	12.093	12.176	12.260	12.343	12.427	12.510
0.4	15.568	15.679	15.790	15.902	16.013	16.124	16.235	16.346	16.458	16.569	16.680
0.5	19.460	19.599	19.738	19.877	20.016	20.155	20.294	20.433	20.572	20.711	20.850
0.6	23.352	23.519	23.686	23.852	24.019	24.186	24.353	24.520	24.686	24.853	25.020
0.7	27.244	27.439	27.633	27.828	28.022	28.217	28.412	28.606	28.801	28.995	29.190
0.8	31.136	31.358	31.581	31.803	32.026	32.248	32.470	32.693	32.915	33.138	33.360
0.9	35.028	35.278	35.528	35.779	36.029	36.279	36.529	36.779	37.030	37.280	37.530
1.0	38.920	39.198	39.476	39.754	40.032	40.310	40.588	40.866	41.144	41.422	41.700
1.1	42.812	43.118	43.424	43.729	44.035	44.341	44.647	44.953	45.258	45.564	45.870
1.2	46.704	47.038	47.371	47.705	48.038	48.372	48.706	49.039	49.373	49.706	50.040
1.3	50.596	50.957	51.319	51.680	52.042	52.403	52.764	53.126	53.487	53.849	54.210
1.4	54.488	54.877	55.266	55.656	56.045	56.434	56.823	57.212	57.602	57.991	58.380
1.5	58.380	58.797	59.214	59.631	60.048	60.465	60.882	61.299	61.716	62.133	62.550
1.6	62.272	62.717	63.162	63.606	64.051	64.496	64.941	65.386	65.830	66.275	66.720
1.7	66.164	66.637	67.109	67.582	68.054	68.527	69.000	69.472	69.945	70.417	70.890
1.8	70.056	70.556	71.057	71.557	72.058	72.558	73.058	73.559	74.059	74.560	75.060
1.9	73.948	74.476	75.004	75.533	76.061	76.589	77.117	77.645	78.174	78.702	79.230
2.0	77.840	78.396	78.952	79.508	80.064	80.620	81.176	81.732	82.288	82.844	83.400

    c. Freedom of movement
    d. Knowledge of vehicle
    e. Reaction time

Evasive Action

Evasive action is an action or combination of actions such as steering or braking taken by a traffic unit with intention to avoid a collision or other hazardous situation.

Evasive Action Distance

Evasive action distance is the distance travelled after the action point to where the traffic unit stops by itself or otherwise avoids a collision or to the point of impact.

True Area

The true area is that area leading up to the point of no escape during which evasive action could be initiated in order to avoid a collision.

Point of No Escape

The point of no escape is the place and time after or beyond which the accident cannot be prevented by a particular traffic unit.[6] Because of committed motion and laws of physics, no action will avoid the collision completely at this point, although action such as braking or steering may reduce the seriousness of injury or damage. The point of no escape may be anywhere along a driver's path before collision depending upon the speeds of vehicles involved, visibility, and so on. This point may be before the point of possible perception, and if so, an accident cannot be avoided.

The point of no escape may be influenced by such factors as:
    a. Visibility of hazard
    b. Roadway alignment
    c. Positioning of traffic-control devices
    d. Driver distractions
    e. Weather and light conditions
    f. Condition of roadway surface, e.g., ruts, holes or other roadway damage, slippery conditions or obstructions, etc.
    g. Type, size and condition of vehicle being operated
    h. Cargo being carried

Encroachment

Encroachment is when a traffic unit intrudes or enters into the rightful path or area of another traffic unit.

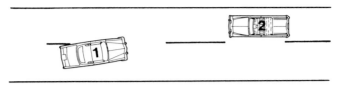

Figure 1-2. Encroachment by vehicle 1.

Point of Impact

The point of impact or collision is the place where a traffic unit strikes another traffic unit or some other object or it overturns (*see* Fig. 1-7).

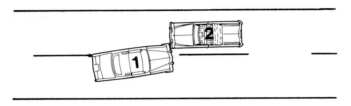

Figure 1-3. Primary or first contact.

Primary Contact

A primary contact is the first contact between two traffic units, between a traffic unit and another object, or first contact of a vehicle with a highway surface during an overturn.

Engagement

Engagement is the penetration of one object into another such as one traffic unit penetrating another traffic unit or object during collision.

Maximum Engagement

Maximum engagement is the point of maximum penetration or engagement by one object into another such as the maximum penetration of one traffic unit into another traffic unit or object during collision.

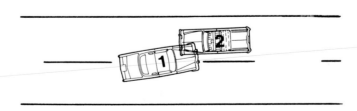

Figure 1-4. Maximum engagement.

Disengagement

Disengagement is the separation of two objects, for example, traffic units, after maximum engagement.

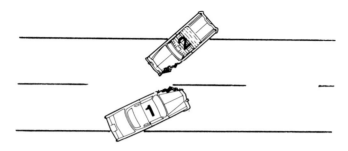

Figure 1-5. Disengagement.

Final Position

The final position of a vehicle or body is the location where it comes to rest after collision. The final position of a vehicle may be controlled or uncontrolled, that is, it may be forced to that location as the result of the collision or it may be steered to that position. In some cases, a vehicle may not have a final position, as in situations where a driver accelerates his vehicle and drives it to a location quite some distance from the point of impact.

1.009 Drivers and witnesses generally describe pre-scene series of events and on-scene series of events forward and lead up to the result. The investigator starts with the result and investigates back through the various series of events as far as necessary to determine where, when, how and why the accident occurred. It may not always be necessary for the investigator to extend his investigation into the pre-scene series of events; however, he should extend his investigation as far back as necessary to determine what a driver may or may not have done before the accident that may have contributed to his action or lack of action at the accident scene.

1.010 The following example illustrates how the on-scene series of events may be applied to traffic accidents. Speed, acceleration, deceleration and other measurements, calculations and determinations are of course necessary in actual investigations and in the application of on-scene series of events. These are covered later in this text.

Example

In Figure 1-6, vehicle 1 was travelling north on First Avenue. At point *A*, the *point of possible perception*, driver 1 saw vehicle 2 approaching an uncontrolled intersection from his right on King Street. Because of a distraction caused by a child playing on the street at point *Y*, driver 1 did not recognize nor perceive vehicle 2 as a hazard.

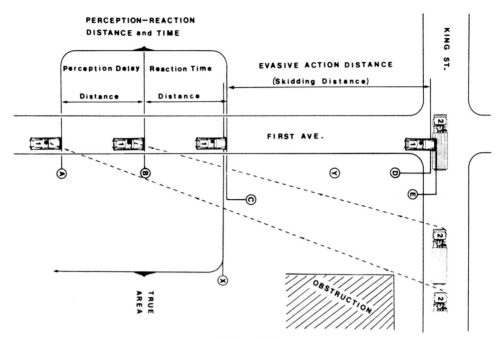

Figure 1-6

There was a perception delay of 0.75 seconds, at which time, at point *B*, driver 1 perceived that vehicle 2 was not likely to stop at the intersection. Driver 1 decided to apply his brakes in an attempt to stop his vehicle before the intersection. It took the driver 0.75 seconds to make his decision and to react to that decision.

At point *C*, the action point, the driver applied his brakes but his vehicle skidded (the evasive action distance) into the intersection and struck vehicle 2.

In this case, the collision or impact was minor. The vehicles did not move after impact and their final positions were relatively the same as at the point of impact.

Had driver 1 perceived the hazard presented by vehicle 2 approaching the intersection at his *point of possible perception*, he would probably have been able to apply his brakes in sufficient time to stop before the intersection. In this case, the *true or safe area* for driver 1 extended to just a very short distance before his *action point* or where he applied his brakes. His action point, however, was past the *point of no escape*, point *X*, and therefore he could not then avoid the collision.

Secondary Contacts

1.011   A collision between two vehicles or a vehicle and another object very often involves a *secondary contact* and a *post-secondary contact*. A secondary contact occurs when a vehicle disengages, rotates and strikes an opposing vehicle a second time (Fig. 1-7B). An example of a post-secondary contact is where a vehicle disengages from a secondary contact and strikes a third vehicle (Fig. 1-7C). In Figure 1-7, post-secondary contact of vehicle 1 with vehicle 3 becomes the primary or first contact of vehicle 3.

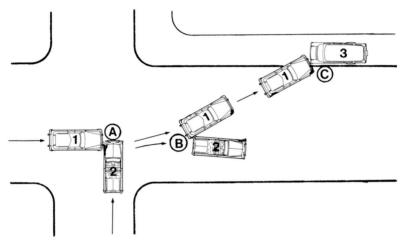

Figure 1-7. Vehicles 1 and 2 have first or *primary contact* at *A*. The point of impact is also at *A*. After disengagement, the vehicles have a *secondary contact* at *B*. After disengagement at *B*, vehicle 1 has a *post-secondary contact* at *C* with vehicle 3. The post-secondary contact of vehicle 1 at *C* is the first or primary contact of vehicle 3.

1.012 Each traffic unit has its own primary and secondary contacts and each must be considered separately.

Incidental (Induced) Damage

1.013 Incidental damage is damage which is incidental to engagement elsewhere on a vehicle, for example, trunk lid being forced open, roof buckling, window breakage, and such.

EXPERT EVIDENCE IN ACCIDENT RECONSTRUCTION

1.014 An investigator may, as the result of his experience and training, be accepted in court as an expert in determining speed from skid marks and other technical aspects of accident reconstruction. Or an accident might be reconstructed by a professional traffic accident reconstructionist based on the information supplied by an investigator. In any event, an investigation must be thorough, and the evidence gathered must be accurate and complete in order that meaningful reconstruction can take place.

1.015 Professional accident reconstructionists are able to apply scientific principles to data and other evidence gathered during field investigations. Unless an investigation is thorough in the initial instance, particularly the

Figure 1-8. Incidental damage.

on-scene investigation, it is difficult for the reconstructionist to arrive at conclusive results in his reconstruction of the accident.

1.016 In accident reconstruction, the police investigator should be prepared to call whatever additional expert evidence might be required to supplement or verify his own findings or to otherwise support his investigation.

FRAUD

1.017 The investigator must be cautious that the accident was not "staged" with intent to defraud insurance companies or to cover up some type of crime such as murder. The possibility of a conspiracy to defraud insurance companies of money should be considered, particularly when there is a lack of witnesses, no reasonable excuse or reason for the accident, a driver or pedestrian states that he or his vehicle suffered injury and the other party involved in the accident freely admits liability.

CLASSIFICATION OF ACCIDENTS

1.018 Classification and legal definitions related to traffic accidents have not been included in this text because of the difference in definitions in various jurisdictions. In all cases, investigators should classify and apply those legal definitions that are accepted or required in their particular jurisdiction.

UNITED STATES (IMPERIAL) AND METRIC MEASUREMENT SYSTEMS

1.019   The metric system was founded by the French during the French revolution. The International System of Units (Système International d'Unites), based on the original metric system, was adopted as the international metric system at a world conference held in 1960. The abbreviation for the international system is SI.

1.020   It is now a general trend by major nations of the world to replace all former measurement systems, including other versions of the metric system, with the international system SI. Because both systems are still used in many places, this text is prepared in such a way as to satisfy the requirements of accident investigation regardless of which measurement system is used. At the same time, the text is also prepared so as to introduce and interpret the international metric system in those areas that have recently or are about to adopt the international system SI.

1.021   In many cases the exact equivalents or conversion factors from United States units to metric units, and vice versa, are carried to six or more decimal places. In this text, some factors are taken to a smaller number of decimal places, and therefore, some corresponding values are approximations. All formulae and tables are, however, worked out in both measurement systems independent of each other so as to avoid any unnecessary confusion. Metric equivalents of United States measurements are shown in brackets immediately following United States measurements.

Abbreviations

United States		*Metric*	
Length			
inch	in	millimeter	mm
		centimeter	cm
foot	ft	meter	m
mile	mi	kilometer	km
Weight			
pound	lb	kilogram	kg
Velocity			
feet per second	ft /sec	meters per second	m/s
miles per hour	mph	kilometers per hour	km/h
Temperature			
degrees Farenheit	°F	degrees Celsius	°C

Conversion Factors

United States		Metric

Acceleration

| 1 ft/sec/sec (ft/sec²) | = | 0.3048 m/s/s (m/s²) |
| 1 m/s/s (m/s²) | = | 3.2808 ft/sec/sec (ft/sec²) |

Acceleration Due to Gravity

| 32.2 ft/sec/sec (ft/sec²) | = | 9.81 m/s/s (m/s²) |

Length

1 inch	= 2.54 centimeters	1 centimeter	= 0.394 inch
1 foot	= 0.3048 meter	1 meter	= 3.281 feet
1 mile	= 1.609 kilometers	1 kilometer	= 0.621 mile

Temperature

$$F = \frac{9C}{5} + 32 \qquad\qquad C = \frac{5 (F - 32)}{9}$$

Velocity

1.467	× miles per hour	=	feet per second
0.6818	× feet per second	=	miles per hour
3.2808	× meters per second	=	feet per second
0.278	× kilometers per hour	=	meters per second
3.6	× meters per second	=	kilometers per hour

Weight (Mass)

| 1 pound = 0.4536 kg | 1 kilogram = 2.205 pounds |

CONSTANTS

1.022   A *constant* is a quantity that retains its value throughout a variety of calculations. In traffic accident investigations, the numbers 5.5 (15.9) and 30 (254) are constants that are frequently used in calculating speeds and distances. The constants 5.5 and 30 represent true constants of 5.47 and 29.94 respectively.

SQUARE ROOTS

1.023   A number that contains two equal factors is a perfect square, for example, 10 × 10 = 100. In this example, *100* is a perfect square because the two factors, *10* and *10,* are equal. The *square root* of a number is the equal factors which multiplied together make the square number. A number multiplied by itself is said to be squared and is written mathematically as, for example, 10². Although a square root table is found in Table 1-V the investigator should know how square roots are derived.

Example 1

Problem: Calculate the square root of 729.

1. Beginning at the decimal point or the right of the number (dividend),

TABLE 1-II-A
INCHES-TO-CENTIMETERS CONVERSION TABLE

Inches	=	Centimeters	Inches	=	Centimeters
1	=	2.54	51	=	129.54
2	=	5.08	52	=	132.08
3	=	7.62	53	=	134.62
4	=	10.16	54	=	137.16
5	=	12.70	55	=	139.70
6	=	15.24	56	=	142.24
7	=	17.78	57	=	144.78
8	=	20.32	58	=	147.32
9	=	22.86	59	=	149.86
10	=	25.40	60	=	152.40
11	=	27.94	61	=	154.94
12	=	30.48	62	=	157.48
13	=	33.02	63	=	160.02
14	=	35.56	64	=	162.56
15	=	38.10	65	=	165.10
16	=	40.64	66	=	167.64
17	=	43.18	67	=	170.18
18	=	45.72	68	=	172.72
19	=	48.26	69	=	175.26
20	=	50.80	70	=	177.80
21	=	53.34	71	=	180.34
22	=	55.88	72	=	182.88
23	=	58.42	73	=	185.42
24	=	60.96	74	=	187.96
25	=	63.50	75	=	190.50
26	=	66.04	76	=	193.04
27	=	68.58	77	=	195.58
28	=	71.12	78	=	198.12
29	=	73.66	79	=	200.66
30	=	76.20	80	=	203.20
31	=	78.74	81	=	205.74
32	=	81.28	82	=	208.28
33	=	83.82	83	=	210.82
34	=	86.36	84	=	213.36
35	=	88.90	85	=	215.90
36	=	91.44	86	=	218.44
37	=	93.98	87	=	220.98
38	=	96.52	88	=	223.52
39	=	99.06	89	=	226.06
40	=	101.60	90	=	228.60
41	=	104.14	91	=	231.14
42	=	106.68	92	=	233.68
43	=	109.22	93	=	236.22
44	=	111.76	94	=	238.76
45	=	114.30	95	=	241.30
46	=	116.84	96	=	243.84
47	=	119.38	97	=	246.38
48	=	121.92	98	=	248.92
49	=	124.46	99	=	251.46
50	=	127.00	100	=	254.00

TABLE 1-II-B
CENTIMETERS-TO-INCHES CONVERSION TABLE

Centimeters	=	Inches	Centimeters	=	Inches
1	=	0.394	51	=	20.094
2	=	0.788	52	=	20.488
3	=	1.182	53	=	20.882
4	=	1.576	54	=	21.276
5	=	1.970	55	=	21.670
6	=	2.364	56	=	22.064
7	=	2.758	57	=	22.458
8	=	3.152	58	=	22.852
9	=	3.546	59	=	23.246
10	=	3.940	60	=	23.640
11	=	4.334	61	=	24.034
12	=	4.728	62	=	24.428
13	=	5.122	63	=	24.822
14	=	5.516	64	=	25.216
15	=	5.910	65	=	25.610
16	=	6.304	66	=	26.004
17	=	6.698	67	=	26.398
18	=	7.092	68	=	26.792
19	=	7.486	69	=	27.186
20	=	7.886	70	=	27.580
21	=	8.274	71	=	27.974
22	=	8.668	72	=	28.368
23	=	9.062	73	=	28.762
24	=	9.456	74	=	29.156
25	=	9.850	75	=	29.550
26	=	10.244	76	=	29.944
27	=	10.638	77	=	30.338
28	=	11.032	78	=	30.732
29	=	11.426	79	=	31.126
30	=	11.820	80	=	31.520
31	=	12.214	81	=	31.914
32	=	12.608	82	=	32.308
33	=	13.002	83	=	32.702
34	=	13.396	84	=	33.096
35	=	13.790	85	=	33.490
36	=	14.184	86	=	33.884
37	=	14.578	87	=	34.278
38	=	14.972	88	=	34.672
39	=	15.366	89	=	35.066
40	=	15.760	90	=	35.460
41	=	16.154	91	=	35.854
42	=	16.548	92	=	36.248
43	=	16.942	93	=	36.642
44	=	17.336	94	=	37.036
45	=	17.730	95	=	37.430
46	=	18.124	96	=	37.824
47	=	18.518	97	=	38.218
48	=	18.912	98	=	38.612
49	=	19.306	99	=	39.006
50	=	19.700	100	=	39.400

TABLE 1-III-A
FEET-TO-METERS CONVERSION TABLE

Feet	=	Meters	Feet	=	Meters
1	=	.3048	51	=	15.5448
2	=	.6096	52	=	15.8496
3	=	.9144	53	=	16.1544
4	=	1.2192	54	=	16.4592
5	=	1.5240	55	=	16.7640
6	=	1.8288	56	=	17.0688
7	=	2.1336	57	=	17.3736
8	=	2.4384	58	=	17.6784
9	=	2.7432	59	=	17.9832
10	=	3.0480	60	=	18.2880
11	=	3.3528	61	=	18.5928
12	=	3.6576	62	=	18.8976
13	=	3.9624	63	=	19.2024
14	=	4.2672	64	=	19.5072
15	=	4.5720	65	=	19.8120
16	=	4.8768	66	=	20.1168
17	=	5.1816	67	=	20.4216
18	=	5.4864	68	=	20.7264
19	=	5.7912	69	=	21.0312
20	=	6.0960	70	=	21.3360
21	=	6.4008	71	=	21.6408
22	=	6.7056	72	=	21.9456
23	=	7.0104	73	=	22.2504
24	=	7.3152	74	=	22.5552
25	=	7.6200	75	=	22.8600
26	=	7.9248	76	=	23.1648
27	=	8.2296	77	=	23.4696
28	=	8.5344	78	=	23.7744
29	=	8.8392	79	=	24.0792
30	=	9.1440	80	=	24.3840
31	=	9.4488	81	=	24.6888
32	=	9.7536	82	=	24.9936
33	=	10.0584	83	=	25.2984
34	=	10.3632	84	=	25.6032
35	=	10.6680	85	=	25.9080
36	=	10.9728	86	=	26.2128
37	=	11.2776	87	=	26.5176
38	=	11.5824	88	=	26.8224
39	=	11.8872	89	=	27.1272
40	=	12.1920	90	=	27.4320
41	=	12.4968	91	=	27.7368
42	=	12.8016	92	=	28.0416
43	=	13.1064	93	=	28.3464
44	=	13.4112	94	=	28.6512
45	=	13.7160	95	=	28.9560
46	=	14.0208	96	=	29.2608
47	=	14.3256	97	=	29.5656
48	=	14.6304	98	=	29.8704
49	=	14.9352	99	=	30.1752
50	=	15.2400	100	=	30.4800

Traffic Accident Investigators' Handbook

TABLE 1-III-B
METERS-TO-FEET CONVERSION TABLE

Meters	=	Feet	Meters	=	Feet
1	=	3.281	51	=	167.331
2	=	6.562	52	=	170.612
3	=	9.843	53	=	173.893
4	=	13.124	54	=	177.174
5	=	16.405	55	=	180.455
6	=	19.686	56	=	183.736
7	=	22.967	57	=	187.017
8	=	26.248	58	=	190.298
9	=	29.529	59	=	193.579
10	=	32.810	60	=	196.860
11	=	36.091	61	=	200.141
12	=	39.372	62	=	203.422
13	=	42.653	63	=	206.703
14	=	45.934	64	=	209.984
15	=	49.215	65	=	213.265
16	=	52.496	66	=	216.546
17	=	55.777	67	=	219.827
18	=	59.058	68	=	223.108
19	=	62.339	69	=	226.389
20	=	65.620	70	=	229.670
21	=	68.901	71	=	232.951
22	=	72.182	72	=	236.232
23	=	75.463	73	=	239.513
24	=	78.744	74	=	242.794
25	=	82.025	75	=	246.075
26	=	85.306	76	=	249.356
27	=	88.587	77	=	252.637
28	=	91.868	78	=	255.918
29	=	95.149	79	=	259.199
30	=	98.430	80	=	262.480
31	=	101.711	81	=	265.761
32	=	104.992	82	=	269.042
33	=	108.273	83	=	272.323
34	=	111.554	84	=	275.604
35	=	114.835	85	=	278.885
36	=	118.116	86	=	282.166
37	=	121.397	87	=	285.447
38	=	124.678	88	=	288.728
39	=	127.959	89	=	292.009
40	=	131.240	90	=	295.290
41	=	134.521	91	=	298.571
42	=	137.802	92	=	301.852
43	=	141.083	93	=	305.133
44	=	144.364	94	=	308.414
45	=	147.645	95	=	311.695
46	=	150.926	96	=	314.976
47	=	154.207	97	=	318.257
48	=	157.488	98	=	321.538
49	=	160.769	99	=	324.819
50	=	164.050	100	=	328.100

TABLE 1-IV-A
MILES-TO-KILOMETERS CONVERSION TABLE

Miles	Kilometers	Miles	Kilometers	Miles	Kilometers	Miles	Kilometers
1.0	1.609	31.0	49.879	61.0	98.149	91.0	146.419
1.5	2.414	31.5	50.684	61.5	98.954	91.5	147.224
2.0	3.218	32.0	51.488	62.0	99.758	92.0	148.028
2.5	4.023	32.5	52.293	62.5	100.563	92.5	148.833
3.0	4.827	33.0	53.097	63.0	101.367	93.0	149.637
3.5	5.632	33.5	53.902	63.5	102.172	93.5	150.442
4.0	6.436	34.0	54.706	64.0	102.976	94.0	151.246
4.5	7.241	34.5	55.511	64.5	103.781	94.5	152.051
5.0	8.045	35.0	56.315	65.0	104.585	95.0	152.855
5.5	8.850	35.5	57.120	65.5	105.390	95.5	153.660
6.0	9.654	36.0	57.924	66.0	106.194	96.0	154.464
6.5	10.459	36.5	58.729	66.5	106.999	96.5	155.269
7.0	11.263	37.0	59.533	67.0	107.803	97.0	156.073
7.5	12.068	37.5	60.338	67.5	108.608	97.5	156.878
8.0	12.872	38.0	61.142	68.0	109.412	98.0	157.682
8.5	13.677	38.5	61.947	68.5	110.217	98.5	158.487
9.0	14.481	39.0	62.751	69.0	111.021	99.0	159.291
9.5	15.286	39.5	63.556	69.5	111.826	99.5	160.096
10.0	16.090	40.0	64.360	70.0	112.630	100.0	160.900
10.5	16.895	40.5	65.165	70.5	113.435	100.5	161.705
11.0	17.699	41.0	65.969	71.0	114.239	101.0	162.509
11.5	18.504	41.5	66.774	71.5	115.044	101.5	163.314
12.0	19.308	42.0	67.578	72.0	115.848	102.0	164.118
12.5	20.113	42.5	68.383	72.5	116.653	102.5	164.923
13.0	20.917	43.0	69.187	73.0	117.457	103.0	165.727
13.5	21.722	43.5	69.992	73.5	118.262	103.5	166.532
14.0	22.526	44.0	70.796	74.0	119.066	104.0	167.336
14.5	23.331	44.5	71.601	74.5	119.871	104.5	168.141
15.0	24.135	45.0	72.405	75.0	120.675	105.0	168.945
15.5	24.940	45.5	73.210	75.5	121.480	105.5	169.750
16.0	25.744	46.0	74.014	76.0	122.284	106.0	170.554
16.5	26.549	46.5	74.819	76.5	123.089	106.5	171.359
17.0	27.353	47.0	75.623	77.0	123.893	107.0	172.163
17.5	28.158	47.5	76.428	77.5	124.698	107.5	172.968
18.0	28.962	48.0	77.232	78.0	125.502	108.0	173.772
18.5	29.767	48.5	78.037	78.5	126.307	108.5	174.577
19.0	30.571	49.0	78.841	79.0	127.111	109.0	175.381
19.5	31.376	49.5	79.646	79.5	127.916	109.5	176.186
20.0	32.180	50.0	80.450	80.0	128.720	110.0	176.990
20.5	32.985	50.5	81.255	80.5	129.525	110.5	177.795
21.0	33.789	51.0	82.059	81.0	130.329	111.0	178.599
21.5	34.594	51.5	82.864	81.5	131.134	111.5	179.404
22.0	35.398	52.0	83.668	82.0	131.938	112.0	180.208
22.5	36.203	52.5	84.473	82.5	132.743	112.5	181.013
23.0	37.007	53.0	85.277	83.0	133.547	113.0	181.817
23.5	37.812	53.5	86.082	83.5	134.352	113.5	182.622
24.0	38.616	54.0	86.886	84.0	135.156	114.0	183.426
24.5	39.421	54.5	87.691	84.5	135.961	114.5	184.231
25.0	40.225	55.0	88.495	85.0	136.765	115.0	185.035
25.5	41.030	55.5	89.300	85.5	137.570	115.5	185.840
26.0	41.834	56.0	90.104	86.0	138.374	116.0	186.644
26.5	42.639	56.5	90.909	86.5	139.179	116.5	187.449
27.0	43.443	57.0	91.713	87.0	139.983	117.0	188.253
27.5	44.248	57.5	92.518	87.5	140.788	117.5	189.058
28.0	45.052	58.0	93.322	88.0	141.592	118.0	189.862
28.5	45.857	58.5	94.127	88.5	142.397	118.5	190.667
29.0	46.661	59.0	94.931	89.0	143.201	119.0	191.471
29.5	47.466	59.5	95.736	89.5	144.006	119.5	192.276
30.0	48.270	60.0	96.540	90.0	144.810	120.0	193.080
30.5	49.075	60.5	97.345	90.5	145.615		

TABLE 1-IV-B
KILOMETERS-TO-MILES CONVERSION TABLE

Kilometers	Miles	Kilometers	Miles	Kilometers	Miles	Kilometers	Miles
1.0	0.621	26.0	16.146	51.0	31.671	76.0	47.196
1.5	0.932	26.5	16.457	51.5	31.982	76.5	47.507
2.0	1.242	27.0	16.767	52.0	32.292	77.0	47.817
2.5	1.553	27.5	17.078	52.5	32.603	77.5	48.128
3.0	1.863	28.0	17.388	53.0	32.913	78.0	48.438
3.5	2.174	28.5	17.699	53.5	33.224	78.5	48.749
4.0	2.484	29.0	18.009	54.0	33.534	79.0	49.059
4.5	2.795	29.5	18.320	54.5	33.845	79.5	49.370
5.0	3.105	30.0	18.630	55.0	34.155	80.0	49.680
5.5	3.416	30.5	18.941	55.5	34.466	80.5	49.991
6.0	3.726	31.0	19.251	56.0	34.776	81.0	50.301
6.5	4.037	31.5	19.562	56.5	35.087	81.5	50.612
7.0	4.347	32.0	19.872	57.0	35.397	82.0	50.922
7.5	4.658	32.5	20.183	57.5	35.708	82.5	51.233
8.0	4.968	33.0	20.493	58.0	36.018	83.0	51.543
8.5	5.279	33.5	20.804	58.5	36.329	83.5	51.854
9.0	5.589	34.0	21.114	59.0	36.639	84.0	52.164
9.5	5.900	34.5	21.425	59.5	36.950	84.5	52.475
10.0	6.210	35.0	21.735	60.0	37.260	85.0	52.785
10.5	6.521	35.5	22.046	60.5	37.571	85.5	53.096
11.0	6.831	36.0	22.356	61.0	37.881	86.0	53.406
11.5	7.142	36.5	22.667	61.5	38.192	86.5	53.717
12.0	7.452	37.0	22.977	62.0	38.502	87.0	54.027
12.5	7.763	37.5	23.288	62.5	38.813	87.5	54.338
13.0	8.073	38.0	23.598	63.0	39.123	88.0	54.648
13.5	8.384	38.5	23.909	63.5	39.434	88.5	54.959
14.0	8.694	39.0	24.219	64.0	39.744	89.0	55.269
14.5	9.005	39.5	24.530	64.5	40.055	89.5	55.580
15.0	9.315	40.0	24.840	65.0	40.365	90.0	55.890
15.5	9.626	40.5	25.151	65.5	40.676	90.5	56.201
16.0	9.936	41.0	25.461	66.0	40.986	91.0	56.511
16.5	10.247	41.5	25.772	66.5	41.297	91.5	56.822
17.0	10.557	42.0	26.082	67.0	41.607	92.0	57.132
17.5	10.868	42.5	26.393	67.5	41.918	92.5	57.443
18.0	11.178	43.0	26.703	68.0	42.228	93.0	57.753
18.5	11.489	43.5	27.014	68.5	42.539	93.5	58.064
19.0	11.799	44.0	27.324	69.0	42.849	94.0	58.374
19.5	12.110	44.5	27.635	69.5	43.160	94.5	58.685
20.0	12.420	45.0	27.945	70.0	43.470	95.0	58.995
20.5	12.731	45.5	28.256	70.5	43.781	95.5	59.306
21.0	13.041	46.0	28.566	71.0	44.091	96.0	59.616
21.5	13.352	46.5	28.877	71.5	44.402	96.5	59.927
22.0	13.662	47.0	29.187	72.0	44.712	97.0	60.237
22.5	13.973	47.5	29.498	72.5	45.023	97.5	60.548
23.0	14.283	48.0	29.808	73.0	45.333	98.0	60.858
23.5	14.594	48.5	30.119	73.5	45.644	98.5	61.169
24.0	14.904	4910	30.429	74.0	45.954	99.0	61.479
24.5	15.215	49.5	30.740	74.5	46.265	99.5	61.790
25.0	15.525	50.0	31.050	75.0	46.575	100.0	62.100
25.5	15.836	50.5	31.361	75.5	46.886	100.5	62.411

TABLE 1-IV-B *(Continued)*
KILOMETERS-TO-MILES CONVERSION TABLE

Kilometers	Miles	Kilometers	Miles	Kilometers	Miles	Kilometers	Miles
101.0	62.721	126.0	78.246	151.0	93.771	176.0	109.296
101.5	63.032	126.5	78.557	151.5	94.082	176.5	109.607
102.0	63.342	127.0	78.867	152.0	94.392	177.0	109.917
102.5	63.653	127.5	79.178	152.5	94.703	177.5	110.228
103.0	63.963	128.0	79.488	153.0	95.013	178.0	110.538
103.5	64.274	128.5	79.799	153.5	95.324	178.5	110.849
104.0	64.584	129.0	80.109	154.0	95.634	179.0	111.159
104.5	64.895	129.5	80.420	154.5	95.945	179.5	111.470
105.0	65.205	130.0	80.730	155.0	96.255	180.0	111.780
105.5	65.516	130.5	81.041	155.5	96.566	180.5	112.091
106.0	65.826	131.0	81.351	156.0	96.876	181.0	112.401
106.5	66.137	131.5	81.662	156.5	97.187	181.5	112.712
107.0	66.447	132.0	81.972	157.0	97.497	182.0	113.022
107.5	66.758	132.5	82.283	157.5	97.808	182.5	113.333
108.0	67.068	133.0	82.593	158.0	98.118	183.0	113.643
108.5	67.379	133.5	82.904	158.5	98.429	183.5	113.954
109.0	67.689	134.0	83.214	159.0	98.739	184.0	114.264
109.5	68.000	134.5	83.525	159.5	99.050	184.5	114.575
110.0	68.310	135.0	83.835	160.0	99.360	185.0	114.885
110.5	68.621	135.5	84.146	160.5	99.671	185.5	115.196
111.0	68.931	136.0	84.456	161.0	99.981	186.0	115.506
111.5	69.242	136.5	84.767	161.5	100.292	186.5	115.817
112.0	69.552	137.0	85.077	162.0	100.602	187.0	116.127
112.5	69.863	137.5	85.388	612.5	100.913	187.5	116.438
113.0	70.173	138.0	85.698	163.0	101.223	188.0	116.748
113.5	70.484	138.5	86.009	163.5	101.534	188.5	117.059
114.0	70.794	139.0	86.319	164.0	101.844	189.0	117.369
114.5	71.105	139.5	86.630	164.5	102.155	189.5	117.680
115.0	71.415	140.0	86.940	165.0	102.465	190.0	117.990
115.5	71.726	140.5	87.251	165.5	102.776	190.5	118.301
116.0	72.036	141.0	87.561	166.0	103.086	191.0	118.611
116.5	72.347	141.5	87.872	166.5	103.397	191.5	118.922
117.0	72.657	142.0	88.182	167.0	103.707	192.0	119.232
117.5	72.968	142.5	88.493	167.5	104.018	192.5	119.543
118.0	73.278	143.0	88.803	168.0	104.328	193.0	119.853
118.5	73.589	143.5	89.114	168.5	104.639	193.5	120.164
119.0	73.899	144.0	89.424	169.0	104.949	194.0	120.474
119.5	74.210	144.5	89.735	169.5	105.260	194.5	120.785
120.0	74.520	145.0	90.045	170.0	105.570	195.0	121.095
120.5	74.831	145.5	90.356	170.5	105.881	195.5	121.406
121.0	75.141	146.0	90.666	171.0	106.191	196.0	121.716
121.5	75.452	146.5	90.977	171.5	106.502	196.5	122.027
122.0	75.762	147.0	91.287	172.0	106.812	197.0	122.337
122.5	76.073	147.5	91.598	172.5	107.123	197.5	122.648
123.0	76.383	148.0	91.908	173.0	107.433	198.0	122.958
123.5	76.694	148.5	92.219	173.5	107.744	198.5	123.268
124.0	77.004	149.0	92.529	174.0	108.054	199.0	123.579
124.5	77.315	149.5	92.840	174.5	108.365	199.5	123.890
125.0	77.625	150.0	93.150	175.0	108.675	200.0	124.200
125.5	77.936	150.5	93.461	175.5	108.986		

divide it into groups of two digits each. The answer or quotient has one digit for each group. In this particular example, group 1 in the dividend has only one digit.

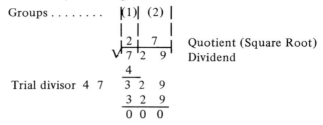

2. Find the largest number which, when squared or multiplied by itself, equals or nearly equals the group 1 digit of 7. In this example, 2 is the number. Place the 2 over the 7. Square the 2 (2 × 2 = 4) and subtract the 4 from the 7, which equals 3. Bring down the group 2 digits and place them to the right of the 3, making a new dividend of 329.

3. Multiply the partial quotient 2 by 2 (2 × 2 = 4). Place the 4 to the left of the new dividend 329. The 4 now becomes a partial new trial divisor. Allow for one more digit to be placed to the immediate right of the 4 to complete the new divisor. To find out what the missing number is, ignore the last number in the dividend 32<u>9</u>, and determine how many times 4 goes into 32, with a little to spare to allow for the unknown number. We know that 4 × 8 = 32, so the number must be less than 8. It should be 7. Place the 7 above 29 in group 2 and also place it to the immediate right of the partial trial divisor 4 as the unknown number. The number 47 now becomes the new divisor.

4. Multiply the new divisor 47 by the partial quotient 7 (7 × 47 = 329). The remainder is 0. Therefore, the quotient 27 is the exact square root of 729. The number 729, as we now see, is a perfect square.

Example 2

To find the square root of a number that is not a perfect square, it is necessary to take the answer (quotient) to the required or desired number of decimal places. Two decimal places satisfy most requirements.

Problem: Find the square root of 9203.1 to two decimal places.

```
Groups . . . . . . .   |(1) | (2) | (3)| (4)|
                        |  |   |  |   |  |   |  |
                        | 9 |  5 | 9 | 3 |     Quotient (Square Root)
                      √  9 2 0 3.1 0 0 0       Dividend
                         8 1
        1 8 5            1 1 0 3
                           9 2 5
        1 9 0 9          1 7 8 1 0  (a)
                         1 7 1 8 1
        1 9 1 8 3          6 2 9 0 0
                           5 7 5 4 9
```

TABLE 1-V
SQUARES AND SQUARE ROOTS

n	n^2	$\sqrt{n}$	n	n^2	$\sqrt{n}$	n	n^2	$\sqrt{n}$	n	n^2	$\sqrt{n}$
1	1	1.000	51	2601	7.141	101	10,201	10.050	151	22,801	12.288
2	4	1.414	52	2704	7.211	102	10,404	10.100	152	23,104	12.329
3	9	1.732	53	2809	7.280	103	10,609	10.149	153	23,409	12.369
4	16	2.000	54	2916	7.348	104	10,816	10.198	154	23,716	12.410
5	25	2.236	55	3025	7.416	105	11,025	10.247	155	24,025	12.450
6	36	2.449	56	3136	7.483	106	11,236	10.296	156	24,336	12.490
7	49	2.646	57	3249	7.550	107	11,449	10.344	157	24,649	12.530
8	64	2.828	58	3364	7.616	108	11,664	10.392	158	24,964	12.570
9	81	3.000	59	3481	7.681	109	11,881	10.440	159	25,281	12.610
10	100	3.162	60	3600	7.746	110	12,100	10.488	160	25,600	12.649
11	121	3.317	61	3721	7.810	111	12,321	10.536	161	25,921	12.689
12	144	3.464	62	3844	7.874	112	12,544	10.583	162	26,244	12.728
13	169	3.606	63	3969	7.937	113	12,769	10.630	163	26,569	12.767
14	196	3.742	64	4096	8.000	114	12,996	10.677	164	26,896	12.806
15	225	3.873	65	4225	8.062	115	13,225	10.724	165	27,225	12.845
16	256	4.000	66	4356	8.124	116	13,456	10.770	166	27,556	12.884
17	289	4.123	67	4489	8.185	117	13,689	10.817	167	27,889	12.923
18	324	4.243	68	4624	8.246	118	13,924	10.863	168	28,224	12.961
19	361	4.359	69	4761	8.307	119	14,161	10.909	169	28,561	13.000
20	400	4.472	70	4900	8.367	120	14,400	10.954	170	28,900	13.038
21	441	4.583	71	5041	8.426	121	14,641	11.000	171	29,241	13.077
22	484	4.690	72	5184	8.485	122	14,884	11.045	172	29,584	13.115
23	529	4.796	73	5329	8.544	123	15,129	11.091	173	29,929	13.153
24	576	4.899	74	5476	8.602	124	15,376	11.136	174	30,276	13.191
25	625	5.000	75	5625	8.660	125	15,625	11.180	175	30,625	13.229
26	676	5.099	76	5776	8.718	126	15,876	11.225	176	30,976	13.267
27	729	5.196	77	5929	8.775	127	16,129	11.269	177	31,329	13.304
28	784	5.292	78	6084	8.832	128	16,384	11.314	178	31,684	13.342
29	841	5.385	79	6241	8.888	129	16,641	11.358	179	32,041	13.379
30	900	5.477	80	6400	8.944	130	16,900	11.402	180	32,400	13.416
31	961	5.568	81	6561	9.000	131	17,161	11.446	181	32,761	13.454
32	1024	5.657	82	6724	9.055	132	17,424	11.489	182	33,124	13.491
33	1089	5.745	83	6889	9.110	133	17,689	11.533	183	33,489	13.528
34	1156	5.831	84	7056	9.165	134	17,956	11.576	184	33,856	13.565
35	1225	5.916	85	7225	9.220	135	18,225	11.619	185	34,225	13.601
36	1296	6.000	86	7396	9.274	136	18,496	11.662	186	34,596	13.638
37	1369	6.083	87	7569	9.327	137	18,769	11.705	187	34,969	13.675
38	1444	6.164	88	7744	9.381	138	19,044	11.747	188	35,344	13.711
39	1521	6.245	89	7921	9.434	139	19,321	11.790	189	35,721	13.748
40	1600	6.325	90	8100	9.487	140	19,600	11.832	190	36,100	13.784
41	1681	6.403	91	8281	9.539	141	19,881	11.874	191	36,481	13.820
42	1764	6.481	92	8464	9.592	142	20,164	11.916	192	36,864	13.856
43	1849	6.557	93	8649	9.644	143	20,449	11.958	193	37,249	13.892
44	1936	6.633	94	8836	9.695	144	20,736	12.000	194	37,636	13.928
45	2025	6.708	95	9025	9.747	145	21,025	12.042	195	38,025	13.964
46	2116	6.782	96	9216	9.798	146	21,316	12.083	196	38,416	14.000
47	2209	6.856	97	9409	9.849	147	21,609	12.124	197	38,809	14.036
48	2304	6.928	98	9604	9.899	148	21,904	12.166	198	39,204	14.071
49	2401	7.000	99	9801	9.950	149	22,201	12.207	199	39,601	14.107
50	2500	7.071	100	10,000	10.000	150	22,500	12.247	200	40,000	14.142

1. Beginning at the decimal point, divide the dividend into groups of two digits each. The answer or quotient will have one digit for each group.
2. Follow the same procedures outlined in Example 1. Remember to double the partial quotient each time to find the trial divisor. Note that if the first group to the right of the decimal contains only one digit, it is necessary to add zeros to the dividend and divide them into groups to meet the required number of decimal places in the quotient or answer. In this example, in group 3, 10 is brought down, *not* just the 1 by itself.

ABBREVIATIONS AND SYMBOLS

1.024   In this text, the following abbreviations and symbols are used. Each is accompanied by a definition so that the reader will understand their meaning as he comes across them. In some cases, definitions are enlarged upon elsewhere in the text.

a = Acceleration in feet per second per second (ft/sec/sec or ft/sec^2) or meters per second per second (m/s/s or m/s^2). Negative acceleration is deceleration.

C = Chord. A chord is a straight line measured from one end of a circular arc to the other.

CG = Center of gravity.

C/M = Center of mass.

e = Grade, slope, bank or superelevation in feet per foot or meters per meter of horizontal distance.

f = Coefficient of friction or drag factor.

F = Force.

g = Accelerating force of gravity.

H = Height.

n = Braking capability or efficiency.

M = Middle ordinate. A middle ordinate is the distance measured at a right angle from the middle of the chord to the arc of a circle.

R = Radius.

S = Speed. Speed is a common term applied to vehicle movement; for the purposes of this text, speed and velocity have the same meaning.

t = Time in seconds, minutes or hours.

V = Velocity. A vector quantity. Movement measured in ft/sec (m/s) where rapidity and direction are elements.

$\bar{S}$ = Average speed. The small bar indicates *average* for the component it is attached to.

S_0 = Original or initial speed. The small dropped zero indicates *original* or *initial* for the component it is attached to.

V_1 = First or number one vehicle. A dropped *1, 2,* and so on indicates the first or number one, number two, and so on for the component it is attached to.

∴. = Therefore.

+ = Plus.

− = Minus.

± = Plus or minus.

′ = Prime. Prime indicates a second value. For example, S' = speed after collision, where an initial speed, S, was being considered in a calculation.

Chapter 2

THE INVESTIGATION

RECEIVING THE CALL

2.001 When the report of a traffic accident is received, obtain the exact location and seriousness. Arrange for any additional assistance that might be required or have it stand by when necessary:

    a. Ambulance
    b. Doctor
    c. Fire fighting equipment
    d. Torch or cutting equipment
    e. Tow truck
    f. Rescue squad

Figure 2-1. Some traffic accidents disrupt traffic flow for considerable periods of time and sometimes require professional, expensive assistance in their investigation or control.

44

2.002 Record name and address of person reporting the traffic accident. Determine the extent of his knowledge of the occurrence. If report is not made in person, obtain the telephone number from which the report is made. If prank call is suspected, call the person back immediately. When more than one report is received on what appears to be the same accident, examine the details very closely, as another accident may have occurred nearby.

PROCEEDING TO THE SCENE

2.003 The seriousness of the accident should always be considered in determining the urgency with which the investigator should proceed to the scene. Proceed to the scene as safely as possible. Do not cause or become involved in yet another accident. Do not depend solely on the siren and emergency lights to get to the scene safely. Always use reasonable care and comply with local legislation respecting the use of emergency vehicles.

2.004 Proceed to the scene as quickly as possible. Be knowledgeable of the main arteries and shortcuts of the patrol area. Avoid possible traffic congestion and highway obstacles. Drivers and witnesses may leave the scene and valuable temporary evidence may be lost if the investigator is unduly delayed.

2.005 Record licence numbers of damaged or suspicious vehicles leaving the scene or parked at or near the scene. Such information may be valuable during follow-up investigation in locating witnesses or a hit-and-run vehicle.

ARRIVAL AT THE SCENE

2.006 Park the police vehicle in a safe, convenient position at the scene. Provide a safeguard for persons and vehicles by utilizing the flashing emergency lights and other safety devices. Bear in mind that there should be easy access to emergency and first aid equipment. Do not position the vehicle so that it might be boxed in by other traffic.

2.007 Care for or make arrangements for immediate care of injured persons.

2.008 Determine whether the accident is a hit-and-run accident and decide upon investigational procedures to be followed.

2.009 Make observations for potentially dangerous results of the accident, for example:

   a. Spilled gasoline
   b. Explosives or other dangerous substances spilled on highway or in loaded vehicle at the scene
   c. Downed electrical wires

2.010   Make arrangements for any additional assistance that might be required such as utility company personnel.

PROTECTION OF THE SCENE

2.011   Place sufficient warning devices on or near the highway approaching the scene and at the scene to warn drivers and ensure orderly and safe passage of traffic. The extent and use of such warning devices depends upon the location and severity of the accident, traffic volume, weather conditions, visibility, terrain and so forth.

2.012   Where a fire hazard exists, such as from spilled gasoline, use caution in placing flares. Ensure that individuals in the area refrain from smoking.

2.013   Restore normal traffic flow as soon as possible. It may be necessary to direct vehicular and pedestrian movements. Detour traffic onto alternate routes when the roadway is blocked, when it is necessary to safeguard the scene or to allow for a detailed on-scene investigation.

2.014   When assistance is required of civilian bystanders in directing traffic, ask those who appear to be responsible, competent and capable of carrying out the task. Do not request civilians to perform duties that are potentially dangerous. Give volunteers specific instructions about what is expected of them and how their task is to be performed.

2.015   Carry out crowd control at the scene in order to protect onlookers and other pedestrians and to facilitate an orderly investigation. Be polite but firm in the instructions given.

THE ON-SCENE INVESTIGATION

2.016   Question drivers and obtain statements in compliance with local legislation and departmental policy.

2.017   Examine and obtain driver's licence data. Where a driver's licence is restricted to operating with certain safety devices, check to see whether the driver had employed the devices stipulated.

2.018   In locating drivers and witnesses, it should be remembered that drivers are quite often near their cars writing down information or inspecting damages. Witnesses are often describing the accident to others and may wish to stand close by when a driver is being questioned. They often speak up, either agreeing or disagreeing with statements made by a driver.

2.019   Interview witnesses either at the scene or during follow-up investigation as warranted by circumstances. Obtain written statements where necessary. Be cautious of information supplied by witnesses who are prejudiced or biased, one who might be trying to gain attention or favor or witnesses who are relatives or friends of a driver suspected of having committed a driving violation.

2.020 Once the on-scene investigation has been completed, ensure that the area is cleared of any dangerous substance deposited as the result of the accident: all debris such as glass and metal fragments are removed; spilled oil is covered with sand or dirt; and flares are removed unless they are specifically required further. Where possible, remove all indications to other motorists that there has been an accident, otherwise a driver's attention might be diverted causing another accident.

Highway

2.021 For the purposes of this text, a *highway* means a *trafficway*.

Trafficway. A trafficway is any land way open to the public as a matter of right or custom for moving persons or property from one place to another.

Roadway. A roadway is that part of a trafficway designed, improved, and ordinarily used for motor vehicle travel or, where various classes of motor vehicle travel or motor vehicles are segregated, that part of a trafficway used by a particular class. Separate roadways may be provided for northbound and southbound traffic or for trucks and automobiles. Exclusions are bridle paths and bicycle paths.

Shoulder. A shoulder is that part of a trafficway contiguous with the roadway for emergency use, for the accommodation of stopped road vehicles, and for lateral support of the roadway structure.[7]

2.022 The investigator must consider the physical conditions of the highway and adjacent properties encountered by the driver involved in an accident. Observations should be made from the driver's line of sight. If necessary, return to the scene on a following day at the same time as the accident occurred.

2.023 Examine an accident scene for:

  a. Obstructions alongside the highway that limit a driver's ability to see existing or potential hazards or traffic-control devices. Particular attention should be given to billboards, cars parked too close to corners, building proximities to highway, hedges, trees, embankments, etc.
  b. Obstructions or defects on the roadway or shoulder which might cause a vehicle to go out of control, e.g., soft shoulders, shoulder lip, potholes, ruts, etc.
  c. Inadequate or improper roadway design, alignment, grade, width of pavement or shoulder, superelevation of curves, etc.

Figure 2-2. Buildings, parked vehicles and improperly placed traffic-control signs can affect a driver's ability to safely approach or enter an intersection.

d. Improperly placed, defective or inadequate traffic-control devices, i.e., traffic lights, stop signs, yield signs, etc.

e. Lack of street lighting. This is particularly important in pedestrian accidents.

f. Glare from fixed lights that impairs a driver's view of traffic-control devices or other traffic, including pedestrians. Elderly persons are generally more seriously affected by glare.[8]

g. Slippery roadway surface caused by inclement weather, spilled oil, warm tar or asphalt, wooden surfaces such as bridges and moisture on dusty pavement or dirt roads.

h. Roadway alignment with position of the sun or oncoming headlights. These conditions can adversely affect a driver's ability to see hazardous or potentially hazardous situations.

2.024 All physical features that can be adjusted to eliminate or minimize accidents, and their existence should be brought to the attention of local highway department officials for remedial action.

Driver

2.025 The physical and mental conditions of drivers and pedestrians can be contributing factors in traffic accidents. Such conditions should be

Figure 2-3. Roadway defects can cause a vehicle to go out of control.

Figure 2-4. When a wheel drops off a pavement lip, the driver may be unable to steer the vehicle onto the roadway; if he oversteers, the vehicle may veer across the highway out of control.

noted and related to the events leading up to the collision and to the collision itself. For example, inattentiveness or deficient eyesight may delay perception of a hazard, and once a hazard is perceived, slow reactions or a physical handicap may delay corrective or evasive action, resulting in a collision.

2.026 *Alcohol and other drug use* impairs a driver's ability to drive a motor vehicle. Persons under the influence of alcohol or a drug are more likely to become involved in a traffic accident than are other drivers.

2.027 The actions of impaired drivers fall into three general classes:

1. Mechanical abnormalities
   a. Failure to dim headlights when meeting oncoming traffic
   b. Driving during darkness without headlights turned on
   c. Failure to signal turns or leaving signal light on after turn completed
   d. Inside vehicle light left on while driving
   e. Excessive use of horn
   f. Problems in putting vehicle into proper gear or driving range, e.g., putting shift into reverse gear when wanting to go forward
   g. Attempting to start car when motor already running
2. Erratic driving
   a. Weaving in and out of driving lane
   b. Driving in wrong lane or wrong direction on one-way street
   c. Driving too fast or too slow
   d. Failure to comply with normally familiar traffic ordinances, e.g., stop signs, yield signs, etc.
3. Traffic accidents
   a. As many as 75 per cent of drivers involved in single-car accidents have been drinking.
   b. A majority of head-on and hit-and-run accidents involve impaired drivers.

2.028 Some symptoms that may be present in the impaired or drinking driver are:

   a. Odor of liquor on driver's breath
   b. Unkempt clothing
   c. Dampness on trousers or clothing
   d. Leaning on objects for support
   e. Incoherent speech
   f. Slow movements
   g. Flushed face or pallor
   h. Provocative attitude
   i. Stumbling or falling

   j. Fumbling for driver's license
   k. Profanity
   l. Sleepiness
  m. Talkative and laughing
   n. Excitement
   o. Crying

2.029 *Attitudes and emotions* are major factors in human behavior. The attitudes of persons who tend to "show off," those who are worried over family or financial problems, impatient, and so on, can contribute to traffic accidents.

2.030 *Judgement* can be related to skills, maturity and experience. A person's ability to make a proper judgement should be investigated when he fails to cope with road conditions or fails to properly analyze illegal or unsafe actions on the part of other highway users.

2.031 *Fatigue or drowsiness* seriously impairs a driver's ability to perceive potential traffic hazards, to control the vehicle and to take evasive action in the face of a hazardous situation. This condition can be inferred from testimony of witnesses that the vehicle was driven at generally slow, uneven speeds; evidence of "stay awake" pills in the vehicle or on the driver's person; the distance of the trip; and other information supplied by passengers or witnesses. Suspect an "asleep" accident when the driver fails to negotiate a curve by driving straight ahead, leaves the roadway and fails to apply brakes just prior to the accident.

2.032 *Carbon monoxide poisoning* is usually characterized by drowsiness, dizziness, headache, confusion and weakness. Carbon monoxide poisoning has several outward symptoms similar to the effects of alcohol or drugs. When carbon monoxide poisoning is suspected, ensure that the victim is given prompt first aid attention.

2.033 *Mind and nerves* play a very important role in a person's ability to perceive hazardous conditions, make proper decisions and coordinate body movements to meet emergent situations. The investigator should examine closely the apparent condition of the mind and nerves of a driver involved in a traffic accident, particularly in the case of a very young or old driver.

2.034 *Sensory conditions,* particularly deficient eyesight or hearing, may prevent or drastically reduce a person's ability to perceive road and traffic hazards. Sight deficiency is often the cause of a driver's failure to see or comprehend the meaning of a traffic-control device such as a stop sign.

2.035 *Driving skills* are necessary in order to drive safely and make the vehicle behave under a variety of conditions. A lack of driving skill often results in a driver losing control of his vehicle during a skid or other vehicle maneuver that would normally be controlled by an experienced driver.

2.036 *Physical limitations* seem to be a contributing factor in a very small percentage of traffic accidents. Drivers with physical disabilities often compensate for their handicap by more cautious driving and also by developing relative driving skills.

2.037 *Maximum visual acuity* takes place in a very small portion of the visual field. The following angles can be used as practical limits:

    a. Cone of clearest vision is 5°.
    b. Limit of fairly clear vision is 10°.

These figures indicate 2.5° and 5° on each side of the centerline of regard. Beyond the 10° boundary is a person's peripheral vision. Studies have shown that some individuals have a peripheral field limited to 60° to 80° on each side, and in some cases limited to 20°. This limited field is sometimes referred to as *tunnel vision.*[9]

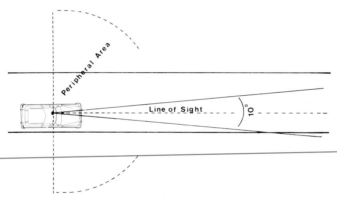

Figure 2-5. Cone of clear vision and normal peripheral view area when looking straight ahead.

2.038 For *peripheral vision* when both eyes are focused forward, the normal driver can see objects 90° or more to each side. These objects, however, are without clear detail or color. This peripheral area is sensitive to motion and brightness and serves the driver with a warning capability.[10]

2.039 *Color blindness* is the situation where an individual cannot or has difficulty in distinguishing some colors, usually red and green. Color blindness may be a factor in accidents or violations involving traffic-control lights.

2.040 *Night blindness* (nyctalopia) is the inability of the eye to adjust to darkness or reduced illumination.[11] Elderly persons are most commonly affected by this condition. Tinted windshields and tinted eyeglasses adversely affect this deficiency in eyesight.

2.041 Various deficiencies such as blackouts or fainting spells, strokes, muscle spasms, heart ailments, epilepsy and others may cause accidents. When these deficiencies are suspected, either by statements of witnesses or as the result of circumstances surrounding the accident, the investigator should seek the advice and assistance of the medical profession in drawing proper conclusions.

2.042 *Reaction time* is the length of time from when a person perceives a given situation to when he reacts to his perception. The reaction time of a driver may properly be referred to as a *perception-reaction* time. When an individual's actual reaction time is unknown, a reaction time of 0.75 second may be used for investigational purposes.

2.043 *Simple reaction* is a response to an expected situation, such as responding to a traffic light. Approximately .55 second is required for this response.[12]

2.044 *Complex reaction* is a reaction involving a decision, such as when the driver has to decide quickly whether to step on the accelerator or the brake pedal. Reaction time in these situations may be as high as 3 seconds or more.

2.045 Simple reaction time involving an uncomplex response such as touching the horn may be as low as 0.25 second. The reaction time required to apply the brake pedal after a situation is perceived is from 0.50 to 0.70 second for most people.[13]

2.046 Older drivers have longer reaction times than do young drivers. At about forty years of age, simple reaction times begin to increase to the extent that at about seventy years of age, a driver's reaction time may increase by as much as 50 percent.[14]

2.047 In addition to age, the type of situation or stimulus, that is, strong or weak, the driver's health or physical condition and habits developed through experience and training have a bearing on his reaction time.

2.048 In cases where it is necessary to establish the identity of a driver, as in cases where there are no witnesses to the accident, all occupants are killed or where occupants do not admit who was driving, the investigator should:

    a. Note the color of the clothing, particularly upper clothing such as shirts or jackets, and other noticeable features of persons involved. There are cases where witnesses who saw erratic driving of a vehicle prior to an accident also noted the color or kind of clothing worn by the driver or other features, for example, eyeglasses or color of hair.

    b. Take fingerprints from steering wheel when possible and fingerprints of individuals involved for comparison purposes where permitted by law.

Figure 2-6. A shoe may be forced from a foot upon impact. A shoe left in an automobile may establish the seating position of the person who was wearing it. Identification of a driver may also be assisted by matching shoe sole with accelerator, clutch and brake pedal imprints.

   c. Examine brake, clutch and accelerator pedals and shoe soles for matching imprints. Not only may the driver's identity be established in this way, but the last pedal to be touched with the shoe may be determined.

   d. Check for personal injuries that would be compatible with a particular seating arrangement.

Pedestrians

2.049 Accident causes for pedestrians are generally the same as for drivers. The investigator must, however, take a special interest in specific items when investigating accidents involving pedestrians.

   a. *Age.* Elderly people are likely to have deficient eyesight, hearing and agility and are prone to becoming confused in traffic.

   b. *Children* are likely to run into the path of a car during play, particularly in their own neighborhood, where they have a false sense of security.

c. *Attitude.* A great number of pedestrians do not consider a driver's reaction time and the distance required to change the course of direction or stop the vehicle.

d. *Judgement.* Elderly people, the mentally deficient and very young children often fail to make a proper judgement concerning traffic movement and traffic-control devices. Improper judgement sometimes leads to confusion and consequently an irrational or unexpected act.

d. *Clothing.* Dark clothing during darkness makes it very difficult for a pedestrian to be seen. Notes should be made of a pedestrian's hair color and the type and color of clothing worn in order that they might be matched to material found on a suspect vehicle.

Weather Conditions

2.050 Darkness and adverse weather or atmospheric conditions and combinations of these can seriously reduce visibility.

a. *Rain* can reduce visibility, particularly if it is a heavy rain where windshield wipers are unable to keep the windshield clear.

b. *Snow* can freeze on the windshield or on windshield wiper blades, resulting in an unclear windshield and obstructed view. An inadequate or malfunctioning defroster can be a contributing factor in this problem.

c. *Fog* is most usually found in low areas. A driver proceeding into a fog patch often slows down suddenly. This sudden deceleration is often a factor in rear-end collisions and can cause a following driver to swerve into an opposing lane to avoid a rear-end collision.

d. *Smoke,* like fog, is often found in patches, although not necessarily in low areas. Smoke may be blown across the highway where there is an adjacent lumber mill or other similar industry, or where grass, brush or waste is being burned. As in fog, drivers often slow down suddenly in smoke patches, with the same dangers being prevalent.

e. *Darkness* can be a contributing factor in accidents involving vehicles with deficient lights or pedestrians wearing dark clothing.

f. *Sun.* The investigator should always note the position of the sun in relation to a driver's direction of travel and his seated position in the vehicle. Driving directly toward the sun as well as sun glare off water, tin rooftops and other objects that reflect sunlight can impair a driver's view of traffic-control devices and other highway traffic.

Vehicle Inspection

2.051 A vehicle inspection should determine whether the conditions found contributed to the cause of the accident or resulted because of the accident. A vehicle defect may have been a contributing factor, and therefore, the investigator should carry out as thorough an investigation at the scene as circumstances and his experience permit. A follow-up and more detailed inspection may be conducted at a subsequent and more suitable location.

2.052 In-depth inspections or examinations of such items as braking systems or headlight filaments should normally be carried out by persons with the expertise to qualify them to testify as an expert witness, for example, mechanical engineers and laboratory technicians.

2.053 Vehicle inspections should cover the following points with a view toward relating their condition, position and existence to the accident:

    a. Accelerator
    b. Brakes
    c. Door locks
    d. Exhaust system
    e. Gadgets, that is, steering wheel knob, window or windshield stickers, ornaments both inside and outside of vehicle, etc.
    f. Gear shift lever
    g. Horn
    h. Lights, e.g., headlights, taillights, signal lights, clearance lights, reflectors, etc.
    i. Loads and binders
    j. Mirrors
    k. Radio
    l. Shocks and springs
    m. Speedometer
    n. Steering
    o. Tires and wheels
    p. Windows and windshield
    q. Windshield wipers

2.054 *Accelerator.* Operate the accelerator to check for a malfunction where it might have been a contributing factor in a vehicle going out of control. Examine the linkage from the accelerator pedal through to the carburetor. Make both a visual and a manual examination. To conduct the manual examination, grasp the throttle linkage and open and close the throttle several times to check for obstructions or bindings that might have caused the throttle to stick open or otherwise malfunction. Check visually for bent linkage rods, worn connections, defective retrieval spring or evidence of binding that could have caused the accelerator to malfunction.

2.055 *Brakes.* Examine the braking system in an effort to determine whether brakes were deficient prior to the collision. This is particularly

Figure 2-7. Master cylinder and fluid reservoir, *A*. Power brake unit, *B*.

important if there are no signs of braking on the roadway leading up to the collision point when there is no apparent reason for the driver to have not applied the brakes.

2.056   Brake failure usually occurs as the result of brake fluid loss; there are a number of tests that can be carried out to determine the cause and the general condition of the braking system without removing the wheels and other parts of the system.

2.057   Brake fluid lines may crack through normal wear and tear, be broken by outside forces, such as rocks or collision, or be worn by rubbing against a wheel or other vehicle part. If brake line failure is evident, check roadway leading up to the point of collision for evidence of fluid loss caused through the application of the brakes. Similarly, the collision point should be examined for fluid loss that would indicate fluid lines were broken and fluid was lost as a direct result of the collision.

2.058   If there is low pedal reserve, determine whether full brake pedal reserve can be restored and, if so, how many strokes are required to restore it to normal. This could very well have a bearing on why brakes were not activated because of the time necessary to restore braking efficiency by pumping the brake pedal. Check the fluid level in the master cylinder. Inspect all fluid lines from the master cylinder to all wheels. Inspect the

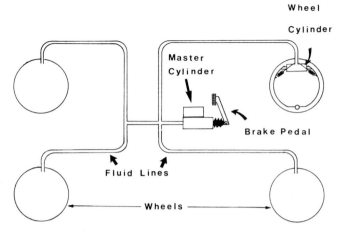

Figure 2-8. Brake fluid line system.

inner side of each wheel for fluid stains. If stains are evident, the wheel cylinder in that wheel should be examined for a leak. Stains usually indicate that the wheel cylinder has been defective or leaking for a long period of time. Fresh fluid on the inside of a wheel indicates a recent break in the wheel cylinder or at least that the brakes were recently applied.

Figure 2-9. Fluid stains on inside of wheel indicate that wheel cylinder may be leaking.

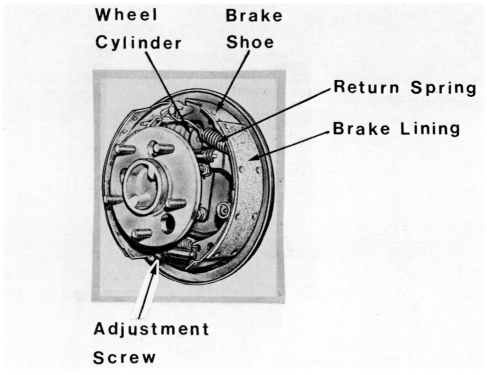

Wheel Cylinder

Brake Shoe

Return Spring

Brake Lining

Adjustment Screw

Figure 2-10. Brake wheel assembly.

2.059 Wet or damp brake linings caused by water, grease or oil often cause braking deficiencies such as maladjustment of the individual brake on each wheel. When there is evidence of brake maladjustment, for example, pulling to the right or left, hard pedal effort, or brake fading, check immediately for wet or damp brake drums and tires and water on the roadway leading up to the point of collision. A later examination can be made of brake linings for oil or grease.

2.060 When brakes are applied constantly over extended periods of time, for example on long steep hills, the brake linings become hot and may result in "fading" or loss of full braking efficiency without the usual evidence of brake failure available to the investigator.

2.061 In a "parked-runaway" accident, check the adequacy of the emergency or hand brake of the vehicle involved.

2.062 Some modern vehicles are equipped with anti-skid brakes which, upon hard application, effect a 10 to 20 percent slip ratio in an action similar to pumping the brakes on and off. Complete wheel stoppage does not occur; therefore, skid marks are not evident. This system works on the basis of electric sensors attached to a computer. The computer is programmed so that when the rear wheels approach lockup, the amount of

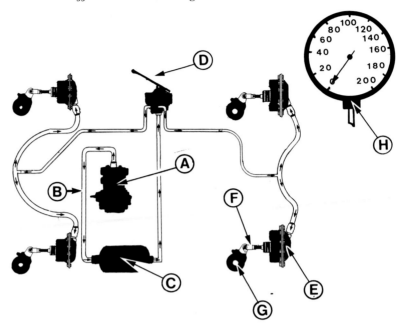

Figure 2-11. Typical air brake system. Air is pumped by the compressor, *A*, through line *B* to the reservoir, *C*. Air pressure in the reservoir is indicated on an air pressure gauge, *H*. Air pressure from the reservoir is available at the foot brake valve and is released upon application of the brake pedal, *D*, through lines to the brake chambers, *E*. The brake chamber pushrods, *F*, move the slack adjusters, *G*. The slack adjusters rotate the brake cams, which force brake shoes against brake drums.

hydraulic fluid in the lines to the rear brakes is controlled so that the slip ratio is maintained. When there are no skid marks, the investigator should determine whether the vehicle was equipped with an anti-skid braking system. Caution must be used in attempting to determine initial speeds of vehicles so equipped. In such instances, it may be necessary to use the momentum equation in calculating speed.

2.063 *Power-assisted brakes* consist of a diaphragm located between the master cyclinder and the brake pedal. The diaphragm receives vacuum from the intake manifold and provides a boost or assist to the pressure applied to the brake pedal by the driver. To check the adequacy of a power-assisted braking system, carry out the normal hydraulic braking system inspection procedures but include the power-assist unit as well.

2.064 An *air brake system* consists of five main components:
  1. Compressor
  2. Reservoir
  3. Foot valve (brake pedal)
  4. Brake chambers
  5. Brake shoes and drums

Figure 2-12. Air brake rear axle assembly. Air pressure is delivered through air line, *A*, into brake chamber, *B*. Brake chamber pushrod, *C*, moves slack adjuster, *D*, which in turn rotates the brake cam, *E*.

The compressor pumps air into the reservoir, where it is stored. The foot valve draws the compressed air from the reservoir when the brake is applied. Upon brake application, the compressed air is transferred through a series of lines and valves to the brake chambers, transferring the force exerted by the compressed air to mechanical linkages and the brake shoes and drums.

2.065 An air pressure gauge indicating the air pressure in the main reservoir system is usually mounted on the dashboard of the vehicle cab. Local legislation usually governs the minimum and maximum amounts of air pressure required for vehicle operation.

2.066 Slack adjusters (Fig. 2-12D) take up the slack in the brake linkages. If slack adjusters are not properly adjusted, braking efficiency can be substantially reduced or totally ineffective.

2.067 When possible, an on-scene air brake system examination should include:
   a. Check of reservoir pressure
   b. Pushrod travel on all chambers
   c. Audible air leaks
   d. Damaged or broken lines and connections

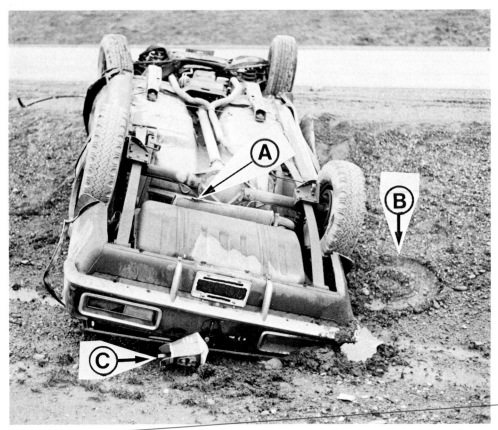

Figure 2-13. Examination of an overturned vehicle reveals vehicle defects such as defective muffler, A. Wheel imprint at B shows the direction in which the vehicle rolled. Empty beer case at C indicates a possible liquor involvement.

2.068 In situations where a vehicle is badly damaged or where a detailed technical examination of the braking system is required, the investigator should obtain the assistance of a qualified mechanic.

2.069 The *exhaust system* carries engine exhaust from the exhaust manifold to the rear of the vehicle in the case of passenger vehicles or to other outside positions in the case of many commercial vehicles. Engine exhaust contains carbon monoxide, which is a colorless, odorless, poisonous gas. This gas can escape through damaged or corroded parts of the exhaust system and improperly fitted connections. The gas frequently finds its way into the passenger compartment through holes in the underportions of the vehicle body caused by corrosion, trunk openings or ill-fitting floor matting and interior upholstery.

2.070 Inhalation of carbon monoxide in the form of fumes from automobile engine exhaust deprives the blood, and consequently the brain,

Figure 2-14. An overturned vehicle provides an opportunity to examine for mechanical conditions and what happened on the roadway. Slide marks on tires at *A* and *B* indicate that wheels were locked on roadway. Underbody is corroded at *C*, leaving an opening into the passenger compartment. Steering linkage, *D*, and brake fluid lines, *E*, can be inspected. For vehicle placement on highway prior to overturn, roadway gouges or chip marks could be matched up to damaged body part at *F*, and roadway scrapes or scratches could be matched up to scratches on gas tank at *G*.

of sufficient oxygen. Severe exposure may bring death by asphyxiation. Most victims, however, sink into a deep coma that is usually followed by confusion and delirium.[15]

2.071 Some automobile air conditioners do not draw in clean, fresh outside air during *maximum cooling* setting. Rather, they recirculate air within the vehicle and at the same time suck in carbon monoxide gas through openings in the vehicle body.

2.072 Drivers may be affected by carbon monoxide in exhaust fumes from other vehicles, particularly when driving with windows open in heavy traffic.[16]

2.073 *Fires.* The traffic accident investigator may not have the training nor the expertise to conduct an investigation which, by itself, will lead to a definite conclusion that a vehicle fire was accidental or that it was deliberately caused. He must, however, be able to recognize suspicious circumstances that would warrant additional investigation by himself to gather

Figure 2-15. Body erosion allows exhaust fumes or carbon monoxide to penetrate passenger compartment.

evidence that would allow an experienced arson investigator to draw proper conclusions as to the origin and cause of the fire, or recognize the need to request the immediate assistance of an arson investigator.

2.074   When a vehicle is destroyed or damaged by fire, particularly in cases of single-car accidents, for example, rollovers, running off the roadway, and so forth, the investigator should consider the possibility of deliberate setting of the fire. Motives for destroying a vehicle by fire are many:

   a. Vehicle damaged in accident and owner wishes to have it replaced by insurance rather than having it repaired.
   b. Vehicle in poor condition and too costly to repair.
   c. Owner wishes to collect money from insurance on vehicle to pay a debt, lien or mortgage.
   d. Vehicle destroyed by a spouse because of jealousy, revenge or other domestic problem.

Figure 2-16. White flame, *A*, indicates extreme heat such as that caused by a fire accelerant. Gas tank cover is removed, *B*. Can, *C*, used to carry gasoline siphoned from gas tank with hose, *D*.

e. Vehicle destroyed to cover up some other type of crime or evidence, e.g., hit-and-run, blood in vehicle, bullet hole, etc.
f. Vehicle destroyed by employee-driver to cover up negligence in repairing vehicle or careless driving.
g. Vehicle destroyed by a mentally deranged owner, driver or other person.

2.075 When arson is suspected, as much information as possible should be obtained before the owner or driver is approached for a statement.

2.076 Vehicles burned because of accident, that is, smouldering cigarette, short circuit, and so on, are seldom destroyed. These types of fires are normally of a low heat intensity. In cases where a fire accelerant such as gasoline or an incendiary device is used, considerable damage is normally sustained because of very intense heat. The roof, trunk lid, hood and seat and axle springs sag noticeably. Window glass and soft metals such as those found in radiators, fuel pumps, carburetors and lead used in body repairs melt, losing their original shape.

2.077 The immediate scene of a vehicle fire should be examined for fire starters and accelerants such as match packages and gasoline or other accelerant containers, as well as devices used to extract or syphon gasoline from the vehicle fuel tank.

2.078   The fuel line or lines from the gas tank through to the fuel pump and carburetor should be examined for breaks, disconnections and other signs of tampering. If, for example, a line were disconnected before a fire was ignited and then reconnected after the vehicle was burned, soot and other debris caused by the fire would show signs of disturbance. Similarly, if a gas tank cap were removed and then replaced after the fire, there would not likely be any sign of burning on the cap.

2.079   The places that an accidental fire under the hood usually starts are in the areas of the fuel pump, carburetor and electrical wiring. Evidence of a fire starting at places on or about the engine that cannot be traced to these sources would indicate that the fire was probably started by using an accelerant.

2.080   When an accelerant is poured or thrown around the inside of a vehicle, the saturated portions of fabric generally burn into a fine ash because of fast burning and intense heat. The actual path or manner in which the accelerant was distributed may be seen upon close examination of the ash trails.

2.081   When a liquid accelerant is used, some of it may drip onto the ground. Ground saturation may be evident, or an odor may be noticeable that would indicate saturation. In these instances, soil samples should be collected for analysis purposes.

2.082   Particular care should be taken to look for rolls of cloth or paper ashes that might have been saturated with an accelerant and placed under a seat, in the glove compartment or trunk of the car or in some other place. In most instances, the ashes of the roll of cloth or paper very closely retain the original shape, and the immediate area suffers intense heat damage. All burned areas should be examined closely to ascertain the degree or intensity of burning in specific areas. It may be found that the greatest degree of burning or heat was in a place where only an accelerant could have been responsible.

2.083   The absence of any indication of an accelerant does not necessarily mean that an accelerant was not used. Accelerants may be consumed or destroyed by fire or, in the case of a liquid, may have totally evaporated prior to the beginning of the investigation.

2.084   Examine all windows to determine whether they were closed, partially open or open. Fire requires oxygen to burn. If windows were open during adverse weather conditions, the possibility would exist that they were opened to facilitate burning.

2.085 A short circuit usually melts the strands of wire and forms a small bead of metal on the ends of the wires. Wires that are cut do not have this bead but show a sharp, clean separation.

2.086 The investigation should determine whether all usual automobile parts and articles such as radio, aerial, mirrors, spare wheel, tape deck, and so on are still with the vehicle or whether they were removed before the vehicle was burned.

2.087 As many photographs as might be necessary should be taken of all damaged areas, and if at all possible, in color. It is far better to have too many photographs than not enough. Photographs should be taken of all evidence from various angles and should be taken before evidence is touched, moved or removed from the vehicle.

2.088 The *gear shift lever* position may corroborate other evidence regarding the speed of a vehicle prior to a collision. In automatic shift vehicles, *low* range indicates a slower speed, whereas *drive* or *high* ranges indicate the possibility of higher speeds.

2.089 In manual shift vehicles, for example, large commercial trucks or farm tractors, unless the investigator is totally familiar with the shifting mechanism, he should have the gear shift lever position explained to him by a competent operator.

2.090 The investigator should bear in mind that the gear shift lever might have moved to a position other than the original position as a result of the collision.

2.091 *Horn.* The adequacy of the horn is important in accidents involving pedestrians, pullout and sideswipe accidents and all other cases where a horn warning might have prevented a collision.

2.092 *Lights and reflectors.* Examine headlight switch to determine whether it was in the *on* or *off* position. Check all lights. If a light is not broken but does not work, check to see if electrical wires attached to the light are broken or whether the light has shorted in some manner as the result of the collision.

2.093 Determine the position of the high-low beam switch and whether the high beam light and indicator was working. This is important in accidents involving oncoming vehicles being forced off the roadway because of *bright* lights, accidents involving pedestrians and accidents attributed to a driver overdriving his headlights.

2.094 In cases involving signals by a driver, determine the position of the signal switch lever and whether signal indicator lights were functioning.

2.095 Check brake lights in all cases of rear-end collisions and other accidents that can be attributed to a driver's sudden braking or deceleration ahead of a following vehicle.

2.096 Most commercial and oversize vehicles require clearance lights and reflectors at their outer extremities. Accidents involving these vehicles should be checked for this equipment, particularly in cases of sideswipe and intersection accidents.

2.097 Where it is important to the investigation to determine whether a light was on or off immediately prior to or at the time of collision, the lamp should be removed from the vehicle and an examination of the filament made by an expert.

2.098 *Loads* on vehicles may contribute to accidents.
    a. A load may shift, throwing a vehicle out of control.
    b. A load or part of a load may fall from a vehicle because of inadequate binders or other constraining devices, causing damage or injury to other highway users.
    c. A driver's view or movements may be obstructed because of the manner in which the load is placed in or on the vehicle.
    d. A load that extends too far to the sides, top or rear may strike objects, i.e., bridges, utility poles, etc., or other highway users.
    e. A load may be so high as to throw the vehicle off balance by displacing the center of mass.

2.099 *Mirror* positioning is very important in pullout, sideswipe and back-up accidents. Examine inside and outside mirror positions in relation to the driver's seated height.

2.100 *Radio.* Determine whether the car radio was turned on or off. If on, the station it was tuned to should be noted. The driver or passenger should be able to recall what was being broadcast at the time of the accident. This information can be useful in determining the exact time of the accident when this information is essential and not otherwise available. Additionally, a radio being played at high volume might be the reason a driver did not hear a siren or horn.

2.101 *Seat belts* and *door locks* should be examined for adjustment and condition in all cases in which an occupant is thrown from a vehicle. Additionally, it should be determined whether a seat belt was worn in all cases of serious injury or death, inasmuch as this can be a factor in injuries sustained. Examine the condition of restraining systems, that is, seat and shoulder belts, for condition of webbing, buckles, locking retractors and inertia reels.

2.102 An investigator should look for obvious indicators in establishing whether or not seat belts were used:*

---

* Reproduced with permission of Marion Oversby, Coordinator, Traffic Accident Research Unit, British Columbia Research Council, Vancouver, British Columbia.

Figure 2-17. Windshield damage with a spider web pattern and an outward bulge indicates contact from the inside of the automobile. This type of damage is common when a driver's or passenger's head strikes the windshield; damage may assist in determining seating arrangement of occupants when related to injuries sustained.

Not Used
1. Belts buckled together in front of, behind or under seat.
2. Shoulder belt is stowed away.
3. Belts not accessible, e.g., pushed down behind seat.
4. Sometimes car deformation as the result of impact intrudes and anchorage is compressed against the seat. If the belt was worn, could it have retracted? If not and it is not visible, it was probably not worn.
5. If there is a windshield impact, perhaps a spider web pattern and bulge, from the inside of the vehicle, it is likely the seat belt was not used.
6. If the steering wheel was damaged by the driver, suspect non-use.
7. If an occupant was ejected from the vehicle, suspect incorrect or non-use of the seat belt.
8. If the upper dashboard (instrument panel) was damaged by an occupant, suspect non-use.
9. Check the injuries of the occupant for injuries compatible with non-use of a seat belt.

Belt Used
1. Belts jammed in the *out* position due to side intrusion preventing belt retraction.

2. Belt webbing was cut to release an occupant. When investigation reveals that a belt is cut, attempt to determine who cut the belt and the reason for it. In many cases, ambulance attendants or other persons present at the scene cut a seat belt to release an occupant.

3. When an occupant remains in an original seating position and his injuries are less than what would be expected from the severity of the accident.

4. Check the injury diagnosis. People wearing lap and shoulder belts show a decreased likelihood of head injury. Belt-associated injuries from shoulder restraints are rib fractures, sternal fracture and clavicle fracture. Seat restraints may result in such injuries as bruises on the chest and abdomen. When the torso is restrained, limbs are still mobile and shins may be bruised from striking the steering column, underneath the dashboard, etc.

5. A laboratory examination may detect belt stretch, which might indicate seat belt use.

6. Marks on the buckle tab may show if the belt was used on a regular basis.

2.103   The *speedometer* reading should be noted and recorded. Generally, the reading is zero. Occasionally, however, the needle sticks at the speed

Figure 2-18. Speedometer reading may indicate speed at time of impact.

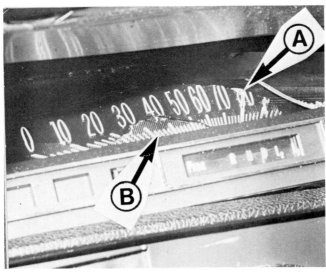

Figure 2-19. On impact, a speedometer needle may bounce to a reading higher than the actual original speed of the vehicle, *A,* and be locked in that position by a broken speedometer face glass, *B,* or by damaged internal speedometer parts.

registered at the time of collision because of impact damage. This evidence corroborates in some cases other evidence of speed such as statements made by witnesses. A stuck speedometer reading should be used with caution unless it can be established that the needle did not bounce and stick at that position at the time of collision.

2.104 *Steering.* A worn or defective steering assembly may cause loss of vehicle control. Check condition of steering assembly by turning the steering wheel as fully as possible in each direction. Quick, short turns on the steering wheel often indicate loose or worn parts. An examination of all steering parts for continuity and of steering column for loose mountings should also be made. An examination can be made most effectively when a tow truck lifts the vehicle in removing it from the accident scene.

2.105 When a power-assisted steering system is involved, check for broken or disconnected hoses; drive belt for tension, slippage or breakage; and pump reservoir for fluid. If power steering belt is missing, check engine compartment or the roadway leading to the point of collision for the belt or its remnants. Belt breakage may have caused loss of steering and braking control.

2.106 Raise and rotate each wheel separately to check for binding. Check for wheel bearing play by grasping either side of the tire of a raised wheel with both hands (one on each side) and attempting to move the wheel in and out. Worn or loose bearings can cause steering difficulty, particularly at high speeds.

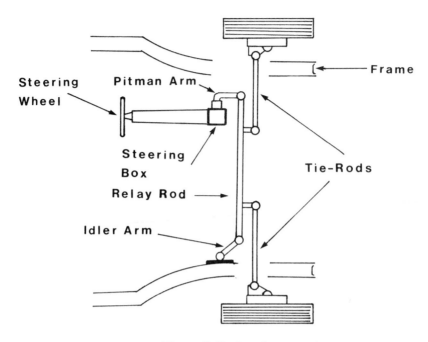

Figure 2-20. Steering assembly.

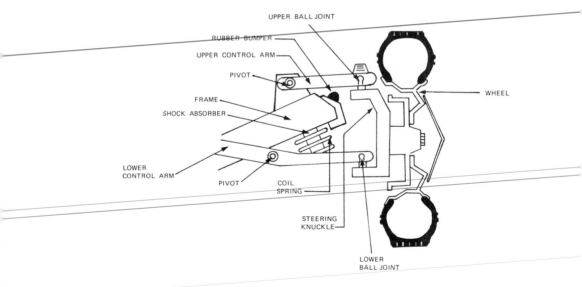

Figure 2-21

Figure 2-22. A power steering examination should include an inspection of the hydraulic pump, *A*, the hydraulic pump drive belt, *B*, and all hoses, *C*.

2.107   Damaged or improper wheel alignment causes a vehicle to steer hard, cause it to pull to one side or the other and may cause the vehicle to wander on the roadway. Worn tires often indicate improper wheel alignment and front suspension problems (*see* Fig. 2-38).

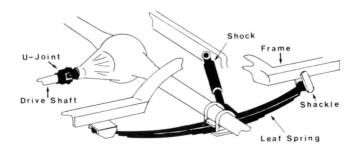

Figure 2-23

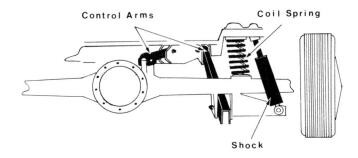

Figure 2-24

2.108 Check the free play of the steering wheel. Steering wheel play in excess of approximately one inch is a possible indication of worn or defective steering linkage or steering box.

2.109 If there is evidence of rear wheel displacement or improper alignment, check rear axle positioning arms and/or struts, axle and drive shaft for breakage or broken or worn supports.

2.110 *Tires.* There are three basic types of tires:
   a. Bias-ply tires (Fig. 2-26)
   b. Bias-belted tires (Fig. 2-27)
   c. Radial tires (Fig. 2-28)

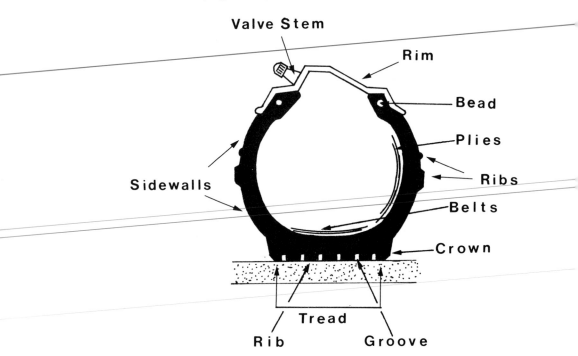

Figure 2-25. Parts of tire.

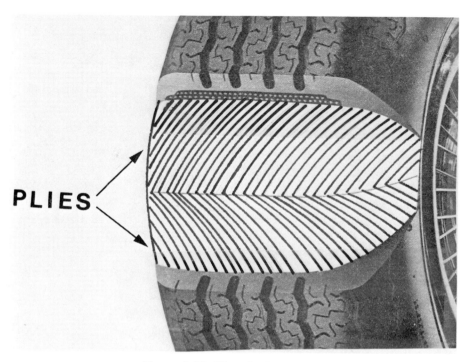

PLIES

Figure 2-26. Bias-ply tire construction.

BELTS

FABRIC

Figure 2-27. Bias-belted tire construction.

Figure 2-28. Radial-ply tire construction.

2.111   *Bias-ply tires* are constructed with polyester, rayon or nylon plies, and in some cases other fabrics. Each ply is placed in a position diagonal to the ply on top of or underneath it. The fabric is placed on the bias at an angle of approximately 30° to 40° to the circumference line.

2.112   A *bias-belted tire* is considered to be a tire that is midway in construction between a bias-ply tire and a radial tire. A bias-belted tire is a bias-ply tire with a pre-formed "belt" of fabric and/or steel belts placed around the circumference between the tread and the bias plies.

2.113   In *radial tire* construction, the fabric plies lead directly from bead to bead at 90° perpendicular to the circumference or rotational line. There are also continuous steel and fabric belts around the circumference under the tread.

2.114   Radial tires should not be mixed with other types of tires on a vehicle. Because of their particular construction, the sidewalls of a *bias*-type tire curl and tuck under when driven into curves at high speeds (Fig. 2-29). When this occurs, only a small portion of the tread is in contact with the roadway and, depending on speed, the sidewall itself may come into contact with the roadway (Fig. 2-30). When the tire tread distorts in this way, the vehicle turns less than it should under normal steering conditions. This action is referred to as *slip angle*. In the case of a bias-constructed tire, the slip angle is extensive. Because of the construction of *radial* tires, the

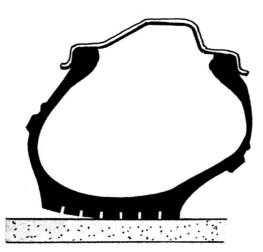

Figure 2-29. Bias-ply tire cornering distortion. Note the inside tire lift.

tread stays in a flat *full contact* position on the roadway, the slip angle is practically eliminated and they react in a positive way to steering (Fig. 2-31). Because of the individual and unique reactions to stress such as cornering and steering, a mix of bias and radial tires on a vehicle can cause a loss of vehicle control.

2.115 The sidewalls of a bias-type tire are constructed very sturdily and can withstand extreme abuse. Radial sidewalls, however, are generally much thinner and are more liable to be cut or damaged when scraping curbs, striking rocks, and so forth and can be damaged by tire chains. Similarly, their sidewalls are more prone to deterioration and subsequent failure because of the inherent longer life of their tread and consequent longer use.

2.116 When a tire suffers air loss, it is important to determine whether the loss occurred prior to or as a result of the collision. Prior air loss can be a contributing factor to a vehicle going out of control. When a tire is found to be flat at a collision scene and there are no roadway marks indicating an air pressure loss leading up to the point of impact, check the tire closely for damage before vehicles are moved, if at all possible. This examination should attempt to determine what damaged the tire or otherwise caused the loss of air pressure.

2.117 If loss of air pressure is caused by damage such as a cut or tear, attempt to determine what caused the damage, for example, broken body part puncturing the tire (Fig. 2-33), foreign objects on the roadway, and so on. Where a tire loses air pressure because of cuts or holes resulting from the collision, the damage should be matched to the object or part that caused it. Such objects may be found on either vehicle involved or any

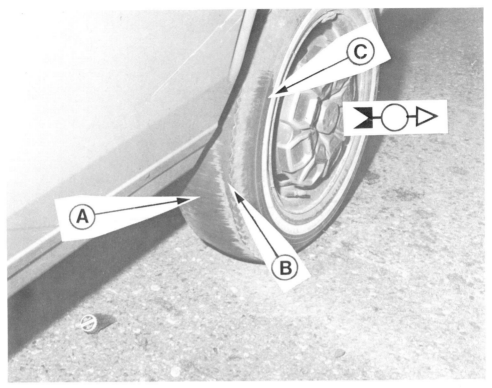

Figure 2-30. Under tremendous sideways force, a tire may slide sideways as indicated at *A* and *B*. If the force is great enough, particularly in the case of a bias-ply tire, the tire may roll or tuck under, and the sidewall may come into contact with the roadway as indicated at *C*.

other item that the vehicle might have come into contact with. In these cases, such matching evidence eliminates any argument or suggestion that the tire was damaged or that it lost air pressure before impact.

2.118   Tires should be checked for fabric or rubber deterioration, tread wear, breaks in casing, cuts, valve stem breakage, nails, glass or other foreign objects embedded in tire tread, particularly in the tire tread grooves, tread separation, bead failure and general condition for wear. Abnormal tire wear may be traced to overall vehicle neglect, which in turn might be traced to the underlying reason that the driver was not able to properly control his vehicle.

2.119   An underinflated tire overheats very rapidly. As heat increases, it melts the tire rubber and weakens tire fabrics. Under these circumstances, particularly on a long trip or travel at high speeds, the tire may burst. Tire tread wear indicates that a tire has been operated underinflated or over-inflated. In accidents where tire failure appears to be a contributing factor, examine the air pressure of all remaining tires to determine whether the

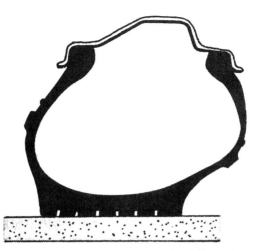

Figure 2-31. Radial-ply tire cornering distortion. Note the full tread contact with roadway.

driver habitually operated on underinflated tires. An underinflated tire may pull loose from the rim on rough roads, striking potholes or driving into curves at high speeds. As the tire is pulled loose from the rim, air loss results, causing loss of vehicle control.

2.120   Poor quality recaps on tires may become loose and fall or tear away from the casing, causing difficulty in vehicle control. When a tire indicates this type of failure, the highway should be examined for tire tread frag-

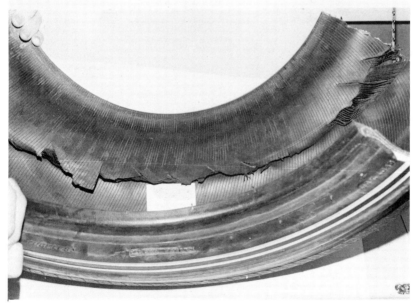

Figure 2-32. Rim damage to tire caused by operating on underinflated tire.

Figure 2-33. Air pressure loss caused from a tire puncture by a broken body part during collision.

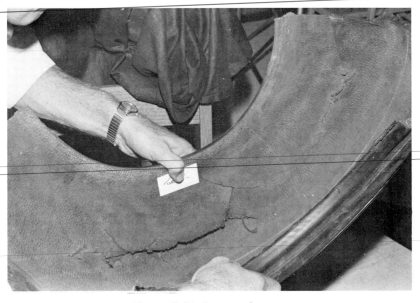

Figure 2-34. Impact damage.

Figure 2-35. Tire tread wear indicator. When a tire is worn to the extent that two or more adjacent grooves form a smooth band, the tire should be replaced.

Figure 2-36. Tire tread wear on edges, *A* and *B*, is caused by underinflation. Tire inspection should include an examination for various deflation causes such as nail puncture, *C*.

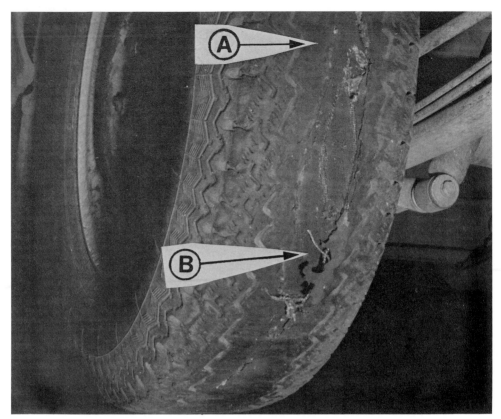

Figure 2-37. Center tread wear, *A*, is caused by overinflation. Note outward directional thrust of tire fabrics at *B*, which indicates a burst or blowout because of thin, weakened tread and plies.

Figure 2-38. Tire tread worn more on one side than the other indicates improper wheel alignment.

Figure 2-39. Bald, worn-out tire. No tread or drainage grooves are left. While traction on dry surfaces may be good, the coefficient of friction on wet surfaces is very poor.

Figure 2-40. Abrasion to part of front-end suspension by oversize tire. Tire wall becomes weak, resulting in tire failure.

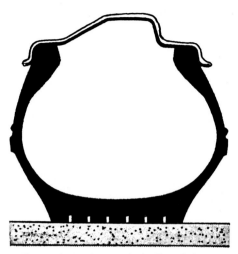

Figure 2-41. Properly inflated tire.

ments leading up to the collision point to determine whether the tire damage or failure occurred before or resulted from collision.

2.121   When driven at high speeds, winter or mud grip tires overheat more readily on hard surfaces because of their heavy, thick rubber tread construction. Therefore, they are more susceptible to blowouts because of rubber and fabric failures than are regular highway tires when driven on hard surfaces.

2.122   When it is necessary to remove a tire from the wheel rim to conduct a deeper analysis of tire failure, mark the tire and rim in such a way that

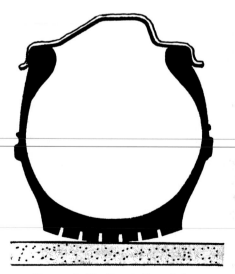

Figure 2-42. Overinflated tire.

Figure 2-43. Underinflated tire.

any tire damage may be related to rim damage or defects after the tire has been removed.

2.123 *Wheels.* Loose wheel lug nuts allow the rim to move back and forth and cause lug nut holes to become elliptical. Lugs eventually wear through and break off. When this happens, a vehicle may go out of control and overturn.

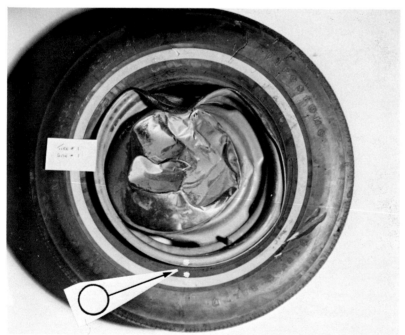

Figure 2-44. Tire and rim marked so that tire and rim damages may be related after tire is removed.

Figure 2-45. Loose lug nuts can lead to wheel failure. Note broken lug and elliptical nut holes.

Figure 2-46. Contact damage suffered to windshield showing radial, *A*, and circular, *B*, cracks in glass.

Figure 2-47. Windshield damage caused by an indirect force (induced damage) generally makes at least two sets of parallel cracks crossing each other in a checkerboard fashion.

2.124 The *windshield and windows* of a vehicle involved in an accident should be examined to determine whether or not their condition did or could have contributed to the accident. Dust, dirt, ice, snow, mud and stickers on windshields or windows obstruct view. Interior fog or conden-

Figure 2-48. Stone impact damage.

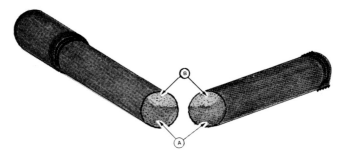

Figure 2-49. Example of broken tie-rod. Note discoloration of old crack, *A*, and shiny, gritty appearance of new break, *B*.

sation or a heavy smoke film on the inside of a windshield can obscure a driver's view. This is particularly true when all windows are closed, not allowing the condensation to dissipate. Under these conditions, when meeting oncoming headlights at night or other bright lights, visibility can be very limited. In such cases, determine the condition of the windshield defroster and whether it was in operation and whether vent windows were open so as to allow fresh air into the driver's compartment.

2.125 The cause of chips, gouges or cracks in a windshield should be determined. A damaged windshield or windows can block a driver's view of other traffic on the highway and cause glare from sunlight, headlights or other bright lights, which also obstructs a driver's view. When these conditions are suspected, the driver's seated height should be established and his sight line related to the windshield damage.

2.126 The positions of all windows, including air vent windows, should be examined as to whether they were open, partially closed or closed. This information can be useful in the event a reason given for the accident is that an object or insect entered the vehicle, striking or distracting the driver, or that a siren or horn of another vehicle was not heard.

2.127 A *broken metal part* should be examined to determine whether it might have contributed to the accident through weakness or breakage. These examinations should pay particular attention to steering, drive shaft, braking and wheel assemblies and any other metal part such as the windshield wiper assembly that, due to the particular type of operation, might have malfunctioned because of breakage or weakness.

2.128 Broken metal has a gritty or rough surface. Old breaks or cracks such as those that often occur as the result of metal fatigue are discolored. New breaks give a shiny appearance. A combination of discoloration and shiny metal in a break usually indicates an old crack and a fresh or recent break. If a part is broken as the result of impact, the part normally shows damage where it was struck.

2.129 When metal fatigue, breakage or damage caused from stress requires examination, a metallurgist or mechanical engineer should be consulted. Examination and analysis should be conducted to determine why a particular part failed and how much force was required to cause the damage or failure. Similar examinations can be made on plastics, glass and other materials.

ACCIDENT INVESTIGATION GUIDE AND REPORT

REFERENCES						FATAL ☐		P.I. ☐		P.D. ☐

LOCATION		NUMBER OR INTERSECTION	

CITY		STATE/PROV.	DAY		TIME	
				19		am / pm

VEH. No.	YEAR	MAKE	TYPE	LICENCE No.	COLOUR	

PARTS DAMAGED				APPROX. AMT. $	

DRIVER		ADDRESS	

PHONE	DRIVER'S LIC.		RESTRICTIONS	EXPIRES	BIRTHDATE

OWNER		ADDRESS	

INSURANCE CO.	AGENT		POLICY No.	EXPIRES

VEH. REMOVED BY	TO		WHOSE REQUEST	OK to Release ☐

KILLED OR INJURED & ADDRESSES	AGE	SEX	SEATED	K	INJURY	HOSPITAL
CHARGES ☐ NO CHARGES ☐	STATUTE, SEC.					

VEH. No.	YEAR	MAKE	TYPE	LICENCE No.	COLOUR	

PARTS DAMAGED				APPROX. AMT. $	

DRIVER		ADDRESS	

PHONE	DRIVER'S LIC.		RESTRICTIONS	EXPIRES	BIRTHDATE

OWNER		ADDRESS	

INSURANCE CO.	AGENT		POLICY No.	EXPIRES

VEH. REMOVED BY	TO		WHOSE REQUEST	OK to Release ☐

KILLED OR INJURED & ADDRESSES	AGE	SEX	SEATED	K	INJURY	HOSPITAL
CHARGES ☐ NO CHARGES ☐	STATUTE, SEC.					

PEDESTRIAN/CYCLIST & ADDRESS	AGE	SEX	PED.	CYCL.	K	INJURY	HOSPITAL

NEXT OF KIN & ADDRESS	PHONE	NOTIFIED TIME am / pm

PROPERTY DAMAGE OTHER THAN VEHICLE	OWNER & ADDRESS

WITNESSES & ADDRESSES	PHONE	AGE	SEX

Figure 2-50

ACCIDENT INVESTIGATION GUIDE AND EVALUATION	
Item	Description and Comments

A. *Area*

Business ☐
        Industrial ☐
        Shopping ☐
Playground ☐
        General ☐
        School ☐
Residential ☐
        Apartment ☐
        Family ☐
Recreational ☐
        Park ☐
        Camping ☐
Rural ☐
        Agriculture ☐
        Other ☐

B. *Highway*

Lanes   1 ☐
           2 ☐
           3 ☐
           4 ☐
Divided ☐
Undivided ☐
Bridge ☐
Exit ☐
        Acceleration lane ☐
        Deceleration lane ☐
Exit ☐
        Ramp ☐
        Intersection ☐
Entrance intersection ☐
Ferry or dock ☐
Parking lot ☐
Tunnel ☐
Off highway ☐

Traffic Flow
1-way ☐
2-way ☐

Speed Zone
_____ mph (km/h)
_____ mph (km/h)

Figure 2-51

Item		Description and Comments
Roadway Type		
Asphalt	☐	
Brick	☐	
Concrete	☐	
Earth	☐	
Gravel	☐	
Gravel (oiled)	☐	
Stone	☐	
Roadway Characteristics		
Horizontal		
Curve	☐	
Acute ☐		
Slight ☐		
Reverse ☐		
Switchback ☐		
Winding ☐		
Straight	☐	
Vertical		
Flat	☐	
Hillcrest	☐	
Hollow	☐	
Roadway Surface		
Dry	☐	
Wet	☐	
Muddy	☐	
Snow	☐	
Ice	☐	
Slush	☐	
Other (mixed)	☐	
C. *Collision*		
Contact point	☐	
On roadway ☐		
Off roadway ☐		
D. *Type of Collision*		
Another vehicle	☐	
Animal	☐	
Bicycle	☐	
Bridge structure	☐	
Building wall	☐	
Crash cushion impact attenuator	☐	

Figure 2-51 *(Continued)*

Item		Description and Comments
D. *Type of Collision (continued)*		
Culvert	☐	
Curbing	☐	
Ditch	☐	
Fence	☐	
Fire	☐	
Fire hydrant	☐	
Guardrail	☐	
Median island	☐	
Overturned	☐	
Pedestrian	☐	
Railroad train	☐	
Ran off roadway	☐	
Rock face	☐	
Rock on road	☐	
Signpost	☐	
Streetcar	☐	
Submersion in water	☐	
Snowbank or drift	☐	
Tree	☐	
Trolley coach	☐	
Utility pole	☐	
E. *Contributing Factors*		
Alcohol involvement	☐	
Animal	☐	
Domestic ☐		
Wild ☐		
Consciousness, loss of	☐	
Driver inexperience	☐	
Driving without due care and attention	☐	
Driving on wrong side of roadway	☐	
Drugs	☐	
Legal ☐		
Illegal ☐		
Failure to signal	☐	
Failure to obey traffic-control device	☐	
Failure to yield right-of-way	☐	
Failure to obey signal	☐	
Peace officer ☐		
Flagman ☐		
Guard ☐		

Figure 2-51 *(Continued)*

Item		Description and Comments
E. *Contributing Factors (continued)*		
Fatigue	☐	
Fell asleep	☐	
Following too closely	☐	
Illness	☐	
Pre-existing disability	☐	
Lighting glare	☐	
Sunlight	☐	
Artificial	☐	
Mechanical defect	☐	
Accelerator	☐	
Brakes	☐	
Brakelights	☐	
Engine	☐	
Headlights	☐	
Safety restraint	☐	
Steering	☐	
Suspension	☐	
Tire	☐	
Tow hitch	☐	
Turn signal	☐	
Windshield	☐	
Pedestrian	☐	
Error	☐	
Confused	☐	
Roadway		
Construction	☐	
Defect	☐	
Markings	☐	
Maintenance	☐	
Traffic-control device	☐	
Obstructed	☐	
Obliterated	☐	
Unsafe passing	☐	
Unsafe speed	☐	
Unsafe turn	☐	
Weather		
Fog	☐	
Hail	☐	
Mist	☐	
Snow	☐	
Rain	☐	

Figure 2-51 *(Continued)*

Item	Description and Comments
E. *Contributing Factors (continued)*	

Vehicle

        Overweight ☐

        Overwidth ☐

Vision obstructed ☐

        Driver's sight ☐

        By passenger ☐

        Window ☐

        Windshield ☐

        Load ☐

        Mirror position ☐

F. *Safety Equipment*

Air bag ☐

Harness only ☐

Lap belt only ☐

Lap belt and harness ☐

Motorcycle helmet ☐

Vehicle equipped but not used ☐

Vehicle not equipped ☐

Ejected from vehicle ☐

        Driver ☐

        Passenger ☐

G. *Vehicle Action*

Avoiding road hazard ☐

Backing ☐

Changing lanes ☐

Entering parking area ☐

Going straight ☐

Making turn ☐

        Left ☐

        Right ☐

        U-turn ☐

Parked ☐

        Legally ☐

        Illegally ☐

Jackknifing ☐

Merging ☐

Overtaking ☐

Figure 2-51 *(Continued)*

Item	Description and Comments
G. *Vehicle Action (continued)*	

G. *Vehicle Action (continued)*

Starting up ☐
        From parked ☐
          position
        From in traffic ☐
Skidding ☐
Slowing ☐
Spinning ☐
Stopping ☐
Yawing ☐

H. *Position of Passengers in Vehicle*

Vehicle 1
Vehicle 2

I. *Pedestrian Action*

Crossing ☐
        With signal ☐
        Against signal ☐
        In X-walk ☐
          Signal ☐
          No signal ☐
        Between inter- ☐
          sections
          X-walk ☐
          No X-walk ☐
Child leaving school bus ☐
Child play on roadway ☐
Emerging from behind ☐
    parked vehicle
Riding or hitching on a ☐
    vehicle
Standing on highway ☐
Standing on roadway ☐
Walking along highway ☐
        On roadway ☐
        With traffic ☐
        Against traffic ☐

Figure 2-51 *(Continued)*

Item		Description and Comments
J. *Injury*		
Not injured	☐	
Killed	☐	
Injured	☐	
Location		
Abdomen	☐	
Ankle	☐	
Arm	☐	
Upper	☐	
Lower	☐	
Back	☐	
Chest	☐	
Foot	☐	
Hand	☐	
Head	☐	
Hip	☐	
Knee	☐	
Leg	☐	
Upper	☐	
Lower	☐	
Neck	☐	
Pelvic area	☐	
Shoulder	☐	
Wrist	☐	
Type		
Abrasion	☐	
Amputation	☐	
Bruise	☐	
Burns	☐	
Concussion	☐	
Dislocation	☐	
Drowning	☐	
Fracture	☐	
Laceration	☐	
Bleeding	☐	
Consciousness		
Agitated	☐	
Dead	☐	
Incoherent	☐	
Normal	☐	
Semiconscious	☐	
Unconscious	☐	

Figure 2-51 *(Continued)*

Item		Description and Comments
K. *Traffic Control*		
Present	☐	
None	☐	
Traffic signal	☐	
Advance flasher ☐		
Stop sign	☐	
Yield sign	☐	
Railroad crossing signal	☐	
Police direction	☐	
Flagman	☐	
School guard	☐	
Color of	☐	
Light ☐		
Sign ☐		
L. *Weather*		
Clear	☐	
Dry	☐	
Cloudy	☐	
Partial ☐		
Total ☐		
Fog	☐	
Hail	☐	
Rain	☐	
Smog	☐	
Snow	☐	
Wind	☐	
M. *Light Conditions*		
Daylight	☐	
Darkness	☐	
Dawn	☐	
Dusk	☐	
Visibility, general	☐	

Figure 2-51 *(Continued)*

MECHANICAL INSPECTION GUIDE
AND
EVALUATION

Examination Requested by:_____

Date of Request: _____

Place of Examination: _____

Examination Conducted by _____

			am
Start:	Date _____	Time _____	pm
			am
Finish:	Date _____	Time _____	pm

Item	Findings, Conclusions and Comments
A. *Vehicle Description*	
Licence plate no.	
State or province	
Make	
Year	
Model/Type	
Color	
Registration no.	
Serial no. (VIN)	
Odometer mileage	
B. *Accelerator*	
Linkage	
Freedom of movement	
Retrieval (spring)	
Pedal tread	
C. *Brakes*	
Type	
Hydraulic	
Power assist	
Air	
Anti-skid device	
2-wheel	
4-wheel	
Not equipped	
Hydraulic pressure	
proportioning valve	
Wheel brake assembly	
Caliper movement	
Disc runout	
Drum surface	
Primary shoes	
Secondary shoes	
Wheel cylinder	
(extension)	
Fluid pressure (psi)	

Figure 2-52

Item	Findings, Conclusions and Comments
Master cylinder	
Fluid level	
Fluid pressure (psi)	
Hand brake	
Emergency braking device	
Pedal tread	
Good condition	
Worn condition	
Lines (fluid, vacuum, air)	
Cracked	
Rock fractures	
Worn	
Leaks	
Collision damage	
Pedal reserve	
D. *Doors*	
Latches	
Handles	
Safety catches	
General operation	
(binding, loose)	
E. *Exhaust System*	
Manifold connection	
Exhaust pipe	
Muffler	
Tailpipe	
Connections	
F. *Air Conditioning Unit*	
Defects (drawing in	
exhaust fumes, etc.)	
G. *Frame*	
Collision damage	
Alignment	
Cross members	
"A" frame	
H. *Horn*	
Switch type (ring, button,	
shroud, spoke)	
Horn type (electrical, vacuum, air)	
General condition	
Audibility	

Figure 2-52 *(Continued)*

Item	Findings, Conclusions and Comments
I. Lights	
Switches	
Headlights	
Dimmer	
Back-up	
Brakelight	
Signal	
Lights, general (type, color, number, location, condition)	
Headlights	
Taillights	
Signal	
Brakelights	
Clearance	
Fog	
Back-up	
High-beam indicator	
J. Power Train	
K. Reflectors	
Reflectors, general (type, color, number, location, condition)	
L. Steering	
Type (power, manual)	
Linkage, general	
Tie-rods	
Idler arm	
Drag links	
Steering box	
Springs	
King pins	
Ball joints	
Steering wheel free play	
M. Suspension	
Springs	
Control arms	
Torsion bars	
Shocks	
N. Tires	
Make	
Name	

Figure 2-52 *(Continued)*

Item	Findings, Conclusions and Comments
Tires (continued)	
Ply	
Size	
Serial number	
Sidewall type	
Load capacity	
Pressure	
Recommended	
Actual	
Tube or tubeless	
Tread type	
Summer	
Snow grip	
Mud grip	
Slick	
Original	
Recap	
Studded	
Chains	
Tread wear pattern	
Sides	
Center	
Uneven	
Tread depth	
New	
Percent worn	
General condition	
Cuts	
Abrasions	
Blowout	
Wear (light, medium, heavy, bald)	
Damage	
Type	
Location related to serial number	
Tire damage related to rim damage	
Tire damage related to vehicle damage	
O. *Wheels*	
Bearings	
Rotation	
Locking uniformity (brake application)	

Figure 2-52 *(Continued)*

Item	Findings, Conclusions and Comments
Wheels (continued)	

Lugs (missing, loose, worn)
    Seals
    Rim
        Condition
        Damage	

P. *Windshield and Windows*
    Clear
    Tinted
    View obstructions
    Damage
    General condition	

Q. *Windshield Wipers*
    Type (electrical, vacuum,
      mechanical)
    Blades and blade arms
    Switch	

R. *Windshield and Window
    Defrosters*
    General Condition
    Type
    Switch	

S. *Speedometer*
    General condition
    Cable	

T. *Mirrors*
    Location
    Position
    Type	

Examiner _____ (Signature)	

Figure 2-52 *(Continued)*

Chapter 3

VEHICLE BEHAVIOR

PHYSICS, VEHICLE MECHANICS AND DYNAMICS

3.001 *Physics* may be defined as the science of matter in motion or under stress. *Mechanics,* as part of physics, is a very broad subject. In accident reconstruction, it is necessary to have some knowledge of that part of mechanics known as *dynamics* as described by Newton's Laws of Motion.

Law 1. Every body remains at rest or moves with constant velocity (in a straight line) unless acted upon by an external force. This law may be partially explained by the term *inertia,* which is the tendency of a body at rest to resist motion and remain at rest, or if in motion to remain in motion. An example of this law is the case of a vehicle under forward acceleration, where the load or passenger has a tendency to be pushed toward the rear. Conversely, under sudden braking, loads can move forward off the seats and passengers may even strike the windshield. Similarly, a vehicle proceeding around a curve has a tendency to push a person towards the outer side of the vehicle, that is, in the direction the vehicle would have travelled in a *straight line* if it had not followed the curve. It can be said that inertia is the *resistance to change* of velocity. A heavy object has more resistance than a light object, due to its mass; it is the mass of an object that gives it inertia. An example of this is a large, heavy truck that requires more braking power than a small, compact vehicle because it has more mass and consequently more inertia.

Law 2. A free body acted upon by a constant force moves with constant acceleration in the direction of the force. The amount of acceleration is directly proportional to the acting force and inversely proportional to the mass of the body. This second law may be considered in application to two vehicles having different masses but propelled by engines of equal size and power. For example, a vehicle weighing 6,000 pounds (2722 kg) has only half the acceleration of a vehicle weighing 3,000 pounds (1361 kg) when driven by the same motor and gear train.

Law 3. To every action there is an equal and opposite reaction. An example of this law is when two vehicles collide with each other. When the collision takes place, the force of vehicle 1 against vehicle 2 is equal and opposite to the reaction force of vehicle 2, even if one is stationary and massive and the other is light and moving quickly. Another example would be a vehicle colliding with a large utility pole. The forces sustained by both objects are equal and opposite, though the effects on each may be quite different.

3.002   *Gravity* is a force defined in Newton's law of gravitation: "Any two bodies in the universe attract each other with a force that is directly proportional to their masses, and inversely proportional to the square of their distance apart." Gravity is the constant vertical attraction on an object downwards towards the center of the earth, referred to by the acceleration it causes the object. On our planet Earth, this acceleration g has the value 32.2 ft/sec/sec (9.81 m/s/s). On Jupiter the acceleration is much higher because of the larger mass of that planet, while on the Moon the gravitational pull is about one-sixth that of the Earth due to the smaller mass of the Moon.

3.003   *Mass* is the amount of matter in a body, which is constant anywhere in the known universe. The difference in mass between substances having the same volume relates to the composition of the molecules and atoms of the material. The heavy elements such as plutonium, which is used in atomic reactors, have large numbers of electrons closely packed together. Light elements such as the gas hydrogen have smaller numbers of atomic particles widely dispersed. On Earth the mass of an object is its weight divided by the gravitational pull of the Earth:

$$\text{Mass} = \frac{\text{Weight}}{g}$$

3.004   *Weight.* The action of the force of gravity acting on the mass of an object gives it weight. The weight of an object is then defined as the product of mass multiplied by the acceleration due to gravity, that is, weight equals mass times gravity. The weight of a body depends on where

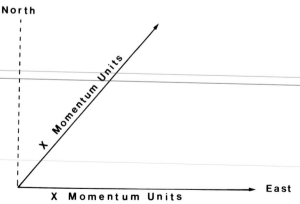

Figure 3-1. Vectors represented by line segments showing magnitude and direction.

it is in the universe. The same object weighs much more on Jupiter and much less on the Moon, but its mass remains the same. For our purposes, the gravitational pull of the Earth is a constant, and while it may seem that the distinction between mass and weight is academic, it is vital when one considers the next important factor in accidents, force.

3.005 *Force* acting on a body is the product of its *mass* multiplied by the acceleration or deceleration of the body. The result of a force acting on a stationary object is to cause it to move. If the body is already moving, the force may cause it to move faster, accelerate. If the direction of the force is opposite to the motion of the body, it causes it to slow down, decelerate. The direction of the force is very important, and force must always be defined both by its size and its direction. This makes force a *vector* quantity.

3.006 *Centrifugal force.* If a body is moving at a constant speed and direction, a force is necessary to change *either* its speed or its direction. When a vehicle is travelling at a constant speed around a curve, its direction is changing all the time, and a force called *centrifugal force* acts on it, tending to maintain it in a tangent direction.

3.007 *Centripetal force.* An object being swung around at the end of a piece of string has a tension force on the string equal to the centrifugal force acting on the object. This equal and opposite force is called a *centripetal force*. In a car travelling round a curve, this force is supplied by the friction between the tires and the road surface and also by other forces brought into play by the superelevation. When a vehicle travels around a curve at too fast a speed, the centrifugal force may be greater than the centripetal force supplied by road friction or superelevation, which can lead to the vehicle running off the curve. When the roads are icy or the superelevation is non-existent, a car may leave the road at a much lower speed or centrifugal force value. In the absence of centripetal force, a body does not travel in a curve. In other words, the centrifugal and centripetal forces must be in equilibrium for an object to travel in a curve.

3.008 *Momentum* is a term describing the inertial qualities of an object. It is defined as the product of the mass multiplied by the velocity of the object. Heavier vehicles have more momentum than lighter vehicles. Faster vehicles have more momentum than slower vehicles of the same mass.

3.009 *Work* is defined in mechanics as the deformation experienced by an object when acted upon by a force. Thus, work is done in expanding an elastic band, but in vehicle crashes work is also done in the bending and crushing of the metal. Work is defined as the product of force applied times the distance through which the force is applied.

3.010 *Kinetic energy.* When a body is in motion, it is said to possess kinetic

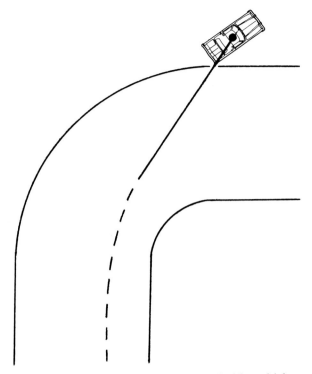

Figure 3-2. When there is insufficient centripetal force to hold a vehicle on the roadway in a curve, centrifugal force causes it to continue in a straight path.

energy. This is defined as the product of ½ times mass times velocity². The reader will recall that force was defined as the product of mass times velocity, so kinetic energy may be seen as the product of force times velocity/2. The expression velocity/2 represents the average distance through which the force acted in the time period. Thus kinetic energy is equivalent to work. In application to car crashes, what this means is that a heavy vehicle at high speed does a great deal of work, that is, damage or smash an object with which it collides, including its occupants. An object possessed of kinetic energy is able to do work, so it is possible to determine the travelling speed of a vehicle from a skilled examination and analysis of the damage caused (work done) in a crash. However, this is usually beyond the scope of investigators in the field.

CENTER OF MASS

3.011 *Center of mass or the center of gravity.* It is necessary and convenient to consider that all the weight or all the mass of a body acts through one particular point called the *center of mass.* In a billiard ball, that point is precisely in the center of the sphere. In a hollow ball, it is also precisely in the center but actually located in air. If a force is applied to such an object with its direction aimed exactly through the center of mass, then the object will move in the direction of the force without other effects. If the force does not quite act through the center of mass, some kind of rotation will also be caused to the object (for example, the action of a cue on a billiard ball).

Calculating Center of Mass

3.012 In a vehicle, the center of mass is located at some point through the central axis, usually halfway between the front and rear axles. Typically the point is about one-third of the height of the vehicle measured from the ground level.[17] For practical investigation purposes, locating the center of mass in this manner is usually sufficient.

3.013 Determining the center of mass can be a complicated and complex procedure and is generally beyond the requirements of the normal investigation. In serious cases where it is considered necessary to determine the center of mass, the vehicle involved or an identical vehicle should be used. The passenger and load distribution should also be duplicated as closely as possible.

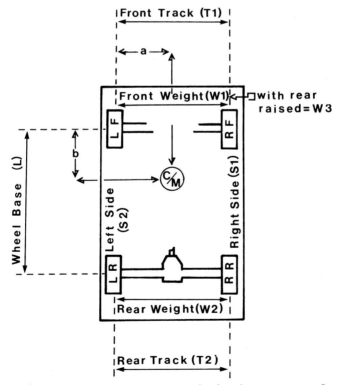

Figure 3-3. Vehicle measurements required to locate center of mass.

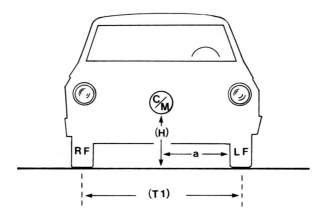

Figure 3-4

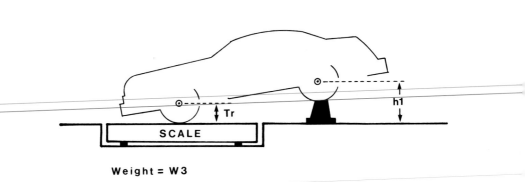

Figure 3-5. Weighing position to locate height of center of mass.

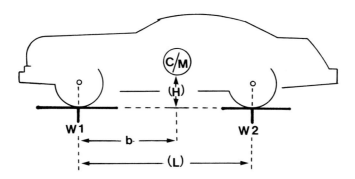

Figure 3-6

3.014 In a large commercial truck, the center of mass position varies with the nature of the loading. In a combination of truck and trailer, the center of mass of the combination varies from individual centers of mass of the separate components.

3.015 The following information is required in order to calculate the center of mass of a vehicle *(C/M):*

a. Wheelbase (The distance between centers of the front and rear axles. *See* Figs. 3-3 and 3-6 distance *L.*)

b. Front track width (The distance between front tire centers. *See* Fig. 3-3 and distance *T1*). Rear track width, distance *T2,* will be required rather than *T1* if front end is to be raised (*see* paragraph d).

c. Weight carried by:
   (1) each individual wheel (LF, RF, LR, RR)
   (2) front wheels combined (LF + RF)
   (3) rear wheels combined (LR + RR)
   (4) left wheels combined (LF + LR)
   (5) right wheels combined (RF + RR)

d. Weight supported by the front wheels with rear wheels raised approximately 3 ft so that there is a weight shift to the front. In this position, the rear end must be supported at the rear axle (*see* Fig. 3-5).

Distance *a* in Figures 3-3 and 3-4 may be calculated by using Formula 3-1:

United States	*Metric*
$a = \dfrac{S1 \times T1}{W}$	$a = \dfrac{S1 \times T1}{W}$

where a = horizontal distance between center of mass and center of tire
S1 = weight supported by *right* wheels
T1 = track width of front tires (center to center)
W = total vehicle weight

Example

S1 = 2,000 lb	S1 = 907 kg
T1 = 60 in	T1 = 152.4 cm
W = 4,000 lb	W = 1814.4 kg
$a = \dfrac{2,000 \times 60}{4,000}$	$a = \dfrac{907 \times 152.4}{1814.4}$
a = 30 in from tread center of left tire	a = 76 cm from tread center of left tire

Distance *b* in Figures 3-3 and 3-6 may be calculated by using Formula 3-2:

United States	*Metric*
$b = \dfrac{W2 \times L}{W}$	$b = \dfrac{W2 \times L}{W}$

where b = horizontal distance between center of front axle and center of mass
W2 = weight supported by *rear* wheels
L = wheelbase
W = total vehicle weight

Example

W2 = 2,000 lb	W2 = 907 kg
L = 120 in	L = 304.8 cm
W = 4,000 lb	W = 1814.4 kg
$b = \dfrac{2,000 \times 120}{4,000}$	$b = \dfrac{907 \times 304.8}{1814.4}$
b = 60 in behind center of front wheels	b = 152 cm behind center of front wheels

The vertical location *H* (Figs. 3-4 and 3-6) may be calculated using Formula 3-3:

$$H = Tr + \frac{(W3 - W1)\ L\ \sqrt{L^2 - (h1 - Tr)^2}}{W\ (h1 - Tr)}$$

where H = height of center of mass
    Tr = front tire radius (Fig. 3-5)
   W3 = weight on front wheels with rear wheels raised (Figs. 3-3 and 3-5)
   W1 = weight carried by front wheels only (rear wheels off of scale)
     L = wheelbase (Figs. 3-3 and 3-6)
    h1 = height to center of rear axle with rear raised (Fig. 3-5)
     W = total vehicle weight

Example

United States	Metric
Tr = 12 in	Tr = 30.48 cm
W3 = 2,100 lb	W3 = 952.56 kg
W1 = 2,000 lb	W1 = 907 kg
L = 120 in	L = 304.8 cm
h1 = 36 in	h1 = 91.44 cm
W = 4,000 lb	W = 1814.4 kg

United States

$$H \;=\; 12 \;+\; \frac{(2100 \;-\; 2000)\; 120\; \sqrt{120^2 \;-\; (36 \;-\; 12)^2}}{4,000\; (36 \;-\; 12)}$$

H = 27 in above ground level

Metric

$$H \;=\; 30.48 \;+\; \frac{(952.56 \;-\; 907)\; 304.8\; \sqrt{304.8^2 \;-\; (91.44 \;-\; 30.48)^2}}{1814.4\; (91.44 \;-\; 30.48)}$$

H = 68 cm above ground level

Assuming the foregoing was an accident vehicle, from these calculations we have determined that the C/M is 30 in (76 cm) towards the center from the tread center of the left front tire; 60 in (152 cm) toward the rear from the center of the front wheels; and 27 in (68 cm) above ground level.

Effect of Center of Mass on Vehicle Movement

3.016   The center of mass of a vehicle and the direction of force in relation to the center of mass determines how the vehicle reacts during a collision. If two vehicles collide with their mass centers in direct line, that is, head on, both vehicles come quickly to a stop and do not rotate (Fig. 3-7). If both vehicles are approximately the same weight and come to rest at the point of impact, their immediate prior speeds would have been approximately equal. A faster vehicle or a heavier vehicle travelling at about the same speed will shove an opposing vehicle back during collision in these cases.

3.017   If vehicle parts momentarily lock during initial engagement, the vehicles tend to rotate about the locked position until they disengage, at which time they rotate about their respective centers of mass.

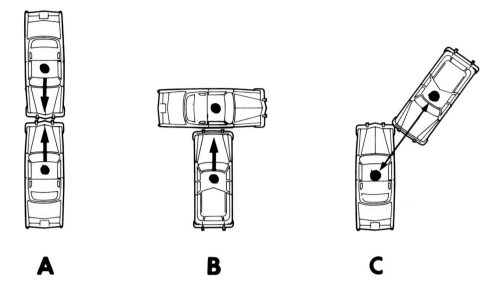

Figure 3-7 (A, B and C). Vehicles that collide with centers of mass in direct line do not rotate.

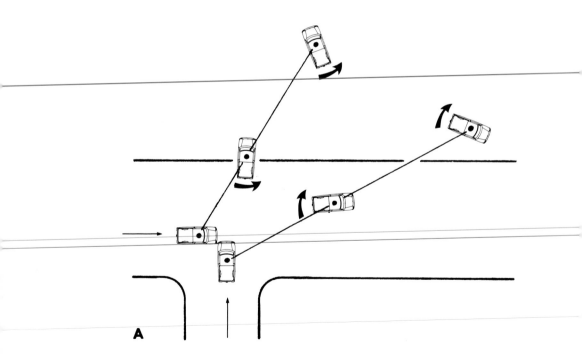

Figure 3-8A

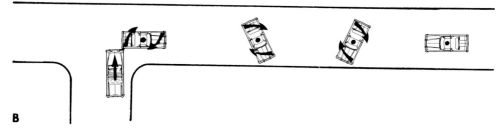

Figure 3-8 (A and B). Intersection collision, with centers of mass and subsequent rotation shown.

3.018 Vehicles that collide slightly off-center (eccentric force) rotate about their centers of mass. If one of the vehicles is much heavier than the other, its rotation and distance travelled after collision is considerably less than the lighter vehicle, provided that their impact speeds were approximately equal. Speed does play a very important part in collisions; therefore, a higher speed by one vehicle has a direct bearing on the extent of rotation and distances travelled after collision of vehicles involved.

3.019 Direction of rotation of a vehicle depends upon where the opposing eccentric force is applied in relation to its center of mass. For example, if the initial contact is with the left side of a vehicle, the right or free side tends to keep going, thereby giving direction to its rotation.

Yaw

3.020 *Yaw* is a term applied to a sideways movement of a vehicle, such as when the rear of a vehicle sideslips and moves in a direction other than the direction in which the vehicle is headed. At high speeds on curves, centrifugal force attempts to overcome centripetal force, that is, the frictional resistance or adhesion between the tires and the roadway, and causes a vehicle to slide in a straight path. If the speed is great enough, the vehicle will sideslip or go into *yaw* and possibly spin or overturn.

3.021 At a safe or reasonable speed on curves, rotating rear tires always track inside the front tires. At excessive speeds, tires slip sideways as the vehicle goes into yaw, and the front tires track inside the rear tires. Similarly, when brakes are applied as a vehicle drives into a curve, the vehicle may skid sideways and the rear wheels may lead to the outside of the curve as in yaw.

Effect of Crosswinds

3.022 *Crosswinds* should be taken into account in accidents where for no other apparent reason, a vehicle shifts sideways from its normal course of

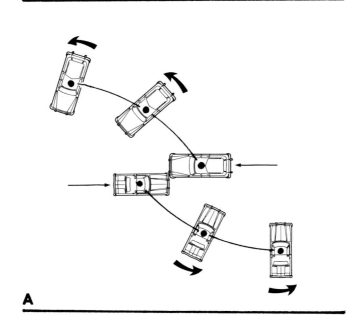

Figure 3-9A

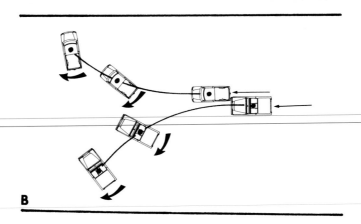

Figure 3-9B

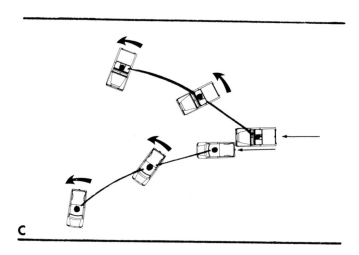

Figure 3-9 (A, B and C). Off-center collisions produce eccentric forces, with centers of mass and subsequent rotation shown.

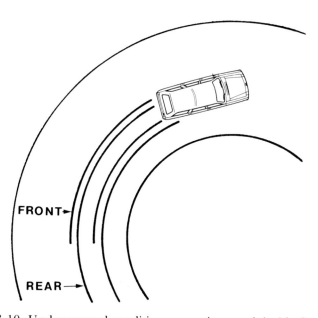

Figure 3-10. Under normal conditions, rear tires track inside front tires.

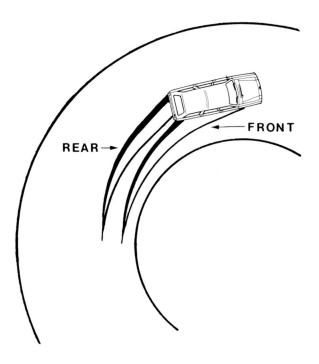

Figure 3-11. Entering a curve at an excessive speed causes a vehicle to go into yaw, under which conditions the rear tires track outside front tires.

travel. This is more likely to happen with rear-engine passenger cars and small, lightweight vehicles.[18]

3.023   When brakes are applied and the wheels cease to rotate, the wheels are said to be *locked.* When one rear wheel fails to lock upon brake application, the vehicle does not rotate or swerve; however, when one front wheel fails to brake upon application, the vehicle swerves to the side of the braked or locked wheel. When only the rear wheels of a vehicle lock during brake application, the vehicle rotates so that the rear of the vehicle moves into a position so as to lead down the roadway. This is particularly true at high speeds.

3.024   A sudden tire deflation, that is, a blowout, causes a vehicle to swerve, particularly if it is a front tire. In the case of a front tire failure, the vehicle pulls or swerves to the side of the defective tire. As soon as the tire flattens, scuff or flop marks become evident on the roadway surface.

Chapter 4

VEHICLE PLACEMENT ON HIGHWAY

HIGHWAY MARKS

4.001 When a vehicle goes out of control and overturns or collides with a vehicle, pedestrian or other object, various marks are left on the highway and on the units involved as a direct result of the collision. It is very important that the investigator be able to recognize and interpret these marks, and to apply meaningful names to them. By so doing, his investigation will be more thorough and he will be in a better position to relate the results of his investigation to others.

4.002 An accident scene should be examined for pre-collision, collision point and post-collision highway marks. The path of travel of a vehicle, possible cause of the accident and what occurred during collision may be determined from such examination. Particular attention should be paid to the underside parts of a vehicle for breakage and abrasions that might be matched up to marks on the highway. Similarly, marks on a highway should be matched up with parts of a vehicle that caused them. In this way a determination may be made of the behavior of the vehicle and its placement or position on the highway during the times of pre-collision, collision and post-collision.

4.003 What happened during the series of events under investigation may be determined from various sources:

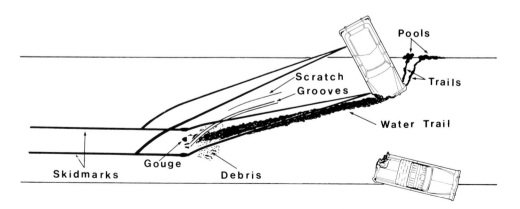

Figure 4-1

117

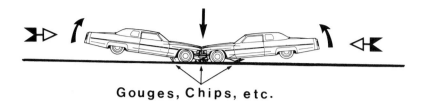

Gouges, Chips, etc.

Figure 4-2

    a. Highway marks (including skid, sideskid, sideslip or yaw tire marks, chips, gouges, scrapes, furrows and other similar highway markings)
    b. Drivers' and witnesses' statements
    c. Matching damages
    d. Vehicle damages that indicate direction of thrust or penetration
    e. Final positions of debris and vehicles

In most cases, each source corroborates other sources, and when all taken together, they often give conclusive results as to vehicle placement on the highway during the series of events under review.

4.004   A *chip* or *gouge* is a concave, chip-like cavity in the pavement caused by a metal protrusion. Edges of the cavity may have striation marks that

Figure 4-3. Matching vehicle damages.

Figure 4-4. Minor scratches on a vehicle can often be matched to objects that caused them.

may be measured and matched to the object that caused them (*see* Fig. 2-14).

4.005 A *groove* is a channel, hollow or rut caused by a metal protrusion such as a piece of broken body part, bolt or metal edge. Groove patterns may appear in sets of two or more. Measurements between these marks will assist in matching the vehicle parts that caused them, which in turn will provide information as to vehicle placement on the highway at the time the groove was caused.

4.006 A groove may be either straight or circular. Straight grooves indicate the direction of travel. Circular grooves indicate that the vehicle was rotating or spinning.

4.007 A *hole* is a cavity in a roadway surface that is round with smooth walls and is usually caused by protruding bolts, broken rods or similar round body objects.

4.008 A *scrape* is a wide superficial wound or a wide, clean graze mark caused by a sharp or angular edge being passed over the highway surface, that is, a vehicle part sliding over roadway.

4.009 A *scratch* is a long, narrow superficial wound on a highway surface.

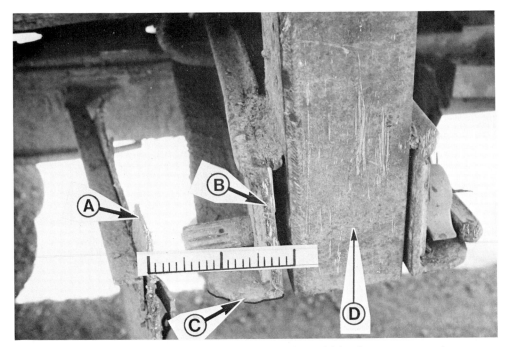

Figure 4-5. An example of the underside parts of a vehicle that can cause damage to roadway. Parts such as *A* and *B* will most probably cause grooves or scratches. *C* will cause a gouge or chip, and *D* will result in scrapes or scratches. Many other parts of an automobile such as tie-rods or cross-members may cause various marks on a roadway when they are forced into contact with the roadway. Measurements of the widths of the parts or the distances between them will assist in matching parts and roadway damage, thereby showing vehicle placement on the highway.

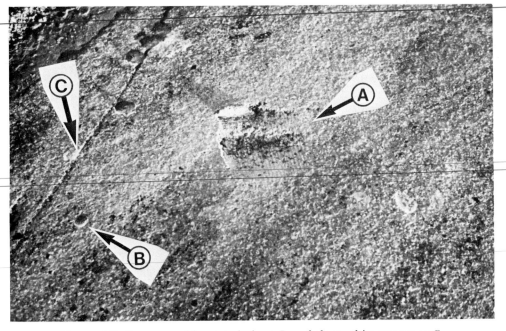

Figure 4-6. Gouge or chip at *A*, hole at *B* and deep, thin groove at *C*.

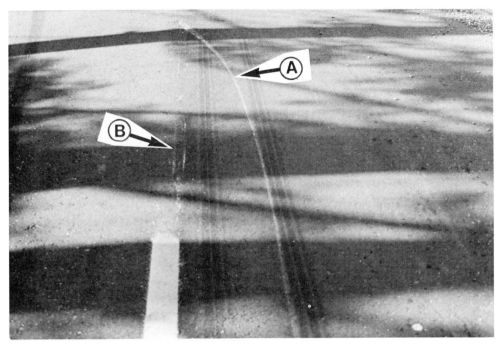

Figure 4-7. Groove at *A* indicates that vehicle was travelling straight and then commenced to rotate. Note parallel scratches at *B*.

Figure 4-8. Scrape marks caused by vehicle body sliding on roadway.

Figure 4-9. Scratches at A and B. The distance between sets of scratches should be measured and matched to parts of vehicle that caused them.

VEHICLE DAMAGE

4.010   When examining vehicle body damage, it is important to distinguish between *incidental* damage and *contact* damage (*see* paragraph 1.013 and Fig. 1-8). To conclude that incidental damage was contact damage could result in erroneous vehicle placement on the highway at the time of primary or secondary contacts.

4.011   Contact damages must be examined closely to determine whether or not older more severe damage is evident that might simply have been scraped or only slightly damaged as a result of the accident under investigation. Recent damage is clean and clear of road grease or discoloration resulting from age, weather effects and traffic. Should older damage not be recognized, improper conclusions could be drawn from the apparent amount of damage in terms of speeds involved, vehicle placement on highway and matching paint of other vehicles involved.

4.012   Tire marks on a vehicle body may be matched up to a tire on a suspect or opposing vehicle. Paint scrapings may match color of suspect or opposing vehicle. Metal or other types of vehicle protrusions such as mirrors may be matched to the damage of another vehicle or to the injury of a pedestrian. The imprint of a pedestrian's clothing who has been struck by a vehicle may be found on the vehicle, particularly on a bumper. The

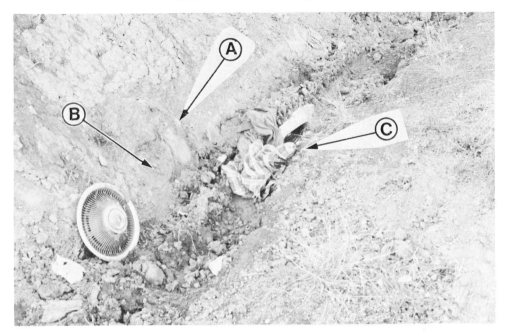

Figure 4-10. A tire or wheel imprint on a vehicle or other place such as an embankment, *A*, can assist in determining the path of travel of a vehicle. Evidence left at the scene, for example a hubcap, matched to hubcap imprint, *B*, and clothing fragments from victim's garment, *C*, found on a vehicle often establish the identity of an offending vehicle.

Figure 4-11. Imprint of clothing on front bumper can be matched to a victim's clothing pattern and place of injury.

Figure 4-12 (A and B). Photographs and measurements should show the direction and angle of thrust. Overhead photographs are helpful for this purpose.

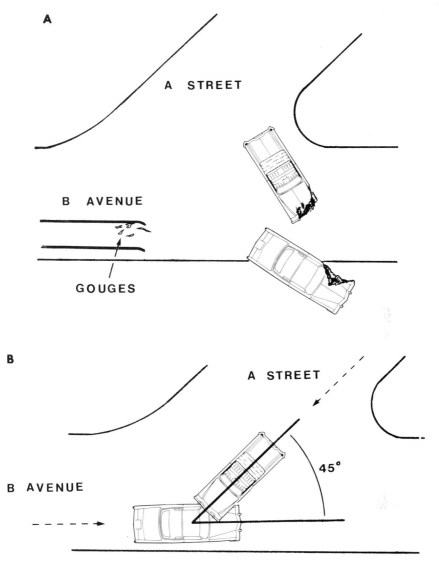

Figure 4-13. After collision, scene A. Careful measurements and a sketch of damages and roadway marks that show direction of thrust make it possible to place vehicles in their positions at time of impact, B.

height of such evidence on a vehicle should be measured and matched to the height of the pedestrian's injury, and the imprint on the vehicle should be matched to the pedestrian's clothing.

4.013 The damage sustained by a vehicle should be matched against the vehicle or object collided with to determine its position compared to the other vehicle or object at the time of *primary* contact. Secondary and post-secondary contact damages should be similarly matched. In attempting to correctly position a vehicle in relation to another vehicle or object collided with at the time of contact, it is very important to first make an examination to determine the *thrust,* that is, the direction and concentration of force applied against the vehicle or object. An overhead view recording the information with photographs and sketches is of considerable benefit in reconstructing the contact positions. Vehicle positions may then be matched up photographically, diagrammatically or a combination of both.

4.014   To diagrammatically reconstruct the positions of vehicles at time of contact, make separate diagrams of vehicles (or vehicle and object), with particular attention being paid to the primary or secondary contact areas as the case may be. Diagrams should be prepared to a scale sufficient to measure and reflect individualisms or characteristics of damaged parts. Use tracing paper so that the two diagrams may be seen at one time when they are brought together. If heavy paper is used, it will be necessary to cut out the damaged areas for matching purposes. Make indentations and other characteristics precisely as they are found on vehicles or objects involved. Then, bring the two diagrams together, maneuvering them into position until the opposing damages match up.

HIGHWAY FIXTURES

4.015   Highway fixtures such as traffic-control devices, signposts, bridge abutments and railings, guardrails, fenceposts, utility poles, and so on should be examined for scrapes, scratches and other damages. These should be matched up with damaged areas of vehicles, with particular emphasis on paint scrapings and chips to determine which vehicle caused the damage and to determine paths of travel of the vehicles.

TIRE MARKS

4.016   An investigator should be able to recognize and interpret the physical appearance of tire marks left on a highway. Unless tire marks are examined and interpreted intelligently, the results could lead to erroneous evidence being relied upon in drawing conclusions based on the investigation.

4.017   It is important to determine whether or not tire marks found on the highway relate to the accident under investigation. Each tire mark should, if possible, be related to the tire that made it. In relating tire marks to the tires that made them, it is often of assistance to count the number of dark lines of the tire mark and relate that number to the number of tire ribs of the tires in question.

4.018   An investigator must not confuse skid marks or other roadway

Figure 4-14. Tire marks, scratches, and so forth on highway fixtures show the path of travel of a vehicle. Such evidence as shown here often answers the question of why a vehicle veered into an opposing lane of traffic.

marks resulting from a damaged vehicle being towed from the accident scene with marks that were caused at the time of the accident. He must be able to interpret and explain these and all other marks found at an accident scene or that appear in photographs.

4.019 A vehicle making skid marks or tire prints at an accident scene is often found at rest a considerable distance from the tire marks. The vehicle involved may be matched up with the tire marks in several ways, all of which corroborate each other. Matching may be done by witnesses' and drivers' statements, tire prints or tread ribs, scrape marks, gouges, and so forth. Of particular importance are specific tire tread and tire mark measurements.

4.020 *Tire prints* are caused by a rotating tire leaving the print of the tire tread pattern on a highway surface (*see* Fig. 4-15).

4.021 An *acceleration mark* is caused by extreme acceleration of the motor that in turn spins a drive wheel. The beginning of the mark is dark with very dark side ridges similar to an overloaded or underinflated tire mark. The tire tread rib marks are often visible (*see* Figs. 4-28 and 4-29).

Figure 4-15. Tire print caused by a rotating tire. A tire print shows the tread pattern, *A*. The number of dark lines, *B*, indicates the number of tire tread ribs. Tire tread ribs often leave similar dark lines in a straight skid but without the tread pattern.

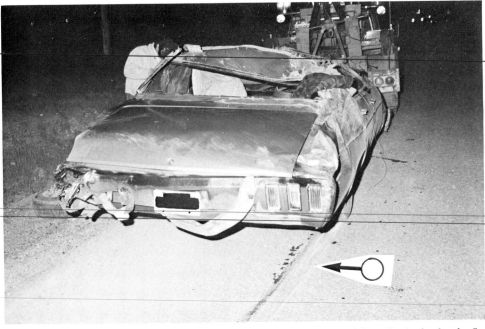

Figure 4-16. During follow-up investigation, a skid mark caused by a locked wheel of a towed vehicle must not be confused with an accident skid mark.

Figure 4-17. An investigator must be able to explain all marks appearing in a photograph. For example, the shadows at *B* and *C* must not be confused with or interpreted as skid marks. Note skid mark at *A*.

Figure 4-18. Crossover tire prints, *A*, caused by passing traffic must not be confused with skid marks such as those at *B*.

Figure 4-19. Reverse-forward acceleration mark at *A*. Dark lines at outer edges of straight acceleration tire mark, *B*, are common. Note dark tread rib marks on face of tire mark at *C*.

4.022　An examination of a tire provides evidence as to whether it skidded or spun to leave a mark. A clean tread for the full tire circumference indicates that the tire had been spinning under acceleration. If the tire was spinning in gravel or on a gritty surface, the tire bears scrape marks from that surface on its circumference. A tire that has skidded has a cleaned or scraped portion for only the area that was in contact with the roadway while the wheel was locked.

4.023　*Striation marks* are a number of parallel, narrow scratches or tire marks caused by (a) tire sideslipping, (b) gravel-like particles caught between a skidding or sideslipping tire on the roadway, or (c) a vehicle part scraping over a roadway surface. Striation marks are very important in showing direction of travel. Similarly, studded tires on a skidding, sideslipping or spinning wheel leave thin, parallel scratches or striation marks.

4.024　A vehicle that enters a curve at an excessive speed will go into *yaw*. Frequently, evidence of the vehicle going into yaw is found in a tire mark on the roadway caused by a rotating tire that is sideslipping at the same time. The tire mark appears as a curved mark with the lead or outside tire marks being much darker than the inside tire marks. Striation marks are very often evident, particularly in the leading outside tire mark. The beginning of a yaw mark is very narrow, widening to at least the width of

Figure 4-20. A spinning tire has a cleaned tread. After spinning in gravel or on a gritty surface, the tread shows scrapes or striation marks on the surface.

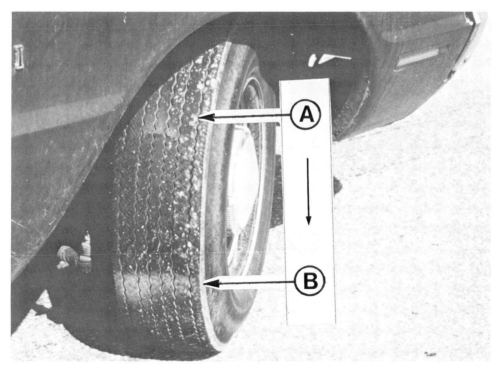

Figure 4-21. Braked wheel causes tire to be cleaned or scraped on the area of the tire that was in contact with the roadway, as indicated in *A* to *B*.

Figure 4-22. Striation marks caused by a vehicle sideslipping on gravel or a gritty surface.

Figure 4-23. Longitudinal striation marks caused by a studded tire.

Figure 4-24. Striations in a tire mark indicate that the wheel causing the mark was rotating and sideslipping. When this type of mark results, the vehicle was in yaw.

Figure 4-25

Figure 4-26. Beginning of a yaw mark.

Figure 4-27. Yaw marks.

Figure 4-28. Underinflated tire mark.

the total tire contact area with the roadway, depending upon the amount of vehicle rotation.

4.025 A rotating *underinflated tire* leaves two parallel marks appearing as fairly straight, dark thin lines at the outer edges of the tire tread. An underinflated tire mark may not necessarily result from tire air pressure less than the recommended amount. The concave or "cupping" appearance of the tire may also result from a shift in weight from the vehicle's load onto that tire or from a shift in weight onto the front tires, for example, during braking action. A good example of a load shift is when a tire on a dual wheel loses air pressure and the remaining tire on that dual wheel unit carries the additional weight, giving it the appearance of an underinflated tire.

4.026 When a tire loses air pressure and becomes flat as in the case of a *blowout,* the tire begins to "flop" under the wheel rim. As the wheel rotates, the tire sidewalls as well as the tread come into contact with the roadway, leaving distinct "flop" tire marks.

4.027 A studded tire or a regular tire skidding or sideslipping on a roadway surface covered with lime, loose gravel or sand leaves scratches on the surface. During rainfall or at other times when the roadway is wet, these scratches are not necessarily evident. Often it is not until the roadway

Figure 4-29. Overloaded tire mark.

dries that the investigator can determine that a vehicle skidded or side-slipped.

4.028   A rotating tire travelling in soft material such as mud or snow causes *ruts*. A skidding or sideslipping tire travelling in soft material causes a *trench* or *furrow*, pushing the material in front of it. A rotating tire travelling over grass causes the grass to flatten for the width of the tire. A skidding or sideslipping tire causes grass roots to be bared and causes a furrow in the soft earth.

4.029   Tire treads pick up loose or soft materials such as sand, dirt and mud and deposit them elsewhere as they rotate or when they come to a stop. The path of a vehicle and the place where it stops can often be traced from these deposits. Grass or other foreign material caught between a tire bead and wheel rim indicates that the vehicle was sideskidding or sideslipping on an earth surface or had struck an abutment of hard material with considerable force. This material is found on the lead side of the tire during the sideskid or sideslip and consequently, assists in determining the direction of travel of the vehicle at that time.

SKID MARKS

4.030   When brakes are applied, brake shoes expand against the inner side of the brake drum. This causes friction between the shoe and drum,

Figure 4-30. Flat-tire "flop" marks.

which in turn causes the wheel to cease rotating. When a brake is applied hard, the drum, wheel and tire as a unit stop and become locked for as long as the brake is firmly applied. While the vehicle remains in motion, the tire skids and in most instances leaves a skid mark.

4.031 Skid marks may be used to determine where brakes were applied, the minimum speed of the vehicle when the skid marks commenced, the location of the vehicle on the roadway (both pre- and post-collision), direction of travel and the number of wheels having braking capability.

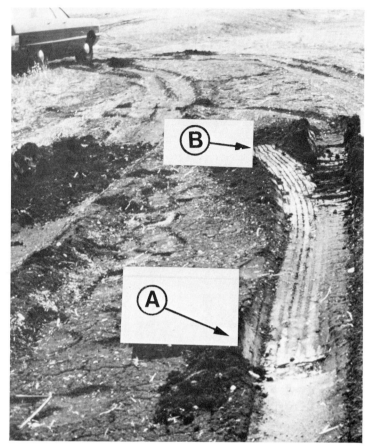

Figure 4-31. A rut caused by a rotating tire. Note tire tread pattern from A to B and material thrown to sides. A skidding tire does not show a tread pattern but may show tread rib marks. A skidding tire throws material to the sides and to the front.

Figure 4-32. A trench or furrow caused by a sideslipping tire.

Figure 4-33. Furrows in grass caused by rotating sideslipping tires.

Figure 4-34. Debris picked up by a skidding tire leaves a deposit where vehicle stops.

Figure 4-35. Grass lodged between tire bead and rim indicates that the vehicle skidded or sideslipped on a turfed area. The direction of movement is toward the side on which the grass is located.

4.032   Some skid marks are very easy to see; others may not be distinguishable. Unless an investigator is aware of how to discover, interpret and record skid marks, a competent investigation cannot normally be carried out. In checking skid marks, the investigator should kneel down so that the eye level is approximately 24 in (60 cm) above the roadway surface. When circumstances permit, a better view of skid marks may be had when the sun is behind the investigator. Polarized sun glasses also provide a clearer view of skid marks during daylight.

4.033   An *impending skid mark* is that portion of a tire mark left by a braked wheel just before there is a complete cessation of rotation. Braking is most effective at that time. The mark left may appear as a cleaning action and leads directly into a skid mark.

4.034   A *skid mark* is a tire mark caused by a locked wheel. Locked wheels need not occur only during pre-collision braking, but may also result from binding during collision.

4.035   During extreme *sideslip* or *sideskid,* a tire may curl under the wheel rim so that the resultant tire mark is caused by the tire sidewall (*see* Fig. 2-30).

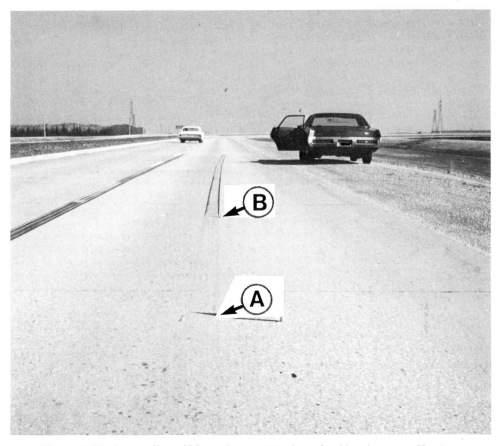

Figure 4-36. Impending skid mark, *A* to *B*, where braking is most effective.

4.036 A *scuff mark* is a friction mark on pavement made by a tire that is both rotating and slipping. There are acceleration scuffs, yaw marks and flat-tire marks.[19]

4.037 A tire *scrub mark* is a tire mark resulting from a wheel that is locked or jammed during collision and moving on the roadway until such time as the vehicle stops or the wheel becomes free to rotate. The beginning of a scrub mark often helps in determining the point of impact. When the direction of the skid is in alignment with the wheel, the scrub mark appears much the same as a straight skid mark. If there is a sideways movement of the vehicle while the wheel is locked, striation marks usually result from tire shoulder ribs.

4.038 Skid marks are usually straight. However, when a vehicle travels on a crowned or superelevated roadway, the tires on the lower side carry more weight because of a natural weight shift to that side. When the wheels lock in a skid, the weight and superelevation tend to cause the vehicle to

Figure 4-37. Front tire skid mark at *A*. Note dark lines at outer edges of skid mark caused by braking. Rear tire skid mark at *B*. Change in direction of front tire mark at *C* indicates point of engagement. Front tire sideskid mark at *D* is caused by vehicle being forced sideways after impact. Tire scrub mark at *E*, where tire slid sideways leaving striation marks, can often be matched to the tire that caused them, thereby giving vehicle position.

Figure 4-38. A crowned or superelevated roadway causes a vehicle in a skid to "drift" to the lower side, *a* and *b*. There are two different roadway surfaces divided at *A* and *B*, each of which may have a different coefficient of friction. Front wheel skid marks are easily identified by dark, thin lines, *C*, at outer edges of tires. Rear tire skid marks, *D* and *E*, are lighter, and in this case slightly offset. Because of the forward shift in weight due to braking and a shift in weight to the right due to the superelevation, the left rear tire skid mark, *E*, appears very faint.

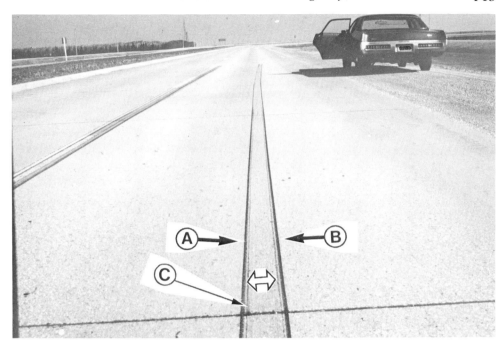

Figure 4-39. Skid mark. Because of the forward shift in weight, front tires "cup," with most of the weight being carried by outer edges of tire. The tire distortion is similar to that of an overloaded or underinflated tire. The outer edges of the tire generate greater heat, leaving two thin parallel lines as indicated at *A* and *B*. At the same time, the rear tires lift slightly, with tire distortion similar to an overinflated tire. In a straight skid, a rear tire leaves an overlapping skid mark that tracks inside the front tire skid mark, as indicated by the two-way arrow.

"drift" to the lower side or to the side that is carrying the most weight, which might be the opposite side if the weight is great enough on that side to compensate for the effect of superelevation.

4.039 When a vehicle brakes abruptly or is in a continuous braking action, there is a forward shift of weight. This extra weight on the front tires has the same effect on the tire tread distortion as an underinflated tire, that is, they "cup," and the extra weight is carried by the outer edges of the tires. Because of the extra weight, more heat is generated on the edges of a tire, resulting in two thin parallel skid lines or streaks at the outer edges of a tire. At the same time, the rear tires lift slightly but normally stay in contact with the roadway. The tire tread distortion of the rear tires is similar to that of an overinflated tire. In a straight skid, the rear tire skid marks track inside the two thin parallel skid lines or streaks caused by the front tires.

4.040 *Spin skid marks* result when a vehicle rotates around its center of mass, as in cases where the rear wheels move in a manner so as to lead the front wheels, and in cases where there is an external force applied to a vehicle at a location other than in direct line with its center of mass.

4.041   If skid marks are not readily evident at an accident scene, an investigator should not conclude on that basis alone that brakes were not applied nor that braking action did not take place. Additionally, if sideslip marks are not evident, it should not be concluded that evasive steering action was not taken. On *hard surfaces,* rubber particles burn or scrape off the skidding tire and stick to the pavement surface. In a similar manner, rubber deposits are left on a roadway surface by a rolling tire that is at the same time skidding sideways, such as driving into a curve. On hard, bituminous concrete surfaces and other hard surfaces such as cement roadway surfaces, a skid mark appears as a scraping or cleaning mark and is often very difficult to see. On these surfaces, the burned-off tire particles usually remain for a very short period of time, possibly only minutes, and may be blown away by wind generated by passing vehicles or destroyed by traffic or adverse weather conditions. Traffic, rain or wind on or over faint skid or sideslip marks often obliterates them within a very short time. Notwithstanding, more prominent scraping or cleaning marks may last for several days.

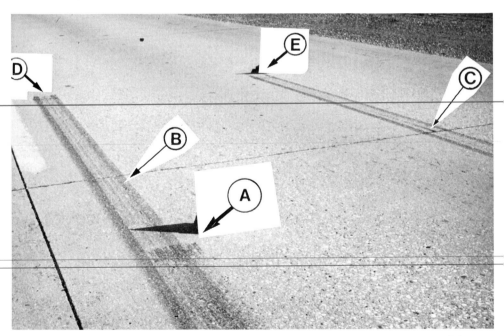

Figure 4-40. Burned-off tire particles, *A* and *B*, are from a tire in a skid. These particles are short-lived evidence. Burned-off tire particles appearing as a short, black streak in the center of skid mark at *C* were caused by a skidding tire striking sharp edge in pavement surface. Direction of travel is indicated by direction the dark streak leaves the sharp edge. Small deposits of burned-off particles will be found at ends of skid marks, *D* and *E*.

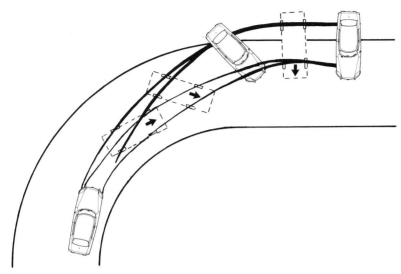

Figure 4-41. Width of and distance between tire marks helps to establish the positions of a vehicle at various locations.

4.042 Skid marks on a bituminous concrete roadway surface are caused by smearing of the asphalt or tar from the heat generated by a skidding tire. Cold bituminous concrete surfaces do not normally soften or smear, and consequently skid marks on these surfaces appear much the same as on cement surfaces.

4.043 Skid marks and sideslip marks are not common on wet, paved roadway surfaces. As mentioned previously, skid marks on bituminous concrete surfaces result because of heat generated by a skidding tire. Water keeps the tire cooled so that heat friction does not develop sufficiently to cause pavement smear. As a tire skids or sideslips on wet pavement, there is a temporary erasing or cleaning action as the tire pushes the water away from its path. The evidence of such skids or sideslips is normally short-lived. Nevertheless, such areas should be marked and examined for any skidding or sideslip action as soon as the pavement dries.

4.044 On paved surfaces covered with foreign material such as dust, dirt or sand, a skidding tire pushes the material aside and leaves a skid mark, and then the material may return as the vehicle passes, covering the skid marks. Under these roadway surface conditions, an investigator should sweep away the material leading to the involved vehicles to determine whether in fact skid marks are evident. In so doing, care must be taken not to destroy other evidence, for example, blood stains. Also, under these surface conditions, a skid mark may appear as a light mark. This is because during the skid, the tire actually cleans the pavement.

Figure 4-42. Skip skid mark caused by dual wheel of truck tractor running over body of animal.

4.045 In a straight skid, a tire leaves a skid mark the width of the tire tread and often leaves parallel tread rib marks, but not any cross pattern. However, a wider skid mark occurs from front tires when the wheels have been turned to either a left or right position, but the vehicle continued to skid in a straight line (*see* Fig. 4-38).

4.046 Vehicles that rotate or spin on a roadway such as after an off-center right-angle collision or when in yaw leave skid marks and sideskid marks of varying widths. These widths are dependent upon the position of the vehicle on the roadway, with resultant variance in amount of tire tread in contact with the roadway and in relation to its direction of travel. The path of the vehicle may be traced from these marks.

4.047 If a vehicle was being steered into a turn before brakes were applied, the skid marks may be slightly curved. When a vehicle is skidding, however, all efforts to change its direction of travel by steering are to no avail.

Figure 4-43. Skip skid marks resulting from a braked dual wheel of an empty or lightly loaded semitrailer.

4.048 *Skip skid marks* occur when a locked wheel bounces on the roadway. The blank spaces between the skid marks are not usually longer than 3 ft (1 m). Bouncing is usually caused by:

a. A wheel striking a hole, bump, rut or body or driving on a wash-board-type surface.
b. A vehicle colliding with another vehicle or object, causing the rear wheels to momentarily lift off the roadway.
c. An unloaded or lightly loaded trailer, particularly in cases of large, semitrailers with a braking system that locks the rear wheels before the front wheels so as to prevent jackknifing. When this occurs, the rear wheels bounce slightly, leaving skip skid marks.

4.049 A defective brake on a single wheel may not hold the wheel constantly locked but rather give total braking action intermittently as the wheel rotates. The resulting skid mark appears similar to a skip skid mark. When circumstances rule out the mark being a skip skid mark, a thorough examination of the wheel brake shoe and drum should be made. If the

Figure 4-44. Intermittent skid marks caused by "pumping" the brake pedal with full application and release.

brake is found to be defective, the vehicle would have had less than 100 percent braking capability.

4.050 Do not confuse *skips* in skid marks with *intermittent skid marks,* which appear with gaps between them. These gaps occur when locked wheels are released and relocked through braking action. Blank spaces or gaps between the intermittent skid marks are usually a minimum of approximately 15 to 20 feet, depending upon the speed of the vehicle and the driver's reaction time.

4.051 Rotation on any type of roadway surface causes a tire to become hot. When brakes are applied and a wheel locks on snow or ice surfaces, the tire sometimes grooves the surface at the same width as the tire contact with it. At freezing temperatures, this groove freezes. At other times, particularly in short skids or at the beginning of a long skid, a skid mark on ice or snow surfaces appears as a smooth, shiny mark.

4.052 An *underinflated tire* in a straight skid leaves two dark, thin parallel

Figure 4-45. Point of impact may be established by following skid marks to *A*, where the front end of vehicle 1 ran under the rear of vehicle 2, causing tire gouges in pavement. Note the clockwise rotation of vehicle 1 as a result of the eccentric force caused by the off-center collision (*see* Fig. 3-9B).

streaks on the roadway (*see* Fig. 4-39). These streaks appear at the outer edges of the tire tread. These lines or streaks are caused by the "cupping" effect of the tire and have an appearance similar to the front tire skid mark of a vehicle in a straight skid. The tire distortion that results in the "cupping" effect causes the majority of the weight to be carried by the outer edges of the tread; consequently, more heat is generated at these two points. The center of the tread may leave only a cleaning appearance on the roadway, with possibly some indication of the tread ribs.

4.053 Skid marks may change direction abruptly due to an impact with another vehicle or object. This change of direction is very important in determining the point of impact. Care must be taken in evaluating such marks to ensure that the driver did not at the last moment release his brake and steer the vehicle in an attempt to avoid collision. Such steering results in a yaw mark, which can be distinguished by its tire striation marks.

4.054 When a vehicle in a skid strikes an object, the front end dips and the rear end first rises and then drops after collision. Resultant tire marks often assist in determining the positions of the front and rear tires at the

Figure 4-46. Approximate point of impact at *A*. Vehicle continued skidding after impact, but skid marks become offset where vehicle was forced to side of roadway due to collision. Debris on the roadway and vehicle must be closely examined to determine whether the debris fell from the rear wheel area or from the front end. Improper conclusions could misplace the point of impact.

Figure 4-47. Approximate point of impact may be established at point where pedestrian was apparently lifted out of his shoes. Caution must be taken in establishing the point of impact in this manner, as shoes may have been carried or thrown to this location.

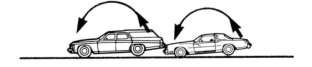

Figure 4-48. Both vehicles braking.

Figure 4-49. Spatter at *A* as the result of violent release of radiator water. Water trails form at *B* as water flows on roadway. Liquid trails flowing from vehicle often form pools at lower side of roadway.

time of collision. The front tires are forced against the roadway surface with tremendous pressure, leaving a *scrub mark*. The rear tires often lift sufficiently to leave a bounce or skip skid mark, depending on the speed and force of collision. The braking action leading to the point of impact often causes the front bumper to strike the other vehicle at a much lower point than would be the case if brakes were not applied. This should be considered when investigating front and rear vehicle damages that do not appear to match up.

VEHICLE DEBRIS

4.055   Vehicle *debris* may be solids or liquids. Generally, it is broken or loosened vehicle parts, portions of load, paint, rust, dirt, mud, radiator water, battery acid, and so on that falls off or from a vehicle during or as the result of collision. Debris may assist in tracing the approximate positions of a vehicle at times of primary and secondary contacts and the path following collision. However, when seeking this type of evidence or information, it must be determined whether the debris fell or rolled to its final position; any conclusions should be based on this determination.

4.056   Underbody debris, particularly dirt from the undersides of fend-

Figure 4-50. Liquid trails from the final position of a vehicle may often be traced back to locate the point of impact.

ers, falls forward at the time of collision. The concentration of this debris is heavy close to where it departed the vehicle. As it travels forward, the path widens into a fan pattern and becomes more thinly spread. This pattern not only assists in determining the approximate position of the vehicle at the time of impact, but it also indicates the direction of travel. Caution must be taken, however, that *deflected debris* is not confused with debris that would otherwise indicate the direction of travel of a vehicle.

4.057 Debris may assist in determining the point of impact and vehicle placement on the highway. Although it does not normally prove these points conclusively, it corroborates other evidence such as tire marks, scratches, gouges and witnesses' statements.

4.058 Broken radiators allow the violent release of water at time of collision. Water marks on the roadway result almost immediately, and as the vehicle rolls away from the point of impact, *water trails* are caused by water running out of the radiator onto the roadway to the point where the vehicle comes to rest. Release of oil from broken parts such as motor or transmission and acid from a broken battery leave evidence in a similar fashion. As the vehicle rests, the liquid flows in trails to form *pools*. Pools and water trails may be used to locate the original and rest positions of a vehicle and, frequently, the approximate point of impact.

4.059 Vehicle parts found at an accident scene may help in identifying vehicles involved. For example, headlamp rings, hubcaps, body ornaments and paint chips may be identified as belonging to a certain make, model and type of vehicle. These items may be matched to broken parts of vehicles at the scene or may assist in determining the vehicle involved in hit-and-run situations (*see* Fig. 4-10).

Chapter 5

SPEED ESTIMATES

COEFFICIENT OF FRICTION

5.001 *Coefficient of friction* (*f* value) represents the resistance of one body to another when they are sliding or rubbing against each other, for example, a tire sliding over a level roadway surface. The term *drag factor* represents the horizontal force required to cause an object to move in the direction of the force divided by the weight of the object being moved. The terms *coefficient of friction* and *drag factor* as used in this text are synonymous.

5.002 Coefficient of friction is actually the stopping force expressed as a numerical value of slipperiness, usually as a decimal fraction. In traffic accident investigation, the stopping force is commonly used to express the friction, drag, traction or adhesion between a tire and a highway surface and is frequently used in calculating speed from skid marks or a vehicle in yaw.

5.003 Coefficient of friction, in terms of vehicle tires and a highway surface, is the ratio of pounds or kilograms force (F) required to move a vehicle at a *constant* speed over the surface divided by the weight of the vehicle. For example, if a force of 2,000 pounds or kilograms is required to move a 4,000 pound or kilogram vehicle with its brakes locked, the coefficient of friction between the tires and the highway surface would be 2,000 divided by 4,000, or .50 (Fig. 5-1).

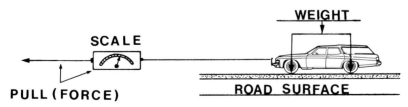

Figure 5-1A

155

SKID - YAW SPEED GUIDE AND REPORT

REPORT No._____

ACCIDENT DATA	TEST DATA

Date	Time	am / pm	Date	Time	am / pm

ACCIDENT DATA		TEST DATA	
Weather Temp		Weather Temp	
Location		Location	
VEHICLE		**VEHICLE**	
Licence no. VIN		Driver	
Make Yr. Model		Licence no.	
Odometer reading		Make Yr. Model	
		Odometer reading	
		Speed-O calibration date 19_____	

ROADWAY	DIRECTION OF TRAVEL	ROADWAY	DIRECTION OF TRAVEL
Type		Type	
Condition		Condition	
Grade		Grade	

ACCIDENT SKID DATA

	Impending		Skid		Totals
RF		+		=	
LF		+		=	
RR		+		=	
LR		+		=	
			Total		
			Average		

Longest skid mark [＿＿＿＿＿]

TEST SKID DATA

Test no.	1	2	3
Speed			
RF			
LF			
RR			
LR			
Total			
Average			

Total for f value [＿＿＿＿＿＿＿]

f = _____%

YAW DATA
Length
Chord
Middle ordinate

MEASUREMENT METhOD
Tape   Wheel   Paced   Other

MEASUREMENT METHOD
Tape   Wheel   Paced   Other

FORMULAE *(United States)*

$$f = \frac{S^2}{30D}$$

$$R = \frac{C^2}{8M} + \frac{M}{2}$$

$$S = 5.5 \sqrt{Df} \qquad \text{Skid}$$

$$S = 3.87 \sqrt{(f \pm e)\ R} \quad \text{Yaw}$$

Calculated Speed_____

FORMULAE *(Metric)*

$$f = \frac{S^2}{254D}$$

$$R = \frac{C^2}{8M} + \frac{M}{2}$$

$$S = 15.9 \sqrt{Df} \qquad \text{Skid}$$

$$S = 11.27 \sqrt{(f \pm e)\ R} \quad \text{Yaw}$$

Investigator: _____

Figure 5-1B

5.004   Coefficient of friction is calculated by using Formula 5-1:

United States

$$f = \frac{S^2}{30D}$$

Metric

$$f = \frac{S^2}{254D}$$

where   f = coefficient of friction
          S = speed in making test skids
          D = average skid distance

The numbers 30 and 254 represent the squares of 5.5 and 15.9 respectively, which are constants in calculating speed.

5.005   The coefficient of friction is not restricted to a braked skidding tire. It may also be applied to a tire sideslipping in a turn or driving into a curve, the friction between the drive wheels under acceleration, or a body or vehicle part moving over a highway surface.

TESTING FOR COEFFICIENT OF FRICTION

5.006   The coefficient of friction, f value, may be determined by conducting test skids. Under no circumstances, however, should test skids ever be made where there is a danger of causing yet another accident. Use the coefficient of friction table, Table 5-I, when actual tests cannot be made or are not necessary.

TABLE 5-I
COEFFICIENTS OF FRICTION OF VARIOUS ROADWAY SURFACES

COEFFICIENTS OF FRICTION OF VARIOUS ROADWAY SURFACES

DESCRIPTION OF ROAD SURFACE	DRY				WET			
	Less than 30 mph		More than 30 mph		Less than 30mph		More than 30mph	
	From	To	From	To	From	To	From	To
PORTLAND CEMENT								
New, Sharp	.80	1.20	.70	1.00	.50	.80	.40	.75
Travelled	.60	.80	.60	.75	.45	.70	.45	.65
Traffic Polished	.55	.75	.50	.65	.45	.65	.45	.60
ASPHALT or TAR								
New, Sharp	.80	1.20	.65	1.00	.50	.80	.45	.75
Travelled	.60	.80	.55	.70	.45	.70	.40	.65
Traffic Polished	.55	.75	.45	.65	.45	.65	.40	.60
Excess Tar	.50	.60	.35	.60	.30	.60	.25	.55
GRAVEL								
Packed, Oiled	.55	.85	.50	.80	.40	.80	.40	.60
Loose	.40	.70	.40	.70	.45	.75	.45	.75
CINDERS								
Packed	.50	.70	.50	.70	.65	.75	.65	.75
ROCK								
Crushed	.55	.75	.55	.75	.55	.75	.55	.75
ICE								
Smooth	.10	.25	.07	.20	.05	.10	.05	.10
SNOW								
Packed	.30	.55	.35	.55	.30	.60	.30	.60
Loose	.10	.25	.10	.20	.30	.60	.30	.60

Reproduced with permission of the Traffic Institute, Northwestern University, Evanston, Illinois.

5.007   Certain procedures and precautions are necessary in making test skids:

    a. Duplicate actual conditions as closely as possible. Use the same vehicle with its load or a similar vehicle and load. Conduct tests in the same location, travelling in the same direction and under the same weather, temperature and highway surface conditions.

b. If safe, make test skids at approximately the same speed it is believed the accident vehicle was travelling. For safety reasons, test speeds should not, however, exceed 35 mph (56 km/h).

c. If the accident vehicle can be used to make test skids, it does not matter what its braking capability might have been. This is because its own coefficient of fraction will be used in the speed formulae.

d. If the speed limit is 35 mph (56 km/h) or less, make test skids at the speed limit. If the resultant skid marks are shorter than the accident skid marks, the investigator has good evidence that the accident vehicle was travelling in excess of the legal speed limit.

e. Ensure the test vehicle is kept on a straight path. Travel at a constant speed of approximately 3 to 5 mph (5 to 8 km/h) over the speed at which the test is to be made. Decelerate to the test speed and apply brakes quickly and hard and hold firm. Skid to a complete stop. Unless the brakes are applied quickly and hard and held firm, the wheels will slow gradually, with considerable braking effort exerted before a skid mark is commenced. Consequently, an incorrectly high coefficient of friction would be calculated because of a shorter skid mark.

f. Test skids should not be made at less than 15 mph (25 km/h). It is difficult to measure resultant skid marks, and any calculations made therefrom usually result in an excessively high coefficient of friction rather than an average or more accurate *f* value. Additionally, short skids do not normally allow for such factors as tire heat buildup and pavement smear, which occur with longer skids. These and other factors such as patches of mud or sand, gritty surfaces or worn tires are all necessary in determining an average coefficient of friction for a portion of roadway if applicable.

g. Conduct a test skid. Measure the length of all skidmarks and calculate the average skid distance. Conduct a second test skid. If the average skidding distances are ±10 percent, add the two sums and divide by two to obtain the average skid distance of the two tests. If the two tests do not agree ±10 percent, make a further test or tests until two suitably consistent results are obtained.

Example

Two test skids were made at 30 mph (48 km/h). Their average skid distances were not within 10 percent. A third test was made, also at 30 mph (48 km/h), the average result of which was within 10 percent of test

Figure 5-2. Heat buildup in a skidding tire may cause asphalt surfaces to melt and smear.

1. Therefore, tests 1 and 3 should be used to calculate the coefficient of friction.

	Test 1		*Test 2*		*Test 3*
LF —	50 ft (15.2 m)	LF —	44 ft (13.4 m)	LF —	51 ft (15.5 m)
RF —	49 ft (14.9 m)	RF —	45 ft (13.7 m)	RF —	50 ft (15.2 m)
LR —	47 ft (14.3 m)	LR —	42 ft (12.8 m)	LR —	48 ft (14.6 m)
RR —	48 ft (14.6 m)	RR —	40 ft (12.2 m)	RR —	47 ft (14.3 m)
	194 ft (59.0 m)		171 ft (52.1 m)		196 ft (59.6 m)

	Average 1		*Average 2*		*Average 3*
	48.5 ft (14.75 m)		42.75 ft (13.0 m)		49 ft (14.9 m)

Average skid distance of tests 1 and 3 is 49 ft (15 m).

United States

$$f = \frac{30^2}{30 \times 49}$$

$$f = \frac{900}{1470}$$

$$f = .61$$

Metric

$$f = \frac{48^2}{254 \times 15}$$

$$f = \frac{2304}{3810}$$

$$f = .61$$

h. When it is necessary to make test skids on a level surface or when Table 5-1 is used and the accident vehicle skidded upgrade (+), the grade percent is added to the coefficient of friction in the speed formulae. Similarly, if an accident vehicle skidded downgrade (−), the grade percent would then be subtracted in the speed formulae.

5.0071 An alternative method to calculate the f value using a skid test is to use the longest tire mark. The resultant speed estimate using the calculated f value will be conservative.

5.008 Automatic detonators are available that may be attached to a vehicle. Upon brake application, the detonator releases a chalk or dye under tremendous pressure onto the roadway, marking the point of brake application. It is much easier to locate the beginning of skid marks or impending skid marks in this manner.

5.009 Skid tests must be conducted using an accurate speedometer. Speedometer accuracy may be determined through either (1) instrument calibration by a qualified speedometer technician or (2) by driving over a measured mile or kilometer. In driving over a measured mile or kilometer, it is necessary to determine the number of seconds required to drive the distance using a stopwatch. A car moving at 60 mph or km/h takes 60 seconds to travel 1 mile or 1 kilometer. To test a speedometer, travel at a constant speed over the mile or kilometer and divide 3,600 by the number of seconds it takes to travel the mile or kilometer.

Example
It took a vehicle 70 seconds to travel 1 mi or km. The actual speed travelled was 51.43 mph or km/h.

If, in this case, the speedometer registered a constant speed of 55 mph or km/h, the speedometer error would have been approximately 3.5 mph or km/h.

5.010 Alternative methods of measuring the coefficient of friction to that of making test skids are shown in Figures 5-3, 5-4 and 5-5. See also paragraphs 5.011, 5.012 and 5.013. In these examples, the unit should be weighed and pulled with the same scale. Note the pounds (kilograms) pull required to keep it moving. The total weight of the unit and the pounds (kilograms) pull (force) can then be measured and placed into Formula 5-2.

United States	Metric
$f = \dfrac{F}{W}$	$f = \dfrac{F}{W}$

where f = coefficient of friction
    F = pounds or kilograms force to move the unit
    W = total weight of unit

TABLE 5-II
SPEEDOMETER ACCURACY CHECKLIST

Time (in seconds)	Speed (mph or km/h)	Time (in seconds)	Speed (mph or km/h)	Time (in seconds)	Speed (mph or km/h)
40	90.00	88	40.91	136	26.47
41	87.80	89	40.45	137	26.28
42	85.71	90	40.00	138	26.09
43	83.72	91	39.56	139	25.90
44	81.82	92	39.13	140	25.71
45	80.00	93	38.71	141	25.53
46	78.26	94	38.30	142	25.35
47	76.60	95	37.89	143	25.17
48	75.00	96	37.50	144	25.00
49	73.47	97	37.11	145	24.83
50	72.00	98	36.73	146	24.66
51	70.59	99	36.36	147	24.49
52	69.23	100	36.00	148	24.32
53	67.92	101	35.64	149	24.16
54	66.67	102	35.29	150	24.00
55	65.45	103	34.95	151	23.84
56	64.29	104	34.62	152	23.68
57	63.16	105	34.29	153	23.53
58	62.07	106	33.96	154	23.38
59	61.02	107	33.64	155	23.23
60	60.00	108	33.33	156	23.08
61	59.02	109	33.03	157	22.93
62	58.06	110	32.73	158	22.78
63	57.14	111	32.43	159	22.64
64	56.25	112	32.14	160	22.50
65	55.38	113	31.86	161	22.36
66	54.55	114	31.58	162	22.22
67	53.73	115	31.30	163	22.09
68	52.94	116	31.03	164	21.95
69	52.17	117	30.77	165	21.82
70	51.43	118	30.51	166	21.69
71	50.70	119	30.25	167	21.56
72	50.00	120	30.00	168	21.43
73	49.32	121	29.75	169	21.30
74	48.65	122	29.51	170	21.18
75	48.00	123	29.27	171	21.05
76	47.37	124	29.03	172	20.93
77	46.75	125	28.80	173	20.81
78	46.15	126	28.57	174	20.69
79	45.57	127	28.35	175	20.57
80	45.00	128	28.13	176	20.45
81	44.44	129	27.91	177	20.34
82	43.90	130	27.69	178	20.22
83	43.37	131	27.48	179	20.11
84	42.86	132	27.27	180	20.00
85	42.35	133	27.07	181	19.89
86	41.86	134	26.87		
87	41.38	135	26.67		

Example

A tire and wheel weighing 50 lb (22.68 kg) required 30 lb (13.61 kg) pull or force to move it along a roadway surface. The coefficient of friction was (*see* Fig. 5-3):

United States	*Metric*
$f = \dfrac{30}{50}$	$f = \dfrac{13.61}{22.68}$
$f = .60$	$f = .60$

5.011   In cases where a vehicle turns onto its side or top, the coefficient of friction (*f* value) of metal to pavement or metal to an earth-type surface such as gravel or dirt is approximately .30 to .40. The *f* value depends, of course, on the slipperiness of the pavement or consistency of the earth surface. The drag or coefficient of friction can be affected by the metal configuration of the vehicle, for example, protrusions that might scrape or dig into the road surface.

5.012   To determine the coefficient of friction of metal to a roadway, a piece of the same type of metal may be pulled along the roadway as illustrated in Figure 5-5. The weight of the unit and the pounds (kilograms) pull or force required to move it along the roadway surface may then be placed into Formula 5-2 and the coefficient of friction calculated. The pull or force on the unit must be as close as possible to the horizontal so as to avoid any lift on the unit, which would affect the weight resting on the road surface.

5.013   When using the alternative methods of testing the coefficient of friction explained in paragraphs 5.010 and 5.012, the pounds (kilograms) force required to *keep* the unit moving is the force that must be used in the formula rather than the *static* force or the force required to move the unit from its standing position.

Figure 5-3. Method of determining coefficient of friction using a tire and wheel and a spring scale.

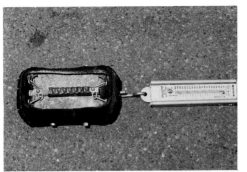

A   *B*

Figure 5-4 A and B. *A* shows method of constructing drag sled using portion of tire with lead weight. Construction must be so that the pull (force) is applied to the center of the mass. *B* shows correct method of measuring force or pull required to determine coefficient of friction.

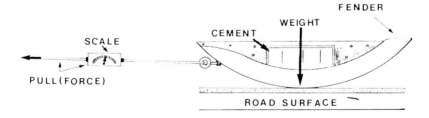

Figure 5-5. Method of determining coefficient of friction between metal and roadway surface.

5.014   To determine the coefficient of friction for a motorcycle requires special calculations. If both the front and rear wheels are locked in a skid, the usual coefficient of friction of the roadway may be used in calculating the speed of the motorcycle from skid marks. However, if only one wheel is locked in a skid, for example, the rear wheel, the motorcycle has only a 50 percent braking capability, and the coefficient of friction must be based on the normal coefficient of friction for the roadway and be calculated on the percentage of the total *loaded* weight of the motorcycle on that wheel. The drag on the remaining free-wheeling wheel is negligible and may be disregarded in speed calculations.

Example

A motorcycle with only the rear wheel locked skidded 175 ft (53 m) to a stop on a roadway having a maximum or usual coefficient of friction of .70. The motorcycle and load (driver) weighed 800 lb (362.88 kg). Of the total weight, 480 lb (217.73 kg) or 60 percent of the total loaded weight of the motorcycle was on the rear wheel during the skid. The coefficient of friction for the motorcycle may be calculated using Formula 5-3:

United States	*Metric*
$f' = fR$	$f' = fR$

where f' = motorcycle coefficient of friction
  f = normal coefficient of friction (from automobile test skids or from chart)
  R = percentage of total weight on rear wheel during skid

Applying Formula 5-3:

$f' = .70 \times .60$	$f' = .70 \times .60$
$f' = .42$	$f' = .42$

5.015   Water, oil, grease, mud, loose gravel, sand and heavy concentrations of salt on paved surfaces as well as mud, snow and icy surfaces give a low coefficient of friction. The best traction is found with dry, clean, gritty or abrasive paved surfaces; consequently, these provide the highest coefficient of friction. Depending upon the type of roadway surface, the coefficient of friction can vary from approximately .05 on extremely icy surfaces to as high as 1.2 on dry, hard, gritty surfaces.

5.016   Since coefficient of friction test skids are to be made under similar weather conditions, *air resistance* should not normally be a factor in determining speed from skid marks. In any event, under speeds of 80 mph (129 km/h), air resistance is negligible. For example, at 60 mph (96.5 km/h), air resistance causes a vehicle to stop as little as 2 ft sooner than it would have stopped without air resistance.

5.017   *Heavy vehicles* require more force to bring them to a stop than do light weight vehicles. They also generate greater friction between the tires and the roadway surface than do lighter vehicles. The important thing to realize is that the stopping distances are the same. This is because when brakes are applied and wheels lock, a vehicle is decelerated by the friction between the tires and the roadway. The extra force required to bring the heavier vehicle to a stop is compensated by the greater friction generated between the tires and the roadway because of the greater weight.

5.018 *Tire pressure* has a negligible effect on coefficient of friction or vehicle stopping distance. However, an underinflated tire provides a greater contact area and under icy conditions provides better traction or *f* value.

5.019 *Smooth tire tread* has a greater coefficient of friction on an ice surface than does a grooved tire. This is because more tire surface comes into contact with the ice surface, thereby providing better traction. However, in mud, snow or other loose material, a *grooved tire* provides more traction. On normal roadway surfaces, smooth tires and grooved tire treads provide approximately the same traction or *f* value.

5.020 *Tire chains* increase the coefficient of friction in mud, snow and ice. However, on hard, paved surfaces, they tend to lower the *f* value compared with standard highway tires.

5.021 *Studded tires* used on glare ice result in a significant reduction in stopping distances compared with standard highway and snow tires. On glare ice, studded tires on all four wheels reduce stopping distance to less than half the stopping distance with studs on rear tires only. On dry or wet *asphalt* surfaces, the type of tire and presence or absence of studs make virtually no significant difference in stopping distances. On both dry and wet *concrete* surfaces, studded tires on the rear wheels only result in a small but significant *increase* in stopping distance compared to standard highway tires. On both dry and wet concrete surfaces, studded tires on all four wheels result in an *increase* in stopping distance compared to that required with standard highway tires. This increase, however, is less than twice that resulting from studded tires on the rear wheels only.[20]

5.022 *Low speeds* usually result in greater *f* values than do *high speeds* on similar surfaces. Regardless of speed, the highest coefficient of friction is after brakes have been applied but just before the tires begin to slide.

5.023 Once a tire begins to slide, particularly on asphalt roadways, tremendous heat builds up between the tire and the roadway surface. Because of the high temperature of the tire, contact with an asphalt surface causes the asphalt to melt and smear (*see* Fig. 5-2). During very hot weather, some asphalt surfaces become soft, and skids at low speeds also cause the pavement to smear. These hot, soft asphalt surfaces may have a much lower coefficient of friction or *f* value than do cold asphalt surfaces.

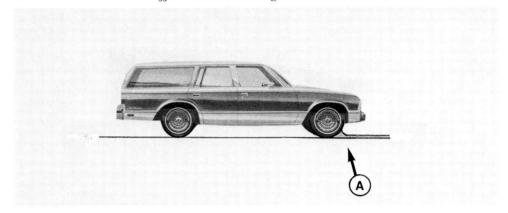

Figure 5-6. At low speeds, a tire pushes water in front of it in the form of a wedge,*A*. At high speeds, a tire may ride upon the film of water, thereby losing all contact with the roadway surface.

5.024 *Hydroplaning* is the situation where tires lose contact with the roadway by riding on a film of water that covers the roadway surface. This phenomenon is most often encountered with the front tires of a vehicle. An investigator must be aware of and consider the effect of hydroplaning on vehicle behavior.

5.025 NASA tests indicate that hydroplaning is not likely to occur unless there is approximately .20 to .30 in of water lying on the roadway.[21]

5.026 Rear-end collisions and failing to negotiate curves are the most common types of accidents resulting from hydroplaning.

5.027 At low speeds, a rotating tire pushes water ahead of itself in the form of a wedge. At high speeds, however, the tire climbs up onto the wedge of water and actually rides on a film of water, losing all contact with the roadway surface.

5.028 Because in hydroplaning the tires tend to lose contact with the roadway surface, it is directly associated with a reduction of the coefficient of friction. As speed increases, the coefficient of friction decreases.

5.029 The effect of hydroplaning is greatest on the front tires. It is the front tires that first encounter the film of water. They push a substantial amount of the water to the sides, clearing the road for contact by the rear tires.

5.030 When the front tires are hydroplaning, they may lose all or most of their rotation. There is no way for a driver to know this has occurred until he applies his brakes or attempts to steer, at which time he loses control of the vehicle. In these situations, only the rear wheels have any braking capability, and the stopping distance is increased by approximately 1.50 times.[22]

5.031 The geometric tire tread design and smoothness of the roadway surface have a considerable bearing on when and the amount of hydroplaning that occurs. Most tire tread patterns are designed so as to allow optimum contact, drainage and adhesion with the roadway surface at all times and under a variety of highway conditions and vehicle maneuvers. Tires with deep longitudinal grooves and adequate cross-drainage channels allow satisfactory drainage in most cases so as to allow roadway contact with the tread at slower speeds. Radial-ply constructed tires prevent most of the distortion that takes place with bias-ply tires. Therefore, there is greater contact with the roadway in curves and less chance of slippage or hydroplaning (*see* Fig. 2-31).

5.032 When tires are hydroplaning, external forces such as crosswinds or improper camber adjustment may cause the vehicle to leave the intended path of travel.

5.033 On well-drained roadways, that is, with significant super-elevation or crowning, hydroplaning is rare except for smooth or well-worn tires driven at fairly high speeds.

SKID MARK MEASUREMENTS AND SPEED

5.034 The purpose in measuring skid marks is to determine how far a vehicle slid. The *motion energy* (inertia) of a vehicle is dissipated during a skid or slide through its contact with the roadway surface or other surface. Therefore, if measurements are not properly taken, speed calculated from skid marks or slides is not accurate.

5.035 It is very difficult to see all of a skid mark because as a wheel starts to lock up, a light shadow is left on the roadway surface that may not be visible to the naked eye and disappears very quickly. It is during this period that a vehicle experiences the greatest braking capability. Because it is difficult to actually see and measure the total skid mark, speed calculated from skid marks does not yield the maximum speed a vehicle was travelling before slowing commenced, but indicates only the amount of speed lost in the distance it can be determined that the vehicle skidded. It does not reflect the amount of speed lost before skidding commenced. Therefore, speed calculated from skid marks is the *minimum initial vehicle speed* required to leave the skid marks.

5.036 Speed from skid marks may be calculated using Formula 5-4:

United States
$$S = 5.5 \sqrt{Df}$$

Metric
$$S = 15.9 \sqrt{Df}$$

where S = minimum initial speed
D = skid distance
f = coefficient of friction (*see* 5.007(h))

The numbers 5.5 and 15.9 are constants in calculating speed (Table 5-III).

TABLE 5-III-A

SPEED FROM SKID MARKS IN MILES PER HOUR

Coefficient of Friction (f)	Skid (feet)													
	5	6	7	8	9	10	11	12	13	14	15	16	17	18
0.05	2.750	3.012	3.254	3.479	3.690	3.888	4.078	4.260	4.434	4.601	4.763	4.919	5.071	5.218
0.10	3.889	4.260	4.602	4.919	5.218	5.500	5.768	6.024	6.270	6.507	6.736	6.957	7.171	7.379
0.15	4.763	5.218	5.636	6.025	6.390	6.732	7.064	7.379	7.680	7.970	8.250	8.521	8.783	9.037
0.20	5.500	6.025	6.508	6.957	7.379	7.777	8.157	8.520	8.868	9.203	9.526	9.839	10.141	10.436
0.25	6.149	6.736	7.276	7.778	8.250	8.695	9.120	9.526	9.915	10.289	10.650	11.000	11.339	11.667
0.30	6.736	7.379	7.971	8.521	9.037	9.526	9.991	10.435	10.861	11.271	11.665	12.050	12.421	12.781
0.35	7.276	7.970	8.609	9.203	9.762	10.285	10.791	11.271	11.731	12.174	12.602	13.015	13.416	13.805
0.40	7.778	8.521	9.203	9.839	10.436	11.000	11.536	12.049	12.541	13.015	13.469	13.914	14.342	14.758
0.45	8.250	9.037	9.761	10.436	11.069	11.665	12.236	12.780	13.302	13.804	14.289	14.758	15.212	15.653
0.50	8.696	9.526	10.290	11.000	11.667	12.298	12.898	13.472	14.022	14.551	15.059	15.556	16.035	16.500
0.55	9.121	9.991	10.792	11.537	12.237	12.897	13.528	14.129	14.706	15.261	15.796	16.316	16.818	17.305
0.60	9.526	10.436	11.272	12.050	12.781	13.469	14.129	14.758	15.360	15.940	16.500	17.041	17.566	18.075
0.65	9.915	10.862	11.732	12.542	13.303	14.019	14.706	15.360	15.987	16.591	17.171	17.737	18.283	18.813
0.70	10.290	11.272	12.175	13.015	13.805	14.547	15.261	15.940	16.591	17.217	17.820	18.407	18.973	19.523
0.75	10.651	11.667	12.602	13.472	14.289	15.059	15.797	16.500	17.173	17.822	18.447	19.053	19.639	20.208
0.80	11.000	12.050	13.015	13.914	14.758	15.554	16.315	17.041	17.736	18.406	19.052	19.677	20.283	20.871
0.85	11.339	12.421	13.416	14.342	15.212	16.032	16.817	17.565	18.282	18.973	19.635	20.283	20.907	21.513
0.90	11.667	12.781	13.805	14.758	15.653	16.500	17.305	18.074	18.812	19.523	20.207	20.871	21.513	22.137
0.95	11.987	13.131	14.183	15.162	16.082	16.951	17.779	18.570	19.328	20.058	20.757	21.443	22.103	22.744
1.00	12.298	13.472	14.552	15.556	16.500	17.391	18.241	19.052	19.830	20.579	21.296	22.000	22.677	23.335
1.05	12.602	13.805	14.911	15.941	16.907	17.820	18.691	19.523	20.320	21.087	21.824	22.543	23.237	23.911
1.10	12.899	14.130	15.262	16.316	17.305	18.238	19.131	19.982	20.798	21.583	22.341	23.074	23.784	24.473
1.15	13.189	14.447	15.605	16.682	17.694	18.650	19.561	20.431	21.265	22.068	22.841	23.592	24.318	25.023
1.20	13.472	14.758	15.941	17.041	18.075	19.052	19.982	20.871	21.723	22.543	23.331	24.100	24.841	25.562
1.25	13.750	15.062	16.269	17.393	18.448	19.442	20.394	21.301	22.171	23.008	23.815	24.597	25.354	26.089
1.30	14.022	15.361	16.591	17.737	18.813	19.827	20.798	21.723	22.610	23.463	24.282	25.084	25.856	26.605

Coefficient of Friction (f)	Skid (feet)													
	19	20	25	30	35	40	45	50	55	60	65	70	75	80
0.05	5.361	5.500	6.149	6.736	7.276	7.778	8.250	8.696	9.121	9.526	9.915	10.290	10.651	11.000
0.10	7.581	7.778	8.696	9.526	10.290	11.000	11.667	12.298	12.899	13.472	14.022	14.552	15.062	15.556
0.15	9.285	9.526	10.651	11.667	12.602	13.472	14.289	15.062	15.798	16.500	17.174	17.822	18.448	19.053
0.20	10.721	11.000	12.298	13.472	14.552	15.556	16.500	17.393	18.241	19.053	19.831	20.579	21.301	22.000
0.25	11.987	12.298	13.750	15.062	16.269	17.393	18.448	19.445	20.395	21.301	22.171	23.008	23.816	24.597
0.30	13.131	13.472	15.062	16.500	17.822	19.053	20.208	21.301	22.341	23.335	24.287	25.204	26.089	26.944
0.35	14.183	14.552	16.269	17.822	19.250	20.579	21.827	23.008	24.131	25.204	26.233	27.224	28.179	29.103
0.40	15.162	15.556	17.393	19.053	20.579	22.000	23.335	24.597	25.797	26.944	28.045	29.103	30.125	31.113
0.45	16.082	16.500	18.448	20.208	21.827	23.335	24.750	26.089	27.362	28.579	29.746	30.869	31.952	33.000
0.50	16.952	17.393	19.445	21.301	23.008	24.597	26.089	27.500	28.842	30.125	31.355	32.538	33.680	34.785
0.55	17.780	18.241	20.395	22.341	24.131	25.797	27.362	28.842	30.250	31.595	32.885	34.127	35.324	36.483
0.60	18.570	19.053	21.301	23.335	25.204	26.944	28.579	30.125	31.595	33.000	34.347	35.644	36.895	38.105
0.65	19.328	19.831	22.171	24.287	26.233	28.045	29.746	31.355	32.885	34.347	35.750	37.100	38.402	39.661
0.70	20.058	20.579	23.008	25.204	27.224	29.103	30.869	32.538	34.127	35.644	37.100	38.500	39.851	41.158
0.75	20.762	21.301	23.816	26.089	28.179	30.125	31.952	33.680	35.324	36.895	38.402	39.851	41.250	42.603
0.80	21.443	22.000	24.597	26.944	29.103	31.113	33.000	34.785	36.483	38.105	39.661	41.158	42.603	44.000
0.85	22.103	22.677	25.354	27.774	29.999	32.070	34.016	35.856	37.606	39.278	40.882	42.425	43.914	45.354
0.90	22.744	23.335	26.089	28.579	30.869	33.000	35.002	36.895	38.696	40.417	42.067	43.655	45.187	46.669
0.95	23.367	23.974	26.804	29.362	31.715	33.904	35.961	37.906	39.756	41.524	43.220	44.851	46.425	47.948
1.00	23.974	24.597	27.500	30.125	32.538	34.785	36.895	38.891	40.789	42.603	44.342	46.016	47.631	49.193
1.05	24.566	25.204	28.179	30.869	33.342	35.644	37.806	39.851	41.796	43.655	45.437	47.153	48.808	50.408
1.10	25.144	25.797	28.842	31.595	34.127	36.483	38.696	40.789	42.780	44.682	46.507	48.262	49.956	51.595
1.15	25.709	26.377	29.490	32.305	34.894	37.303	39.566	41.706	43.741	45.686	47.552	49.347	51.079	52.754
1.20	26.262	26.944	30.125	33.000	35.644	38.105	40.417	42.603	44.682	46.669	48.575	50.408	52.178	53.889
1.25	26.804	27.500	30.746	33.680	36.379	38.891	41.250	43.481	45.604	47.631	49.576	51.448	53.254	55.000
1.30	27.335	28.045	31.355	34.347	37.100	39.661	42.067	44.342	46.507	48.575	50.558	52.467	54.308	56.089

TABLE 5-III-A (*Continued*)
SPEED FROM SKID MARKS IN MILES PER HOUR

Coefficient of Friction (f)	Skid (feet)													
	85	90	95	100	105	110	115	120	125	130	135	140	145	150
0.05	11.339	11.667	11.987	12.298	12.602	12.899	13.189	13.472	13.750	14.022	14.289	14.551	14.809	15.062
0.10	16.035	16.500	16.952	17.393	17.822	18.241	18.651	19.052	19.445	19.831	20.208	20.579	20.943	21.301
0.15	19.639	20.208	20.762	21.301	21.827	22.341	22.843	23.334	23.816	24.287	24.750	25.204	25.650	26.089
0.20	22.677	23.335	23.974	24.597	25.204	25.797	26.377	26.944	27.500	28.045	28.579	29.103	29.618	30.125
0.25	25.354	26.089	26.804	27.500	28.179	28.842	29.490	30.125	30.745	31.355	31.952	32.538	33.114	33.680
0.30	27.774	28.579	29.362	30.125	30.869	31.595	32.305	33.000	33.680	34.347	35.002	35.644	36.275	36.895
0.35	29.999	30.869	31.715	32.538	33.341	34.127	34.893	35.644	36.379	37.099	37.806	38.500	39.181	39.851
0.40	32.070	33.000	33.904	34.785	35.644	36.483	37.303	38.105	38.891	39.661	40.417	41.158	41.887	42.603
0.45	34.016	35.002	35.961	36.895	37.806	38.696	39.566	40.416	41.250	42.067	42.868	43.655	44.427	45.187
0.50	35.856	36.895	37.906	38.891	39.851	40.789	41.706	42.603	43.481	44.342	45.187	46.016	46.831	47.631
0.55	37.606	38.696	39.756	40.789	41.796	42.780	43.741	44.682	45.603	46.507	47.393	48.262	49.117	49.956
0.60	39.278	40.417	41.524	42.603	43.654	44.682	45.686	46.669	47.631	48.575	49.500	50.408	51.301	52.178
0.65	40.882	42.067	43.220	44.342	45.437	46.507	47.552	48.575	49.576	50.558	51.521	52.467	53.395	54.308
0.70	42.425	43.655	44.851	46.016	47.153	48.262	49.347	50.408	51.448	52.467	53.466	54.447	55.411	56.358
0.75	43.914	45.187	46.425	47.631	48.808	49.956	51.079	52.178	53.254	54.308	55.343	56.358	57.356	58.336
0.80	45.354	46.669	47.948	49.193	50.408	51.595	52.754	53.888	55.000	56.089	57.158	58.207	59.237	60.249
0.85	46.750	48.105	49.424	50.707	51.959	53.182	54.378	55.547	56.692	57.815	58.917	59.998	61.060	62.104
0.90	48.105	49.500	50.856	52.178	53.466	54.724	55.953	57.158	58.336	59.492	60.625	61.737	62.830	63.904
0.95	49.424	50.856	52.250	53.607	54.931	56.224	57.487	58.724	59.935	61.122	62.286	63.429	64.552	65.655
1.00	50.707	52.178	53.607	55.000	56.358	57.684	58.980	60.249	61.492	62.710	63.904	65.077	66.229	67.361
1.05	51.960	53.466	54.931	56.358	57.750	59.109	60.437	61.737	63.010	64.258	65.482	66.684	67.864	69.024
1.10	53.182	54.724	56.224	57.684	59.109	60.500	61.859	63.190	64.493	65.770	67.023	68.253	69.461	70.649
1.15	54.378	55.954	57.487	58.980	60.437	61.859	63.250	64.610	65.943	67.249	68.530	69.787	71.022	72.237
1.20	55.547	57.158	58.724	60.249	61.737	63.190	64.610	66.000	67.361	68.695	70.004	71.288	72.550	73.790
1.25	56.693	58.336	59.935	61.492	63.010	64.493	65.943	67.361	68.750	70.112	71.447	72.758	74.046	75.312
1.30	57.815	59.492	61.122	62.710	64.258	65.770	67.249	68.695	70.112	71.500	72.862	74.199	75.512	76.803

Coefficient of Friction (f)	Skid (feet)											
	155	160	165	170	175	180	185	190	195	200	220	240
0.05	15.311	15.556	15.798	16.035	16.269	16.500	16.728	16.952	17.174	17.393	18.241	19.053
0.10	21.654	22.000	22.341	22.677	23.008	23.335	23.656	23.974	24.287	24.597	25.797	26.944
0.15	26.520	26.944	27.362	27.774	28.179	28.579	28.973	29.362	29.746	30.125	31.595	33.000
0.20	30.623	31.113	31.595	32.070	32.538	33.000	33.455	33.904	34.347	34.785	36.483	38.105
0.25	34.237	34.785	35.324	35.856	36.379	36.895	37.404	37.906	38.402	38.891	40.789	42.603
0.30	37.505	38.105	38.696	39.278	39.851	40.417	40.974	41.524	42.067	42.603	44.682	46.669
0.35	40.510	41.158	41.796	42.425	43.044	43.655	44.257	44.851	45.437	46.016	48.262	50.408
0.40	43.307	44.000	44.682	45.354	46.016	46.669	47.313	47.948	48.575	49.193	51.595	53.889
0.45	45.934	46.669	47.393	48.105	48.808	49.500	50.183	50.856	51.521	52.178	54.724	57.158
0.50	48.419	49.193	49.956	50.707	51.448	52.178	52.897	53.607	54.308	55.000	57.684	60.249
0.55	50.782	51.595	52.395	53.182	53.959	54.724	55.479	56.224	56.959	57.684	60.500	63.190
0.60	53.040	53.889	54.724	55.547	56.358	57.158	57.946	58.724	59.492	60.249	63.190	66.000
0.65	55.206	56.089	56.959	57.815	58.660	59.492	60.312	61.122	61.921	62.710	65.770	68.695
0.70	57.290	58.207	59.109	59.998	60.874	61.737	62.589	63.429	64.258	65.077	68.253	71.288
0.75	59.301	60.249	61.184	62.104	63.010	63.904	64.786	65.655	66.514	67.361	70.649	73.790
0.80	61.245	62.225	63.190	64.140	65.077	66.000	66.910	67.809	68.695	69.570	72.966	76.210
0.85	63.130	64.140	65.135	66.114	67.080	68.031	68.970	69.895	70.809	71.711	75.211	78.556
0.90	64.961	66.000	67.023	68.031	69.024	70.004	70.969	71.922	72.862	73.790	77.392	80.833
0.95	66.741	67.809	68.860	69.895	70.912	71.922	72.914	73.893	74.859	75.812	79.513	83.048
1.00	68.474	69.570	70.649	71.711	72.758	73.790	74.808	75.812	76.803	77.782	81.578	85.206
1.05	70.165	71.288	72.393	73.482	74.555	75.612	76.655	77.684	78.700	79.703	83.593	87.310
1.10	71.817	72.966	74.097	75.211	76.309	77.392	78.459	79.513	80.552	81.578	85.560	89.364
1.15	73.431	74.606	75.762	76.902	78.024	79.131	80.223	81.300	82.362	83.412	87.483	91.373
1.20	75.010	76.210	77.392	78.556	79.703	80.833	81.948	83.048	84.134	85.206	89.364	93.338
1.25	76.557	77.782	78.988	80.176	81.346	82.500	83.638	84.761	85.869	86.963	91.207	95.263
1.30	78.073	79.322	80.552	81.763	82.957	84.134	85.294	86.439	87.569	88.685	93.013	97.149

TABLE 5-III-A (*Continued*)

SPEED FROM SKID MARKS ON MILES PER HOUR

Coefficient of Friction (f)	Skid (feet)										
	260	280	300	325	350	375	400	425	450	475	500
0.05	19.831	20.579	21.301	22.171	23.008	23.816	24.597	25.354	26.089	26.804	27.500
0.10	28.045	29.103	30.125	31.354	32.538	33.680	34.785	35.856	36.895	37.906	38.891
0.15	34.347	35.644	36.895	38.402	39.851	41.250	42.603	43.914	45.187	46.425	47.631
0.20	39.661	41.158	42.603	44.342	46.016	47.631	49.193	50.707	52.178	53.607	55.000
0.25	44.342	46.016	47.631	49.576	51.448	53.254	55.000	56.693	58.336	59.935	61.492
0.30	48.575	50.408	52.178	54.308	56.358	58.336	60.249	62.104	63.904	65.655	67.361
0.35	52.467	54.447	56.358	58.660	60.874	63.010	65.077	67.080	69.024	70.916	72.758
0.40	56.089	58.207	60.249	62.710	65.077	67.361	69.570	71.711	73.790	75.812	77.782
0.45	59.492	61.737	63.904	66.514	69.024	71.447	73.790	76.061	78.266	80.411	82.500
0.50	62.710	65.077	67.361	70.112	72.758	75.312	77.782	80.176	82.500	84.761	86.963
0.55	65.770	68.253	70.649	73.534	76.309	78.988	81.578	84.089	86.527	88.898	91.207
0.60	68.695	71.288	73.790	76.803	79.703	82.500	85.206	87.828	90.374	92.851	95.263
0.65	71.500	74.199	76.803	79.939	82.957	85.869	88.684	91.414	94.064	96.642	99.153
0.70	74.199	77.000	79.703	82.957	86.089	89.110	92.033	94.865	97.615	100.290	102.896
0.75	76.803	79.703	82.500	85.869	89.110	92.238	95.263	98.195	101.041	103.810	106.507
0.80	79.322	82.317	85.206	88.685	92.033	95.263	98.387	101.415	104.355	107.215	110.000
0.85	81.763	84.850	87.830	91.414	94.865	98.195	101.415	104.536	107.567	110.514	113.385
0.90	84.134	87.310	90.374	94.064	97.615	101.041	104.355	107.567	110.685	113.718	116.673
0.95	86.439	89.702	92.851	96.642	100.290	103.810	107.215	110.514	113.718	116.835	119.870
1.00	88.685	92.033	95.263	99.153	102.896	106.507	110.000	113.385	116.673	119.870	122.984
1.05	90.875	94.305	97.615	101.601	105.437	109.137	112.716	116.185	119.554	122.830	126.021
1.10	93.013	96.525	99.912	103.992	107.918	111.706	115.369	118.920	122.367	125.720	128.986
1.15	95.104	98.694	102.158	106.329	110.343	114.216	117.962	121.592	125.117	128.546	131.885
1.20	97.149	100.817	104.355	108.616	112.716	116.673	120.499	124.207	127.808	131.311	134.722
1.25	99.153	102.896	106.507	110.856	115.041	119.078	122.984	126.769	130.444	134.018	137.500
1.30	101.116	104.933	108.616	113.051	117.319	121.437	125.419	129.279	133.027	136.673	140.223

Example

A vehicle skidded 50 ft (15.24 m) to a stop on a roadway having a coefficient of friction of .75. Its minimum initial speed was:

United States	Metric
$S = 5.5 \sqrt{50 \times .75}$	$S = 15.9 \sqrt{15.24 \times .75}$
$S = 5.5 \sqrt{37.50}$	$S = 15.9 \sqrt{11.43}$
$S = 5.5 \times 6.123$	$S = 15.9 \times 3.38$
$S = 33.68$	$S = 53.76$
$S = 34$ mph	$S = 54$ km/h

5.037 If any two of the three quantities involved in Formula 5-4 are known, the third quantity may be calculated. To calculate distance, D, use Formula 5-5:

United States

$$D = \frac{S^2}{30f}$$

Metric

$$D = \frac{S^2}{254f}$$

The numbers 30 and 254 represent the squares of 5.5 and 15.9 respectively, which are constants in calculating speeds.

Example

What is the distance a vehicle travelling a 33.68 mph (53.76 km/h) will skid to a stop on a roadway surface having a coefficient of friction of .75?

$D = \dfrac{33.68^2}{30 \times .75}$	$D = \dfrac{53.76^2}{254 \times .75}$
$D = \dfrac{1134.34}{22.5}$	$D = \dfrac{2890.14}{190.5}$
	$D = 15.17$
$D = 50$ ft	$D = 15$ m

To calculate the coefficient of friction, f, use Formula 5-1:

United States

$$f = \frac{S^2}{30D}$$

Metric

$$f = \frac{S^2}{254D}$$

Example

A vehicle travelling at 33.68 mph (53.76 km/h) skidded 50 ft (15.24 m) to a stop. What was the roadway coefficient of friction?

$f = \dfrac{33.68^2}{30 \times 50}$	$f = \dfrac{53.76^2}{254 \times 15.24}$
$f = \dfrac{1134.34}{1500}$	$f = \dfrac{2890.14}{3870.96}$
$f = .75$	$f = .75$

5.038 To ensure accuracy in calculating speed from skid marks:

a. The investigator must know how many wheels were skidding.

b. The vehicle must not have been towing a trailer unless the trailer was

TABLE 5-III-B
SPEED FROM SKID MARKS IN KILOMETERS PER HOUR

Coefficient of Friction (f)	Skid (meters)											
	1	2	3	4	5	6	7	8	9	10	11	12
0.05	3.555	5.028	6.158	7.111	7.950	8.709	9.407	10.056	10.666	11.243	11.792	12.316
0.10	5.028	7.111	8.709	10.056	11.243	12.316	13.303	14.221	15.084	15.900	16.676	17.418
0.15	6.158	8.709	10.666	12.316	13.770	15.084	16.293	17.418	18.474	19.473	20.424	21.332
0.20	7.111	10.056	12.316	14.221	15.900	17.418	18.813	20.112	21.332	22.486	23.584	24.632
0.25	7.950	11.243	13.770	15.900	17.777	19.473	21.034	22.486	23.850	25.140	26.367	27.540
0.30	8.709	12.316	15.084	17.418	19.473	21.332	23.041	24.632	26.126	27.540	28.884	30.168
0.35	9.407	13.303	16.293	18.813	21.034	23.041	24.887	26.606	28.220	29.746	31.198	32.585
0.40	10.056	14.221	17.418	20.112	22.486	24.632	26.606	28.443	30.168	31.800	33.352	34.835
0.45	10.666	15.084	18.474	21.332	23.850	26.126	28.220	30.168	31.998	33.729	35.375	36.948
0.50	11.243	15.900	19.473	22.486	25.140	27.540	29.746	31.800	33.729	35.553	37.289	38.947
0.55	11.792	16.676	20.424	23.584	26.367	28.884	31.198	33.352	35.375	37.289	39.109	40.848
0.60	12.316	17.418	21.332	24.632	27.540	30.168	32.585	34.835	36.948	38.947	40.848	42.664
0.65	12.819	18.129	22.203	25.638	28.664	31.400	33.916	36.258	38.457	40.537	42.516	44.406
0.70	13.303	18.813	23.041	26.606	29.746	32.585	35.196	37.626	39.909	42.067	44.121	46.083
0.75	13.770	19.473	23.850	27.540	30.790	33.729	36.431	38.947	41.309	43.544	45.669	47.700
0.80	14.221	20.112	24.632	28.443	31.800	34.835	37.626	40.224	42.664	44.972	47.167	49.264
0.85	14.659	20.731	25.390	29.318	32.779	35.907	38.784	41.462	43.977	46.356	48.619	50.781
0.90	15.084	21.332	26.126	30.168	33.729	36.948	39.909	42.664	45.252	47.700	50.028	52.253
0.95	15.497	21.917	26.842	30.995	34.653	37.961	41.002	43.833	46.492	49.007	51.399	53.685
1.00	15.900	22.486	27.540	31.800	35.553	38.947	42.067	44.972	47.700	50.280	52.734	55.079
1.05	16.293	23.041	28.220	32.585	36.431	39.909	43.106	46.083	48.878	51.522	54.037	56.439
1.10	16.676	23.584	28.884	33.352	37.289	40.848	44.121	47.167	50.028	52.734	55.308	57.768
1.15	17.051	24.114	29.533	34.102	38.127	41.766	45.112	48.227	51.153	53.920	56.551	59.066
1.20	17.418	24.632	30.168	34.835	38.947	42.664	46.083	49.264	52.253	55.079	57.768	60.336
1.25	17.777	25.140	30.790	35.553	39.750	43.544	47.033	50.280	53.330	56.215	58.959	61.580
1.30	18.129	25.638	31.400	36.258	40.537	44.406	47.964	51.276	54.386	57.328	60.126	62.800

Skid (meters)

Coefficient of Friction (f)	13	14	15	16	17	18	19	20	22	24	26	28
0.05	12.819	13.303	13.770	14.221	14.659	15.084	15.497	15.900	16.676	17.418	18.129	18.813
0.10	18.129	18.813	19.473	20.112	20.731	21.332	21.917	22.486	23.584	24.632	25.638	26.606
1.15	22.203	23.041	23.850	24.632	25.390	26.126	26.842	27.540	28.884	30.168	31.400	32.585
0.20	25.638	26.606	27.540	28.443	29.318	30.168	30.995	31.800	33.352	34.835	36.258	37.626
0.25	28.664	29.746	30.790	31.800	32.779	33.729	34.653	35.553	37.289	38.947	40.537	42.067
0.30	31.400	32.585	33.729	34.835	35.907	36.948	37.961	38.947	40.848	42.664	44.406	46.083
0.35	33.916	35.196	36.431	37.626	38.784	39.909	41.002	42.067	44.121	46.083	47.964	49.775
0.40	36.258	37.626	38.947	40.224	41.462	42.664	43.833	44.972	47.167	49.264	51.276	53.212
0.45	38.457	39.909	41.309	42.664	43.977	45.252	46.492	47.700	50.028	52.253	54.386	56.439
0.50	40.537	42.067	43.544	44.972	46.356	47.700	49.007	50.280	52.734	55.079	57.328	59.492
0.55	42.516	44.121	45.669	47.167	48.619	50.028	51.399	52.734	55.308	57.768	60.126	62.396
0.60	44.406	46.083	47.700	49.264	50.781	52.253	53.685	55.079	57.768	60.336	62.800	65.171
0.65	46.220	47.964	49.648	51.276	52.854	54.386	55.877	57.328	60.126	62.800	65.364	67.832
0.70	47.964	49.775	51.522	53.212	54.849	56.439	57.986	59.492	62.396	65.171	67.832	70.392
0.75	49.648	51.522	53.330	55.079	56.774	58.420	60.021	61.580	64.586	67.458	70.212	72.863
0.80	51.276	53.212	55.079	56.886	58.636	60.336	61.990	63.600	66.704	69.670	72.515	75.253
0.85	52.854	54.849	56.774	58.636	60.441	62.193	63.897	65.557	68.757	71.815	74.747	77.569
0.90	54.386	56.439	58.420	60.336	62.193	63.996	65.750	67.458	70.751	73.897	76.914	79.817
0.95	55.877	57.986	60.021	61.990	63.897	65.750	67.552	69.306	72.689	75.921	79.022	82.005
1.00	57.328	59.492	61.580	63.600	65.557	67.458	69.306	71.107	74.578	77.894	81.074	84.135
1.05	58.744	60.962	63.101	65.171	67.176	69.124	71.018	72.863	76.419	79.817	83.077	86.213
1.10	60.126	62.396	64.586	66.704	68.757	70.751	72.689	74.578	78.218	81.696	85.032	88.241
1.15	61.478	63.798	66.038	68.203	70.302	72.341	74.323	76.254	79.976	83.532	86.943	90.225
1.20	62.800	65.171	67.458	69.670	71.815	73.897	75.921	77.894	81.696	85.328	88.813	92.165
1.25	64.095	66.514	68.849	71.107	73.295	75.420	77.487	79.500	83.381	87.088	90.644	94.066
1.30	65.364	67.832	70.212	72.515	74.747	76.914	79.022	81.074	85.032	88.813	92.439	95.929

TABLE 5-III-B (Continued)

SPEED FROM SKID MARKS IN KILOMETERS PER HOUR

Coefficient of Friction (f)	Skid (meters)											
	30	32	34	36	38	40	42	44	46	48	50	52
0.05	19.473	20.112	20.731	21.332	21.917	22.486	23.041	23.584	24.114	24.632	25.140	25.638
0.10	27.540	28.443	29.318	30.168	30.995	31.800	32.585	33.352	34.102	34.835	35.553	36.258
0.15	33.729	34.835	35.907	36.948	37.961	38.947	39.909	40.848	41.766	42.664	43.544	44.406
0.20	38.947	40.224	41.462	42.664	43.833	44.972	46.083	47.167	48.227	49.264	50.280	51.276
0.25	43.544	44.972	46.356	47.700	49.007	50.280	51.522	52.734	53.920	55.079	56.215	57.328
0.30	47.700	49.264	50.781	52.253	53.685	55.079	56.439	57.768	59.066	60.336	61.580	62.800
0.35	51.522	53.212	54.849	56.439	57.986	59.492	60.962	62.396	63.798	65.171	66.514	67.832
0.40	55.079	56.886	58.636	60.336	61.990	63.600	65.171	66.704	68.203	69.670	71.107	72.515
0.45	58.420	60.336	62.193	63.996	65.750	67.458	69.124	70.751	72.341	73.897	75.420	76.914
0.50	61.580	63.600	65.557	67.458	69.306	71.107	72.863	74.578	76.254	77.894	79.500	81.074
0.55	64.586	66.704	68.757	70.751	72.689	74.578	76.419	78.218	79.976	81.696	83.380	85.032
0.60	67.458	69.670	71.815	73.897	75.921	77.894	79.817	81.696	83.532	85.328	87.088	88.813
0.65	70.212	72.515	74.747	76.914	79.022	81.074	83.077	85.032	86.943	88.813	90.644	92.439
0.70	72.863	75.253	77.549	79.817	82.005	84.135	86.213	88.241	90.225	92.165	94.066	95.929
0.75	75.420	77.894	80.291	82.619	84.883	87.088	89.239	91.339	93.391	95.400	97.367	99.295
0.80	77.894	80.448	82.924	85.328	87.667	89.944	92.165	94.334	96.454	98.529	100.560	102.552
0.85	80.291	82.924	85.476	87.954	90.365	92.712	95.002	97.237	99.423	101.561	103.655	105.708
0.90	82.619	85.328	87.954	90.504	92.984	95.400	97.756	100.056	102.305	104.505	106.660	108.773
0.95	84.883	87.667	90.365	92.984	95.532	98.014	100.435	102.798	105.109	107.369	109.583	111.753
1.00	87.088	89.944	92.712	95.400	98.014	100.560	103.044	105.469	107.839	110.158	112.430	114.657
1.05	89.239	92.165	95.002	97.756	100.435	103.044	105.588	108.073	110.502	112.879	115.206	117.488
1.10	91.339	94.334	97.237	100.056	102.798	105.469	108.073	110.616	113.103	115.535	117.918	120.253
1.15	93.391	96.454	99.423	102.305	105.109	107.839	110.502	113.103	115.644	118.132	120.567	122.955
1.20	95.400	98.529	101.561	104.505	107.369	110.158	112.879	115.535	118.132	120.673	123.161	125.600
1.25	97.367	100.560	103.655	106.660	109.583	112.430	115.206	117.918	120.568	123.161	125.701	128.190
1.30	99.295	102.552	105.708	108.773	111.753	114.657	117.488	120.253	122.955	125.600	128.190	130.729

Skid (meters)

Coefficient of Friction (f)	54	56	58	60	62	64	66	68	70	75	80	85
0.05	26.126	26.606	27.077	27.540	27.995	28.443	28.884	29.318	29.746	30.790	31.800	32.779
0.10	36.948	37.626	38.292	38.947	39.591	40.224	40.848	41.462	42.067	43.544	44.972	46.356
0.15	45.252	46.083	46.898	47.700	48.488	49.264	50.028	50.781	51.522	53.330	55.079	56.774
0.20	52.253	53.212	54.153	55.079	55.990	56.886	57.768	58.636	59.492	61.580	63.600	65.557
0.25	58.420	59.492	60.545	61.580	62.598	63.600	64.586	65.557	66.514	68.849	71.107	73.295
0.30	63.996	65.171	66.324	67.458	68.573	69.670	70.751	71.815	72.863	75.420	77.894	80.291
0.35	69.124	70.392	71.638	72.863	74.067	75.253	76.419	77.569	78.701	81.463	84.135	86.724
0.40	73.897	75.253	76.585	77.894	79.181	80.448	81.696	82.924	84.135	87.088	89.944	92.712
0.45	78.379	79.817	81.230	82.619	83.985	85.328	86.651	87.954	89.239	92.371	95.400	98.336
0.50	82.619	84.135	85.624	87.088	88.527	89.944	91.339	92.712	94.066	97.367	100.560	103.655
0.55	86.651	88.241	89.803	91.339	92.848	94.334	95.797	97.237	98.657	102.120	105.469	108.715
0.60	90.504	92.165	93.797	95.400	96.977	98.529	100.056	101.561	103.044	106.660	110.158	113.549
0.65	94.200	95.929	97.627	99.295	100.937	102.552	104.142	105.708	107.251	111.016	114.657	118.185
0.70	97.756	99.550	101.312	103.044	104.747	106.423	108.073	109.698	111.300	115.206	118.985	122.647
0.75	101.187	103.044	104.868	106.660	108.424	110.158	111.866	113.549	115.206	119.250	123.161	126.951
0.80	104.505	106.423	108.307	110.158	111.979	113.771	115.535	117.273	118.985	123.161	127.200	131.115
0.85	107.722	109.698	111.640	113.549	115.426	117.273	119.091	120.882	122.647	126.951	131.115	135.150
0.90	110.845	112.879	114.877	116.841	118.772	120.673	122.544	124.386	126.202	130.632	134.916	139.068
0.95	113.882	115.972	118.025	120.042	122.027	123.979	125.901	127.795	129.661	134.211	138.613	142.879
1.00	116.841	118.985	121.091	123.161	125.197	127.200	129.172	131.115	133.029	137.698	142.214	146.591
1.05	119.726	121.923	124.081	126.202	128.288	130.341	132.362	134.353	136.314	141.099	145.726	150.211
1.10	122.544	124.792	127.001	129.172	131.307	133.408	135.477	137.514	139.522	144.419	149.155	153.746
1.15	125.298	127.597	129.855	132.075	134.259	136.407	138.522	140.605	142.658	147.665	152.507	157.201
1.20	127.993	130.341	132.648	134.916	137.146	139.341	141.501	143.629	145.726	150.841	155.788	160.582
1.25	130.632	133.029	135.384	137.698	139.974	142.214	144.419	146.591	148.731	153.951	159.000	163.893
1.30	133.219	135.663	138.065	140.425	142.746	145.030	147.279	149.494	151.676	157.000	162.149	167.139

Coefficient of Friction (f)	Skid (meters)							
	90	95	100	110	120	130	140	150
0.05	33.729	34.653	35.553	37.289	38.946	40.537	42.067	43.544
0.10	47.700	49.007	50.280	52.734	55.079	57.328	59.492	61.580
0.15	58.420	60.021	61.580	64.586	67.458	70.212	72.863	75.420
0.20	67.458	69.306	71.107	74.578	77.894	81.074	84.135	87.088
0.25	75.420	77.487	79.500	83.380	87.088	90.644	94.066	97.367
0.30	82.619	84.883	87.088	91.339	95.400	99.295	103.044	106.660
0.35	89.239	91.684	94.066	98.657	103.044	107.251	111.300	115.206
0.40	95.400	98.014	100.560	105.469	110.158	114.657	118.985	123.161
0.45	101.187	103.960	106.660	111.866	116.841	121.612	126.202	130.632
0.50	106.660	109.583	112.430	117.918	123.161	128.190	133.029	137.698
0.55	111.866	114.932	117.918	123.673	129.172	134.447	139.522	144.419
0.60	116.841	120.042	123.161	129.172	134.916	140.425	145.726	150.841
0.65	121.612	124.944	128.190	134.447	140.425	146.159	151.676	157.000
0.70	126.202	129.661	133.029	139.522	145.726	151.676	157.402	162.927
0.75	130.632	134.211	137.698	144.419	150.841	157.000	162.927	168.645
0.80	134.916	138.613	142.214	149.155	155.788	162.149	168.270	174.176
0.85	139.068	142.879	146.591	153.746	160.582	167.139	173.449	179.536
0.90	143.100	147.021	150.841	158.203	165.238	171.985	178.477	184.741
0.95	147.021	151.050	154.974	162.538	169.765	176.698	183.368	189.804
1.00	150.841	154.974	159.000	166.761	174.176	181.288	188.131	194.734
1.05	154.566	158.801	162.927	170.879	178.477	185.765	192.777	199.543
1.10	158.203	162.538	166.761	174.900	182.677	190.136	197.314	204.239
1.15	161.759	166.191	170.508	178.831	186.783	194.410	201.748	208.829
1.20	165.238	169.766	174.176	182.677	190.800	198.591	206.088	213.321
1.25	168.645	173.266	177.767	186.444	194.734	202.686	210.337	217.720
1.30	171.985	176.698	181.288	190.136	198.591	206.700	214.503	222.031

equipped with brakes that were applied at the same time as those of the towing vehicle.

c. The vehicle must have slid to a complete stop without striking another vehicle or other substantial object that slowed its speed or caused it to come to rest.

5.039   The factors important in calculating speed from skid marks are the coefficient of friction and the length of the skid marks. Other factors such as the vehicle weight and tire pressures have no significant bearing on calculating the speed of a vehicle. The striking of a pedestrian or other light object by a vehicle has no appreciable effect on slowing the vehicle, and any continuous skid mark beyond the point where the pedestrian or other light object was struck should be included in the overall skid mark length.

5.040   The investigator should prepare a diagram, either included in or in addition to his field sketch, showing in precise detail the type of marks such as skid marks, yaw marks and scrub marks and their locations. Although some of the marks may seem unimportant at the time, the information will always be available later in the event it is necessary to prepare a scale diagram or otherwise plot the precise location of the vehicle at particular points along the path of travel. The diagram should also record the time, date, weather conditions, type of roadway surface and condition, temperature and all other pertinent details relating to the skid marks.

5.041   The investigator should observe and record both in writing and photographically all facts at the scene. If his expertise is not such that he can interpret all the evidence, he may call upon a professional reconstructionist or other person having expertise in a specific area to interpret the evidence for him from notes made and photographs taken.

5.042   Measurements should be taken to at least the nearest 6 in (15 cm) in general skid mark measurements. Skid marks often show where a vehicle was located on the roadway, for example, on the wrong side of the center line, as well as the position in relation to lane dividers, curb lines, crosswalks, stop signs, traffic lights, and so on. In these situations, measurements should be as exact as possible.

5.043   When making skid mark measurements, it is helpful to place numbered markers at the specific locations from which or to which measurements are made. Photographs should be taken with the markers in place, which will be helpful in explaining the measurements taken. However, photographs should also be taken before markers or any other type of marking is placed on the roadway in the event they are objected to in court.

Figure 5-7. Impending skid mark.

5.044 Particular attention must be given to finding the *beginning* and *end* of each individual skid mark, including the beginning of an *impending skid mark*. The beginning of an impending skid mark may appear only as a very light shadow or cleaning action on the pavement but that leads directly into the skid mark itself. An impending skid mark is caused by a tire passing over a roadway surface after the brakes are applied but just before the wheel locks up. It is at this time that the tire has the greatest drag or friction and, therefore, the impending skid mark area should always be included as part of the overall skid mark length (*see* Fig. 4-36).

5.045 When it is established that all wheels locked at approximately the same time, the longest visible skid mark should be used as the skidding distance in calculating speed from skid marks. However, if the investigator is required for one reason or another to be conservative in his speed estimate, he may then measure each skid mark individually and obtain an average skid distance from their totals. A speed calculated from an average skid distance is generally much lower than the *actual minimum initial vehicle speed* at the beginning of its skid. In Figure 5-8, the total skid distance was 62 (ft or m). The average skid distance, however, was 56 (ft or m).

5.046 If it is evident from skid marks that all wheels locked during braking action but that locking action was quite uneven in terms of time, leaving skid marks of varying lengths, *each* individual skid mark should be measured and an *average skid mark* length used in calculating the speed of the vehicle.

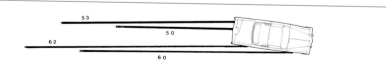

Figure 5-8. When wheels lock at approximately the same time, use the longest skid mark as the skid distance. A conservative measurement of the skid distance may be made by averaging the lengths of all skid marks.

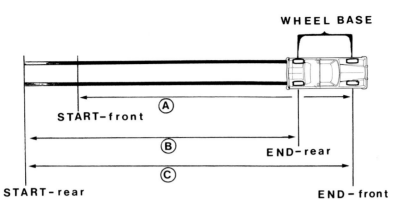

Figure 5-9. When rear skid marks overlap front skid marks, subtract the wheelbase distance from the average length of both skid marks or from the distance from the start to the end of the skid. In this example, C represents the total length of an overlapping skid mark. A and B are the distances the vehicle actually skidded.

Figure 5-10. Dual wheel skid marks. In this example, skid mark A is the same length as skid mark B because the measurement of mark B is taken from the first indication of a skid to the last indication of a skid of that dual wheel unit.

5.047 *Overlaps.* In an overlapping skid mark, the beginning of the mark is caused by the rear tire and the end of the mark is caused by the front tire. In these cases, the true length of the skid is the total length of the skid mark minus the wheelbase of the vehicle (*see* Fig. 4-39).

5.048 *Dual wheel skid marks.* Dual wheels leave two skid marks, one from each tire. The two skid marks are to be measured as one skid mark, starting with the first indication of a skid to the last indication of a skid from the dual unit regardless of which tire made the first or last skid mark.

5.049 *Slight curves.* In measuring skid marks that have a slight curve such as those caused by superelevation, let the tape measure or measuring device follow the path or curvature of the curve.

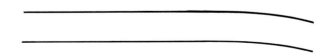

Figure 5-11. Curved skid marks.

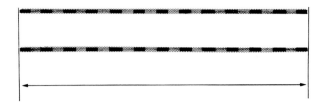

Figure 5-12. Skip skid marks.

5.050 *Skip skid marks.* Skip skid marks are to be measured as a continuous skid mark (*see* Fig. 4-43).

5.051 *Spin skidmarks.* The length of each skid mark should be measured in spin skids. This should be done by letting the tape measure or other measuring device follow the paths or curvatures of the individual skid marks. An average of the number of skid marks measured may then be used as the skid distance. If skid marks are obliterated or are not adequately discernible for measurement purposes, a measurement may be taken from the first indication of the vehicle going into a skid to the last indication of the skid. A straight measurement of this kind in a spin skid is very conservative in determining the skid distance of the vehicle. The investigator should take particular care in examining what appear to be spin skid marks to ensure they are not yaw marks.

5.052 *Intermittent skid marks.* In the case of intermittent skid marks, that is, when brakes are applied and released intermittently leaving spaces or gaps between sets of skid marks, the gaps are disregarded in determining the total skid distance (*see* Fig. 4-44). For example, when two sets of skid marks are separated by a gap, the total skid distance is the sum of the two separate skids. When a skid involves overlapping skid marks, the length of that skid is minus the wheelbase of the vehicle. In Figure 5-14, for example, area A is overlapping skid marks. The actual skid distance is the length of the skid marks minus the wheelbase of the vehicle. Area B is non-overlapping skid marks. The actual skid distance in area B is the length of the longest skid

Figure 5-13. Spin skid marks.

Figure 5-14. Intermittent skid marks.

mark; alternatively, for a conservative estimate, the skid distance may be considered as the average of the lengths of the four skid marks. The total distance of the two sets of skid marks in Figure 5-14 is then the length of skid marks in area *A* minus the wheelbase and plus the length of the longest skid mark in area *B*. The gap distance is disregarded.

VEHICLE BRAKING CAPABILITIES AND SPEED

5.053   If a vehicle swerves significantly to *one side* when all tires are on the same type of roadway surface, it is an indication that braking capability on the *other side* is not effective or does not have equal braking efficiency. If skid marks are straight for a reasonable distance with no indication of swerve, it may be assumed that all wheels have full or equal braking capability. It should be remembered, however, that in long skids, vehicles tend to swerve to the lower side of a crowned or superelevated roadway; such swerves should not be confused with braking efficiency (*see* Fig. 4-38).

5.054   When there is reason to believe that brakes were applied but there is no evidence of skid marks, the investigator should determine whether the vehicle was equipped with anti-skid brakes (*see* paragraph 2.062). If it is evident from some skid marks that brakes were applied but that one or more wheels did not lock up and did not leave skid marks, it is important to establish whether all wheels had braking capability.

5.055   The total braking capability of a vehicle is considered to be 100 percent, and the coefficient of friction formula, Formula 5-1, is based on the assumption that all wheels locked and they had equal braking capability. In cases where one wheel brake does not function, a 4-wheel vehicle would experience not total braking capability, but rather approximately three-quarters or 75 percent of its assumed capability. In determining speed from skid marks of such vehicles, an investigator should use the accident vehicle if possible to make test skids and then calculate the coefficient of friction and speed in the usual manner based on those tests. However, if this is not possible, the investigator should determine the coefficient of friction in one of the methods described in the preceding paragraphs; determine the weight carried on each wheel, and use the following formula to calculate the speed of the vehicle, Formula 5-6:

United States   Metric

$$S = 5.5 \sqrt{Dfn}$$ $$S = 15.9 \sqrt{Dfn}$$

where S = speed
       D = skid distance
       f = coefficient of friction
       n = percentage of total vehicle weight carried on wheels having braking
           capability.

Example

A vehicle with braking capability on only three of its four wheels skidded 50 ft (15.24 m) to a stop. The coefficient of friction was .70. The total weight of the vehicle was evenly distributed on its four wheels. The braking capability of the vehicle was therefore approximately 75 percent.

$S = 5.5 \sqrt{50 \times .70 \times .75}$ $S = 15.9 \sqrt{15.24 \times .70 \times .75}$
$S = 5.5 \sqrt{26.25}$ $S = 15.9 \sqrt{8}$
$S = 5.5 \times 5.12$ $S = 15.9 \times 2.83$
$S = 28.16$ $S = 44.97$
$S = 28$ mph $S = 45$ km/h

For comparison purposes, a vehicle having 100 percent braking capability would have had a minimum initial speed of 32.5 mph (52 km/h).

5.056   Formula 5-6 may be applied to motorcycles having rear wheel braking capability only. In braking, a motorcycle experiences a forward shift of approximately 20% of its *standing* rear wheel weight onto its front wheel. In these cases, use .47 as the *n* value to calculate approximate speed.

SKIDS ON DIFFERENT SURFACES

5.057   When a skid is continuous from one type of surface to one or more other types of surfaces, or when the wheels on one side skid on a different type of surface than the wheels on the other side, the distance the vehicle skidded and the coefficient of friction for each surface must be determined before the speed can be calculated (*see* Fig. 4-38).

5.058   The speed of a vehicle in a continuous skid from one type of surface to another may be calculated using Formula 5-7:

United States   Metric

$$S = 5.5 \sqrt{f_1 D_1 + f_2 D_2}$$ $$S = 15.9 \sqrt{f_1 D_1 + f_2 D_2}$$

where f_1 = coefficient of friction for first surface
       f_2 = coefficient of friction for second surface (f_3 = coefficient of friction for third surface, etc.)
       D_1 = skid distance on first surface
       D_2 = skid distance on second surface
             (D_3 = skid distance on third surface, etc.)

The numbers 5.5 and 15.9 are constants in calculating speed.

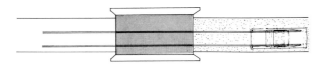

Figure 5-15. Continuous skid on different surfaces: asphalt (f = .70), cement (f = .75) and gravel (f = .50).

Example 1

A vehicle skidded to a stop over three separate sections of roadway, each of which had a different roadway surface (see Fig. 5-15):

Section 1
Asphalt:　　f_1 = .70　　　D_1 = 26 ft (8 m)

Section 2
Cement:　　f_2 = .75　　　D_2 = 26 ft (8 m)

Section 3
Gravel:　　f_3 = .50　　　D_3 = 23 ft (7 m)

In this example, there are three surfaces involved. Therefore, f_3 and D_3 are required in the formula.

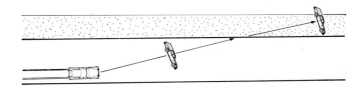

Figure 5-16. Vehicle in skid and slide involving three different surfaces: tires to asphalt, metal to asphalt and metal to gravel.

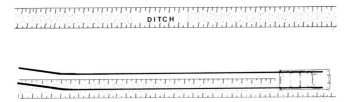

Figure 5-17. Skid where wheels on one side are on different surface than wheels on other side.

United States

$$S = 5.5 \sqrt{(.70 \times 26) + (.75 \times 26) + (.50 \times 23)}$$
$$S = 5.5 \sqrt{18 + 19.5 + 11.5}$$
$$S = 5.5 \sqrt{49}$$
$$S = 5.5 \times 7$$
$$S = 38.5$$
$$S = 39 \text{ mph}$$

Metric

$$S = 15.9 \sqrt{(.70 \times 8) + (.75 \times 8) + (.50 \times 7)}$$
$$S = 15.9 \sqrt{5.6 + 6 + 3.5}$$
$$S = 15.9 \sqrt{15}$$
$$S = 15.9 \times 3.87$$
$$S = 61.5$$
$$S = 62 \text{ km/h}$$

Example 2

A vehicle skidded 50 ft (15.24 m) to a stop. The left wheels were on a paved roadway having a coefficient of friction of .70. The right wheels were on a dirt shoulder (or in a ditch) having a coefficient of friction of .50. In this case, there is a different surface and coefficient of friction for each side of the vehicle. The speed may be calculated by using Formula 5-8:

United States	*Metric*
$S = \sqrt{15(f_1 + f_2)D}$	$S = \sqrt{127(f_1 + f_2)D}$

where f_1 = coefficient of friction for side 1 of the vehicle
$\quad\quad\;\, f_2$ = coefficient of friction for side 2 of the vehicle
$\quad\quad\;\, D$ = distance of skid

The numbers 15 and 127 represent one-half of the squares of the speed constants 5.5 and 15.9 respectively.

$$S = \sqrt{15(.70 + .50)50}$$ $$S = \sqrt{127(.70 + .50)15.24}$$
$$S = \sqrt{15 \times 1.20 \times 50}$$ $$S = \sqrt{127 \times 1.20 \times 15.24}$$
$$S = \sqrt{900}$$ $$S = \sqrt{2322.58}$$
$$S = 30 \text{ mph}$$ $$S = 48 \text{ km/h}$$

COMBINED SPEEDS

5.059 When a skidding vehicle strikes an object such as another vehicle, its speed at the commencement of its skid may be calculated using the *combined speed formula*, Formula 5-9:

United States	*Metric*
$S_c = \sqrt{S_1^2 + S_2^2}$	$S_c = \sqrt{S_1^2 + S_2^2}$

where S_c = speed at commencement of skid
$\quad\quad\;\, S_1$ = skid-to-stop speed calculated on skid mark length
$\quad\quad\;\, S_2$ = estimated or calculated speed at end of skid mark, i.e., at point of collision

Example 1

A vehicle skidded 100 ft (30.5 m) and struck another vehicle broadside. Because of the damage caused by the collision (or because of witnesses' statements), the investigator estimated the speed of the vehicle at time of collision to be 25 mph (40 km/h). The roadway coefficient of friction was .75. The skid-to-stop speed, based on 100 ft (30.5 m) of skid mark, was 47.6 mph (76 km/h). The approximate speed of the vehicle at the commencement of the skid was:

$$S_c = \sqrt{47.6^2 + 25^2}$$
$$S_c = \sqrt{2265.76 + 625}$$
$$S_c = \sqrt{2890.76}$$
$$S_c = 53.77$$
$$S_c = 54 \text{ mph}$$

$$S_c = \sqrt{76^2 + 40^2}$$
$$S_c = \sqrt{5776 + 1600}$$
$$S_c = \sqrt{7376}$$
$$S_c = 85.88$$
$$S_c = 86 \text{ km/h}$$

Example 2

A vehicle skidded 50 ft (15.24 m) to a stop. For the first 33 ft (10 m), the left wheels were on a paved roadway having a coefficient of friction of .70. At the same time and for the same distance, the right wheels were on a gravel shoulder having a coefficient of friction of .50. At 33 ft (10 m), because of the greater drag on the left tires, the vehicle veered to the left, and all four tires skidded the remaining 17 ft (5 m) on the pavement (f = .70) to a stop (Fig. 5-18).

To calculate the speed of the vehicle at the beginning of the skid, it is necessary to:

1. Calculate the skid-to-stop speed based on the distance the left wheels skidded on the pavement and the right wheels on the gravel shoulder.
2. Calculate the skid-to-stop speed based on the distance all tires skidded on the pavement.
3. Place both speeds into the combined speed formula.

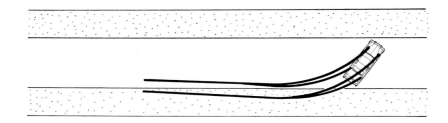

Figure 5-18

Step 1. Calculate skid-to-stop speed using Formula 5-8:

<table>
<tr><td align="center">United States</td><td align="center">Metric</td></tr>
<tr><td>$S = \sqrt{15(.70 + .50)33}$</td><td>$S = \sqrt{127(.70 + .50)10}$</td></tr>
<tr><td>$S = \sqrt{15 \times 1.20 \times 33}$</td><td>$S = \sqrt{127 \times 1.20 \times 10}$</td></tr>
<tr><td>$S = \sqrt{594}$</td><td>$S = \sqrt{1524}$</td></tr>
<tr><td>$S = 24.37$</td><td>$S = 39.04$</td></tr>
<tr><td>$S = 24$ mph</td><td>$S = 39$ km/h</td></tr>
</table>

Step 2. Calculate skid-to-stop speed using Formula 5-4:

<table>
<tr><td align="center">United States</td><td align="center">Metric</td></tr>
<tr><td>$S = 5.5 \sqrt{17 \times .70}$</td><td>$S = 15.9 \sqrt{5 \times .70}$</td></tr>
<tr><td>$S = 5.5 \sqrt{11.9}$</td><td>$S = 15.9 \sqrt{3.5}$</td></tr>
<tr><td>$S = 5.5 \times 3.45$</td><td>$S = 15.9 \times 1.87$</td></tr>
<tr><td>$S = 18.98$</td><td>$S = 29.73$</td></tr>
<tr><td>$S = 19$ mph</td><td>$S = 30$ km/h</td></tr>
</table>

Step 3. Calculate the initial minimum speed of the vehicle using the combined speed formula, Formula 5-9:

<table>
<tr><td align="center">United States</td><td align="center">Metric</td></tr>
<tr><td>$S_c = \sqrt{24.37^2 + 18.98^2}$</td><td>$S_c = \sqrt{39.04^2 + 29.73^2}$</td></tr>
<tr><td>$S_c = \sqrt{593.9 + 360.24}$</td><td>$S_c = \sqrt{1524.12 + 883.87}$</td></tr>
<tr><td>$S_c = \sqrt{954.14}$</td><td>$S_c = \sqrt{2407.99}$</td></tr>
<tr><td>$S_c = 30.89$</td><td>$S_c = 49.07$</td></tr>
<tr><td>$S_c = 31$ mph</td><td>$S_c = 49$ km/h</td></tr>
</table>

SPEED FROM YAW OR SIDESLIP MARKS

5.060   At high speeds in curves, centrifugal force attempts to overcome centripetal force, the frictional resistance or adhesion between the tires and the roadway, and causes a vehicle to slide in a straight line (*see* Fig. 3.2). If the speed is too great, the vehicle will sideslip or go into *yaw* and possibly spin or overturn.

5.061   As a vehicle drives into a curve, the centrifugal force causes a weight shift onto the leading (front) outside tire. It is the outer side of the lead tire tread that carries this excess weight (*see* Fig. 2-29). At the beginning of a sideslip, the outer edge of the tire leaves a very narrow dark mark that appears as a thin line about 2 in (5.08 cm) in width (*see* Fig. 4-26) and widens to the width of that amount of tire tread that is in contact with the roadway as the vehicle goes into yaw and possibly spins. Striation marks caused by the sides of the tire tread are often visible. It is this thin sideslip mark caused by the lead tire that is so important in calculating speed from sideslip or yaw.

5.062   A side scuff mark that appears very similar to a yaw mark can be caused by an underinflated or overloaded tire. Such marks normally follow a path within the lane of travel of the vehicle and continue on for great distances. These types of marks may occur at relatively low speeds and should not be confused with high-speed sideslip or yaw marks.

5.063 Standard construction tires have a greater slip angle than do radial tires and therefore more readily leave a distinct yaw or sideslip mark (*see* Fig. 2-29).[23]

5.064 There are two speed calculations of particular importance to an investigator:

    a. *Critical vehicle curve speed* is the speed at which a vehicle slides off the roadway in driving around a curve.
    b. *Critical curve speed* is the speed above which a vehicle slides out of its lane of travel in driving around a curve.

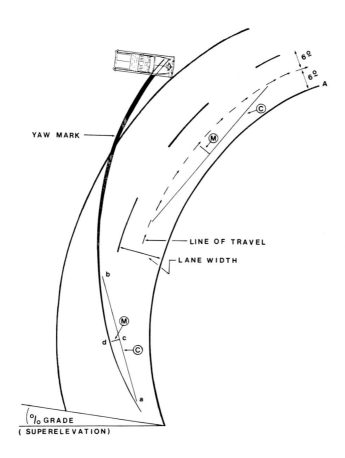

Figure 5-19. Method of plotting the radius of yaw marks, and the roadway line or path of travel.

5.065   To calculate a critical speed it is necessary to have:

1. the radius of the yawmark or the radius of the lane of travel of the vehicle, depending upon the critical speed to be calculated
2. the coefficient of friction
3. roadway superelevation

5.066   To calculate the *critical vehicle curve speed,* use approximately the first one-third of the *yaw mark* or *vehicle center of mass path* as the circumference to calculate the curve radius. To calculate the *critical curve speed,* use the center of the lane of travel (the line of travel) as the circumference. This may be done by first calculating the radius of the curve using the inner roadway edge as the circumference and then adding one-half of the width of the travel lane to the radius.

5.067   The critical speed formula is Formula 5-10:

United States

$$S = 5.5 \sqrt{(f \pm e) \ R/2}$$

Metric

$$S = 15.9 \sqrt{(f \pm e) \ R/2}$$

where S = speed
e = superelevation or bank
R = radius
f = coefficient of friction

The numbers 5.5 and 15.9 are constants in calculating speed.

Example

A vehicle travelled into a curve at a high rate of speed and skidded sideways, leaving a sideslip or yaw mark of 300 ft (91.44 m). Using the first one-third (100 ft or 30.48 m) of the yaw mark as the circumference, a chord was measured at 75 ft (22.86 m) having a middle ordinate of 3 ft (.914 m). The roadway superelevation was measured at +05 percent. Test skids determined that the coefficient of friction was .70.

Step 1. Calculate the radius of the sideslip or yaw mark. Radius may be calculated using Formula 5-11: (see 8.058)

United States

$$R = \frac{C^2}{8M} + \frac{M}{2}$$

Metric

$$R = \frac{C^2}{8M} + \frac{M}{2}$$

where R = radius
C = chord
M = middle ordinate

The number 8 is a constant in calculating radius.

$$R = \frac{75^2}{8 \times 3} + \frac{3}{2}$$

$$R = \frac{5625}{24} + \frac{3}{2}$$

$$R = \frac{22.86^2}{8 \times .914} + \frac{.914}{2}$$

$$R = \frac{522.58}{7.31} + \frac{.914}{2}$$

$$R = 234.38 + 1.5 \qquad\qquad R = 71.49 + .46$$
$$R = 235.88 \qquad\qquad\qquad R = 71.95$$
$$R = 236 \text{ ft} \qquad\qquad\qquad R = 72\text{m}$$

Step 2. Calculate the *critical vehicle curve speed* using Formula 5-10:

<table>
<tr><td align="center">United States</td><td align="center">Metric</td></tr>
</table>

$$S = 5.5 \sqrt{(.70 + .05)\frac{236}{2}} \qquad S = 15.9 \sqrt{(.70 + .05)\frac{72}{2}}$$
$$S = 5.5 \sqrt{.75 \times 118} \qquad\qquad S = 15.9 \sqrt{.75 \times 36}$$
$$S = 5.5 \sqrt{88.5} \qquad\qquad\quad S = 15.9 \sqrt{27}$$
$$S = 5.5 \times 9.41 \qquad\qquad\quad S = 15.9 \times 5.2$$
$$S = 51.76 \qquad\qquad\qquad\quad S = 82.68$$
$$S = 52 \text{ mph} \qquad\qquad\qquad S = 83 \text{ km/h}$$

5.068   Do not use Formula 5-10 to calculate critical speeds if all wheels are not on the same surface, if the vehicle was steered away from its curve path, or if the vehicle was braked. Similarly, this formula should not be used to calculate speed from sideslip of heavily loaded trucks because the behavior of the load and its effect on the center of gravity of a vehicle in yaw plays a large part in the direction and radius of the yaw.

5.069   If the path of a vehicle around a curve cannot be adequately established or is confusing, an investigator may use the *critical curve speed*. The critical curve speed is much less than the *critical vehicle curve speed* because of the shorter radius and is normally much higher than the recommended curve speed. Therefore, using the critical curve speed is frequently sufficient to prove that the vehicle was travelling at an excessive rate of speed (*see* paragraph 8.062 and Fig. 8-44).

Sideslip Speed Using Center of Mass Path

5.070   Some investigators prefer to use the *center of mass path* of the vehicle rather than yaw marks in calculating speed from yaw. In using this method, careful measurements must also be made of all tire marks at the accident scene, identifying the tire that made each mark. The location of the center of mass of the vehicle must be determined and measurements taken from the center of mass to the contact areas of all tires, which in turn must be related to the tire marks on the roadway. The positions of the vehicle on the roadway must then be plotted at sufficient locations to determine the path followed by the center of mass, from which a radius may be calculated. Plotting may be done at the scene using colored chalk to plot vehicle positions at various locations, from which a circumference, chord, *C*, and middle ordinate, *M*, may be calculated. Alternatively, all measurements may be placed on a scale diagram and the positions of the vehicle plotted at various locations and calculations carried out using the scale diagram.

TABLE 5-IV-A

SPEED FROM SIDESLIP OR YAW MARKS IN MILES PER HOUR

(Formula 5-10)

Coefficient of Friction (f)	Radius (feet)											
	20	25	30	35	40	45	50	60	70	80	90	100
0.10	5.500	6.149	6.736	7.276	7.778	8.250	8.696	9.526	10.290	11.000	11.667	12.298
0.15	6.736	7.531	8.250	8.911	9.526	10.104	10.651	11.667	12.602	13.472	14.289	15.062
0.20	7.778	8.696	9.526	10.290	11.000	11.667	12.298	13.472	14.552	15.556	16.500	17.393
0.25	8.696	9.723	10.651	11.504	12.298	13.044	13.750	15.062	16.269	17.393	18.448	19.445
0.30	9.526	10.651	11.667	12.602	13.472	14.289	15.062	16.500	17.822	19.053	20.208	21.301
0.35	10.290	11.504	12.602	13.612	14.552	15.434	16.269	17.822	19.250	20.579	21.827	23.008
0.40	11.000	12.298	13.472	14.552	15.556	16.500	17.393	19.053	20.579	22.000	23.335	24.597
0.45	11.667	13.044	14.289	15.434	16.500	17.501	18.448	20.208	21.827	23.335	24.750	26.089
0.50	12.298	13.750	15.062	16.269	17.393	18.448	19.445	21.301	23.008	24.597	26.089	27.500
0.55	12.899	14.421	15.798	17.063	18.241	19.348	20.395	22.341	24.131	25.797	27.362	28.842
0.60	13.472	15.062	16.500	17.822	19.053	20.208	21.301	23.335	25.204	26.944	28.579	30.125
0.65	14.022	15.677	17.174	18.550	19.831	21.033	22.171	24.287	26.233	28.045	29.746	31.355
0.70	14.552	16.269	17.822	19.250	20.579	21.827	23.008	25.204	27.224	29.103	30.869	32.538
0.75	15.062	16.840	18.448	19.926	21.301	22.594	23.816	26.089	28.179	30.125	31.952	33.680
0.80	15.556	17.393	19.053	20.579	22.000	23.335	24.597	26.944	29.103	31.113	33.000	34.785
0.85	16.035	17.928	19.639	21.212	22.677	24.053	25.354	27.774	29.999	32.070	34.016	35.856
0.90	16.500	18.448	20.208	21.827	23.335	24.750	26.089	28.579	30.869	33.000	35.002	36.895
0.95	16.952	18.953	20.762	22.426	23.974	25.428	26.804	29.362	31.715	33.904	35.961	37.906
1.00	17.393	19.445	21.301	23.008	24.597	26.089	27.500	30.125	32.538	34.785	36.895	38.891
1.05	17.822	19.926	21.827	23.576	25.204	26.733	28.179	30.869	33.342	35.644	37.806	39.851
1.10	18.241	20.395	22.341	24.131	25.797	27.362	28.842	31.595	34.127	36.483	38.696	40.789
1.15	18.651	20.853	22.843	24.673	26.377	27.977	29.490	32.305	34.894	37.303	39.566	41.706
1.20	19.053	21.301	23.335	25.204	26.944	28.579	30.125	33.000	35.644	38.105	40.417	42.603
1.25	19.445	21.741	23.816	25.724	27.500	29.168	30.746	33.680	36.379	38.891	41.250	43.481
1.30	19.831	22.171	24.287	26.233	28.045	29.746	31.355	34.347	37.100	39.661	42.067	44.342
1.35	20.208	22.594	24.750	26.733	28.579	30.312	31.952	35.002	37.806	40.417	42.868	45.187

Radius (feet)

Coefficient of Friction (f)	110	120	130	140	150	160	170	180	190	200	220	240
0.10	12.899	13.472	14.022	14.552	15.062	15.556	16.035	16.500	16.952	17.393	18.241	19.053
0.15	15.798	16.500	17.174	17.822	18.448	19.053	19.639	20.208	20.762	21.301	22.341	23.335
0.20	18.241	19.053	19.831	20.579	21.301	22.000	22.677	23.335	23.974	24.597	25.797	26.944
0.25	20.395	21.301	22.171	23.008	23.816	24.597	25.354	26.089	26.804	27.500	28.842	30.125
0.30	22.341	23.335	24.287	25.204	26.089	26.944	27.774	28.579	29.362	30.125	31.595	33.000
0.35	24.131	25.204	26.233	27.224	28.179	29.103	29.999	30.869	31.715	32.538	34.127	35.644
0.40	25.797	26.944	28.045	29.103	30.125	31.113	32.070	33.000	33.904	34.785	36.483	38.105
0.45	27.362	28.579	29.746	30.869	31.952	33.000	34.016	35.002	35.961	36.895	38.696	40.417
0.50	28.842	30.125	31.355	32.538	33.680	34.785	35.856	36.895	37.906	38.891	40.789	42.603
0.55	30.250	31.595	32.885	34.127	35.324	36.483	37.606	38.696	39.756	40.789	42.780	44.682
0.60	31.595	33.000	34.347	35.644	36.895	38.105	39.278	40.417	41.524	42.603	44.682	46.669
0.65	32.885	34.347	35.750	37.100	38.402	39.661	40.882	42.067	43.220	44.342	46.507	48.575
0.70	34.127	35.644	37.100	38.500	39.851	41.158	42.425	43.655	44.851	46.016	48.262	50.408
0.75	35.324	36.895	38.402	39.851	41.250	42.603	43.914	45.187	46.425	47.631	49.956	52.178
0.80	36.483	38.105	39.661	41.158	42.603	44.000	45.354	46.669	47.948	49.193	51.595	53.889
0.85	37.606	39.278	40.882	42.425	43.914	45.354	46.750	48.105	49.424	50.707	53.182	55.547
0.90	38.696	40.417	42.067	43.655	45.187	46.669	48.105	49.500	50.856	52.178	54.724	57.158
0.95	39.756	41.524	43.220	44.851	46.425	47.948	49.424	50.856	52.250	53.607	56.224	58.724
1.00	40.789	42.603	44.342	46.016	47.631	49.193	50.707	52.178	53.607	55.000	57.684	60.249
1.05	41.796	43.654	45.437	47.153	48.808	50.408	51.960	53.466	54.931	56.358	59.109	61.737
1.10	42.780	44.682	46.507	48.262	49.956	51.595	53.182	54.724	56.224	57.684	60.500	63.190
1.15	43.741	45.686	47.552	49.347	51.079	52.754	54.378	55.954	57.487	58.981	61.860	64.610
1.20	44.682	46.669	48.575	50.408	52.178	53.889	55.547	57.158	58.724	60.249	63.190	66.000
1.25	45.604	47.631	49.576	51.448	53.254	55.000	56.693	58.336	59.935	61.492	64.493	67.361
1.30	46.507	48.575	50.558	52.467	54.308	56.089	57.815	59.492	61.122	62.710	65.770	68.695
1.35	47.393	49.500	51.521	53.466	55.343	57.158	58.917	60.625	62.286	63.904	67.023	70.004

TABLE 5-IV-A (Continued)

SPEED FROM SIDESLIP OR YAW MARKS IN MILES PER HOUR

Radius (feet)

Coefficient of Friction (f)	260	280	300	325	350	375	400	450	500	550	600	650
0.10	19.831	20.579	21.301	22.171	23.008	23.816	24.597	26.089	27.500	28.842	30.125	31.355
0.15	24.287	25.204	26.089	27.154	28.179	29.168	30.125	31.952	33.680	35.324	36.895	38.402
0.20	28.045	29.103	30.125	31.355	32.538	33.680	34.785	36.895	38.891	40.789	42.603	44.342
0.25	31.355	32.538	33.680	35.056	36.379	37.656	38.891	41.250	43.481	45.604	47.631	49.576
0.30	34.347	35.644	36.895	38.402	39.851	41.250	42.603	45.187	47.631	49.956	52.178	54.308
0.35	37.100	38.500	39.851	41.479	43.044	44.555	46.016	48.808	51.448	53.959	56.358	58.660
0.40	39.661	41.158	42.603	44.342	46.016	47.631	49.193	52.178	55.000	57.684	60.249	62.710
0.45	42.067	43.655	45.187	47.032	48.808	50.521	52.178	55.343	58.336	61.184	63.904	66.514
0.50	44.342	46.016	47.631	49.576	51.448	53.254	55.000	58.336	61.492	64.493	67.361	70.112
0.55	46.507	48.262	49.956	51.996	53.959	55.853	57.684	61.184	64.493	67.641	70.649	73.534
0.60	48.575	50.408	52.178	54.308	56.358	58.336	60.249	63.904	67.361	70.649	73.790	76.803
0.65	50.558	52.467	54.308	56.526	58.660	60.718	62.710	66.514	70.112	73.534	76.803	79.939
0.70	52.467	54.447	56.358	58.660	60.874	63.010	65.077	69.024	72.758	76.309	79.703	82.957
0.75	54.308	56.358	58.336	60.718	63.010	65.222	67.361	71.447	75.312	78.988	82.500	85.869
0.80	56.089	58.207	60.249	62.710	65.077	67.361	69.570	73.790	77.782	81.578	85.206	88.685
0.85	57.815	59.998	62.104	64.640	67.080	69.434	71.711	76.061	80.176	84.089	87.828	91.414
0.90	59.492	61.737	63.904	66.514	69.024	71.447	73.790	78.266	82.500	86.527	90.374	94.064
0.95	61.122	63.429	65.655	68.336	70.916	73.405	75.812	80.411	84.761	88.898	92.851	96.642
1.00	62.710	65.077	67.361	70.112	72.758	75.312	77.782	82.500	86.963	91.207	95.263	99.153
1.05	64.258	66.684	69.024	71.843	74.555	77.172	79.703	84.537	89.110	93.460	97.615	101.601
1.10	65.770	68.253	70.649	73.534	76.309	78.988	81.578	86.527	91.207	95.659	99.912	103.992
1.15	67.249	69.787	72.237	75.186	78.024	80.763	83.412	88.471	93.257	97.809	102.158	106.329
1.20	68.695	71.288	73.790	76.803	79.703	82.500	85.206	90.374	95.263	99.912	104.355	108.616
1.25	70.112	72.758	75.312	78.387	81.346	84.201	86.963	92.238	97.227	101.973	106.507	110.856
1.30	71.500	74.199	76.803	79.939	82.957	85.869	88.685	94.064	99.153	103.992	108.616	113.051
1.35	72.862	75.612	78.266	81.462	84.537	87.504	90.374	95.856	101.041	105.973	110.685	115.205

Radius (feet)

Coefficient of Friction (f)	700	750	800	850	900	1000	1100	1200	1300	1400	1500	1600
0.10	32.538	33.680	34.785	35.856	36.895	38.891	40.789	42.603	44.342	46.016	47.631	49.193
0.15	39.851	41.250	42.603	43.914	45.187	47.631	49.956	52.178	54.308	56.358	58.336	60.249
0.20	46.016	47.631	49.193	50.707	52.178	55.000	57.684	60.249	62.710	65.077	67.361	69.570
0.25	51.448	53.254	55.000	56.693	58.336	61.492	64.493	67.361	70.112	72.758	75.312	77.782
0.30	56.358	58.336	60.249	62.104	63.904	67.361	70.649	73.790	76.803	79.703	82.500	85.206
0.35	60.874	63.010	65.077	67.080	69.024	72.758	76.309	79.703	82.957	86.089	89.110	92.033
0.40	65.077	67.361	69.570	71.711	73.790	77.782	81.578	85.206	88.685	92.033	95.263	98.387
0.45	69.024	71.447	73.790	76.061	78.266	82.500	86.527	90.374	94.064	97.615	101.041	104.355
0.50	72.758	75.312	77.782	80.176	82.500	86.963	91.207	95.263	99.153	102.896	106.507	110.000
0.55	76.309	78.988	81.578	84.089	86.527	91.207	95.659	99.912	103.992	107.918	111.706	115.369
0.60	79.703	82.500	85.206	87.828	90.374	95.263	99.912	104.355	108.616	112.716	116.673	120.499
0.65	82.957	85.869	88.685	91.414	94.064	99.153	103.992	108.616	113.051	117.319	121.437	125.419
0.70	86.089	89.110	92.033	94.865	97.615	102.896	107.918	112.716	117.319	121.748	126.021	130.154
0.75	89.110	92.238	95.263	98.195	101.041	106.507	111.706	116.673	121.437	126.021	130.444	134.722
0.80	92.033	95.263	98.387	101.415	104.355	110.000	115.369	120.499	125.419	130.154	134.722	139.140
0.85	94.865	98.195	101.415	104.536	107.567	113.385	118.920	124.207	129.279	134.159	138.868	143.422
0.90	97.615	101.041	104.355	107.567	110.685	116.673	122.367	127.808	133.027	138.049	142.894	147.580
0.95	100.290	103.810	107.215	110.514	113.718	119.870	125.720	131.311	136.673	141.832	146.810	151.625
1.00	102.896	106.507	110.000	113.385	116.673	122.984	128.986	134.722	140.223	145.516	150.624	155.563
1.05	105.437	109.137	112.716	116.185	119.554	126.021	132.172	138.049	143.686	149.110	154.343	159.405
1.10	107.918	111.706	115.369	118.920	122.367	128.986	135.282	141.298	147.067	152.619	157.975	163.156
1.15	110.343	114.216	117.962	121.592	125.117	131.885	138.323	144.473	150.372	156.049	161.526	166.823
1.20	112.716	116.673	120.499	124.207	127.808	134.722	141.298	147.580	153.607	159.405	165.000	170.411
1.25	115.041	119.078	122.984	126.769	130.444	137.500	144.211	150.624	156.774	162.692	168.402	173.925
1.30	117.319	121.437	125.419	129.279	133.027	140.223	147.067	153.607	159.879	165.914	171.737	177.370
1.35	119.554	123.750	127.808	131.742	135.561	142.894	149.869	156.533	162.924	169.075	175.009	180.748

TABLE 5-IV-A (*Continued*)

SPEED FROM SIDESLIP OR YAW MARKS IN MILES PER HOUR

Radius (feet)

Coefficient of Friction (f)	1700	1800	1900	2000
0.10	50.707	52.178	53.607	55.000
0.15	62.104	63.904	65.655	67.361
0.20	71.711	73.790	75.812	77.782
0.25	80.176	82.500	84.761	86.963
0.30	87.828	90.374	92.851	95.263
0.35	94.865	97.615	100.290	102.896
0.40	101.415	104.355	107.215	110.000
0.45	107.567	110.685	113.718	116.673
0.50	113.385	116.673	119.870	122.984
0.55	118.920	122.367	125.720	128.986
0.60	124.207	127.808	131.311	134.722
0.65	129.279	133.027	136.673	140.223
0.70	134.159	138.049	141.832	145.516
0.75	138.869	142.894	146.810	150.624
0.80	143.422	147.580	151.625	155.563
0.85	147.836	152.122	156.291	160.351
0.90	152.122	156.533	160.822	165.000
0.95	156.291	160.822	165.229	169.521
1.00	160.351	165.000	169.521	173.925
1.05	164.311	169.075	173.708	178.220
1.10	168.178	173.053	177.796	182.414
1.15	171.957	176.943	181.791	186.514
1.20	175.656	180.748	185.701	190.526
1.25	179.278	184.476	189.531	194.454
1.30	182.828	188.129	193.284	198.305
1.35	186.311	191.713	196.966	202.083

TABLE 5-IV-B

SPEED FROM SIDESLIP OR YAW MARKS IN
KILOMETERS PER HOUR

(Formula 5-12)

Coefficient of Friction (f)	Radius (meters)											
	8	10	12	14	16	18	20	22	24	26	30	35
0.05	7.128	7.969	8.730	9.429	10.080	10.692	11.270	11.820	12.346	12.850	13.803	14.909
0.10	10.080	11.270	12.346	13.335	14.256	15.120	15.938	16.716	17.459	18.172	19.520	21.084
0.15	12.346	13.803	15.120	16.332	17.459	18.518	19.520	20.473	21.383	22.256	23.907	25.823
0.20	14.256	15.938	17.459	18.858	20.160	21.383	22.540	23.640	24.691	25.700	27.606	29.818
0.25	15.938	17.819	19.520	21.084	22.540	23.907	25.200	26.430	27.606	28.733	30.864	33.337
0.30	17.459	19.520	21.383	23.097	24.691	26.189	27.606	28.953	30.241	31.475	33.810	36.519
0.35	18.858	21.084	23.097	24.947	26.670	28.287	29.818	31.273	32.664	33.997	36.519	39.445
0.40	20.160	22.540	24.691	26.670	28.511	30.241	31.876	33.432	34.919	36.345	39.040	42.168
0.45	21.383	23.907	26.189	28.287	30.241	32.075	33.810	35.460	37.037	38.549	41.409	44.726
0.50	22.540	25.200	27.606	29.818	31.876	33.810	35.639	37.378	39.040	40.635	43.649	47.146
0.55	23.640	26.430	28.953	31.273	33.432	35.460	37.378	39.203	40.946	42.618	45.779	49.447
0.60	24.691	27.606	30.241	32.664	34.919	37.037	39.040	40.946	42.767	44.513	47.815	51.646
0.65	25.700	28.733	31.475	33.997	36.345	38.549	40.635	42.618	44.513	46.331	49.767	53.754
0.70	26.670	29.818	32.664	35.281	37.717	40.005	42.168	44.227	46.193	48.079	51.646	55.784
0.75	27.606	30.864	33.810	36.519	39.040	41.409	43.649	45.779	47.815	49.767	53.458	57.742
0.80	28.511	31.876	34.919	37.717	40.321	42.767	45.080	47.280	49.383	51.399	55.211	59.635
0.85	29.389	32.857	35.993	38.877	41.562	44.083	46.467	48.735	50.902	52.981	56.911	61.471
0.90	30.241	33.810	37.037	40.005	42.767	45.361	47.815	50.148	52.378	54.517	58.561	63.253
0.95	31.069	34.736	38.052	41.101	43.939	46.604	49.125	51.523	53.814	56.011	60.165	64.986
1.00	31.876	35.639	39.040	42.168	45.080	47.815	50.401	52.861	55.211	57.466	61.728	66.674
1.05	32.664	36.519	40.005	43.210	46.193	48.995	51.646	54.166	56.575	58.885	63.253	68.321
1.10	33.432	37.378	40.946	44.227	47.280	50.148	52.861	55.441	57.906	60.271	64.741	69.929
1.15	34.184	38.218	41.866	45.221	48.343	51.275	54.049	56.687	59.208	61.625	66.196	71.500
1.20	34.919	39.040	42.767	46.193	49.383	52.378	55.211	57.906	60.481	62.951	67.620	73.038
1.25	35.639	39.845	43.649	47.146	50.401	53.458	56.350	59.100	61.728	64.249	69.014	74.544
1.30	36.345	40.635	44.513	48.079	51.399	54.517	57.466	60.271	62.951	65.521	70.381	76.020

TABLE 5-IV-B (Continued)

SPEED FROM SIDESLIP OR YAW MARKS IN KILOMETERS PER HOUR

Radius (meters)

Coefficient of Friction (f)	40	45	50	55	60	65	70	75	80	85	90	95
0.05	15.938	16.905	17.819	18.689	19.520	20.317	21.084	21.824	22.540	23.234	23.907	24.562
0.10	22.540	23.907	25.200	26.430	27.606	28.733	29.818	30.864	31.876	32.857	33.810	34.736
0.15	27.606	29.280	30.864	32.371	33.810	35.191	36.519	37.801	39.040	40.242	41.409	42.543
0.20	31.876	33.810	35.639	37.378	39.040	40.635	42.168	43.649	45.080	46.467	47.815	49.125
0.25	35.639	37.801	39.845	41.790	43.649	45.431	47.146	48.801	50.401	51.952	53.458	54.923
0.30	39.040	41.409	43.649	45.779	47.815	49.767	51.646	53.458	55.211	56.911	58.561	60.165
0.35	42.168	44.726	47.146	49.447	51.646	53.754	55.784	57.742	59.635	61.471	63.253	64.986
0.40	45.080	47.815	50.401	52.861	55.211	57.466	59.635	61.728	63.753	65.715	67.620	69.473
0.45	47.815	50.715	53.458	56.068	58.561	60.952	63.253	65.473	67.620	69.701	71.722	73.687
0.50	50.401	53.458	56.350	59.100	61.728	64.249	66.674	69.014	71.278	73.471	75.601	77.673
0.55	52.861	56.068	59.100	61.985	64.741	67.385	69.929	72.383	74.757	77.057	79.291	81.464
0.60	55.211	58.561	61.728	64.741	67.620	70.381	73.038	75.601	78.081	80.484	82.817	85.087
0.65	57.466	60.952	64.249	67.385	70.381	73.255	76.020	78.688	81.269	83.770	86.199	88.561
0.70	59.635	63.253	66.674	69.929	73.038	76.020	78.890	81.659	84.337	86.933	89.453	91.904
0.75	61.728	65.473	69.014	72.383	75.601	78.688	81.659	84.525	87.297	89.984	92.592	95.130
0.80	63.753	67.620	71.278	74.757	78.081	81.269	84.337	87.297	90.160	92.935	95.629	98.250
0.85	65.715	69.701	73.471	77.057	80.484	83.770	86.933	89.984	92.935	95.795	98.572	101.273
0.90	67.620	71.722	75.601	79.291	82.817	86.199	89.453	92.592	95.629	98.572	101.430	104.209
0.95	69.473	73.687	77.673	81.464	85.087	88.561	91.904	95.130	98.250	101.273	104.209	107.065
1.00	71.278	75.601	79.691	83.581	87.297	90.862	94.292	97.601	100.802	103.904	106.917	109.846
1.05	73.038	77.468	81.659	85.645	89.453	93.105	96.620	100.011	103.291	106.470	109.557	112.559
1.10	74.757	79.291	83.581	87.660	91.558	95.296	98.894	102.365	105.722	108.976	112.135	115.208
1.15	76.437	81.074	85.459	89.630	93.616	97.438	101.116	104.665	108.098	111.425	114.655	117.797
1.20	78.081	82.817	87.297	91.558	95.629	99.534	103.291	106.917	110.423	113.821	117.121	120.331
1.25	79.691	84.525	89.097	93.446	97.601	101.586	105.421	109.121	112.700	116.169	119.536	122.812
1.30	81.269	86.199	90.862	95.296	99.534	103.598	107.509	111.282	114.932	118.469	121.904	125.244

Coefficient of Friction (f)	Radius (meters)											
	100	110	120	130	140	150	160	170	180	190	200	220
0.05	25.200	26.430	27.606	28.733	29.818	30.864	31.876	32.857	33.810	34.736	35.639	37.378
0.10	35.639	37.378	39.040	40.635	42.168	43.649	45.080	46.467	47.815	49.125	50.401	52.861
0.15	43.649	45.779	47.815	49.767	51.646	53.458	55.211	56.911	58.561	60.165	61.728	64.741
0.20	50.401	52.861	55.211	57.466	59.635	61.728	63.753	65.715	67.620	69.473	71.278	74.757
0.25	56.350	59.100	61.728	64.249	66.674	69.014	71.278	73.471	75.601	77.673	79.691	83.581
0.30	61.728	64.741	67.620	70.381	73.038	75.601	78.081	80.484	82.817	85.087	87.297	91.558
0.35	66.674	69.929	73.038	76.020	78.890	81.659	84.337	86.933	89.453	91.904	94.292	98.894
0.40	71.278	74.757	78.081	81.269	84.337	87.297	90.160	92.935	95.629	98.250	100.802	105.722
0.45	75.601	79.291	82.817	86.199	89.453	92.592	95.629	98.572	101.430	104.209	106.917	112.135
0.50	79.691	83.581	87.297	90.862	94.292	97.601	100.802	103.904	106.917	109.846	112.700	118.201
0.55	83.581	87.660	91.558	95.296	98.894	102.365	105.722	108.976	112.135	115.208	118.201	123.970
0.60	87.297	91.558	95.629	99.534	103.291	106.917	110.423	113.821	117.121	120.331	123.457	129.482
0.65	90.862	95.296	99.534	103.598	107.509	111.282	114.932	118.469	121.904	125.244	128.498	134.770
0.70	94.292	98.894	103.291	107.509	111.567	115.483	119.270	122.941	126.505	129.972	133.348	139.857
0.75	97.601	102.365	106.917	111.282	115.483	119.536	123.457	127.256	130.946	134.534	138.029	144.766
0.80	100.802	105.722	110.423	114.932	119.270	123.457	127.505	131.430	135.240	138.946	142.555	149.513
0.85	103.904	108.976	113.821	118.469	122.941	127.256	131.430	135.475	139.402	143.222	146.943	154.115
0.90	106.917	112.135	117.121	121.904	126.505	130.946	135.240	139.402	143.444	147.374	151.203	158.583
0.95	109.846	115.208	120.331	125.244	129.972	134.534	138.946	143.222	147.374	151.413	155.346	162.928
1.00	112.700	118.201	123.457	128.498	133.348	138.029	142.555	146.943	151.203	155.346	159.382	167.161
1.05	115.483	121.120	126.505	131.671	136.641	141.437	146.076	150.572	154.937	159.183	163.318	171.289
1.10	118.201	123.970	129.482	134.770	139.857	144.766	149.513	154.115	158.583	162.928	167.161	175.320
1.15	120.857	126.756	132.393	137.799	143.000	148.019	152.874	157.579	162.147	166.590	170.918	179.260
1.20	123.457	129.482	135.240	140.762	146.076	151.203	156.162	160.968	165.634	170.173	174.594	183.116
1.25	126.002	132.152	138.029	143.665	149.088	154.321	159.382	164.287	169.050	173.682	178.194	186.892
1.30	128.498	134.770	140.762	146.510	152.041	157.377	162.538	167.541	172.398	177.122	181.723	190.593

TABLE 5-IV-B (Continued)
SPEED FROM SIDESLIP OR YAW MARKS IN KILOMETERS PER HOUR

Coefficient of Friction (f)	Radius (meters)											
	240	260	280	300	330	360	390	420	450	480	510	540
0.05	39.040	40.635	42.168	43.649	45.779	47.815	49.767	51.646	53.458	55.211	56.911	58.561
0.10	55.211	57.466	59.635	61.728	64.741	67.620	70.381	73.038	75.601	78.081	80.484	82.817
0.15	67.620	70.381	73.038	75.601	79.291	82.817	86.199	89.453	92.592	95.629	98.572	101.430
0.20	78.081	81.269	84.337	87.297	91.558	95.629	99.534	103.291	106.917	110.423	113.821	117.121
0.25	87.297	90.862	94.292	97.601	102.365	106.917	111.282	115.483	119.536	123.457	127.256	130.946
0.30	95.629	99.534	103.291	106.917	112.135	117.121	121.904	126.505	130.946	135.240	139.402	143.444
0.35	103.291	107.509	111.567	115.483	121.120	126.505	131.671	136.641	141.437	146.076	150.572	154.937
0.40	110.423	114.932	119.270	123.457	129.482	135.240	140.762	146.076	151.203	156.162	160.968	165.634
0.45	117.121	121.904	126.505	130.946	137.337	143.444	149.301	154.937	160.375	165.634	170.732	175.682
0.50	123.457	128.498	133.348	138.029	144.766	151.203	157.377	163.318	169.050	174.594	179.967	185.185
0.55	129.482	134.770	139.857	144.766	151.832	158.583	165.058	171.289	177.301	183.116	188.751	194.224
0.60	135.240	140.762	146.076	151.203	158.583	165.634	172.398	178.906	185.185	191.258	197.144	202.860
0.65	140.762	146.510	152.041	157.377	165.058	172.398	179.437	186.211	192.747	199.068	205.194	211.143
0.70	146.076	152.041	157.780	163.318	171.289	178.906	186.211	193.240	200.023	206.583	212.940	219.114
0.75	151.203	157.377	163.318	169.050	177.301	185.185	192.747	200.023	207.043	213.833	220.414	226.804
0.80	156.162	162.538	168.674	174.594	183.116	191.258	199.068	206.583	213.833	220.846	227.643	234.243
0.85	160.968	167.541	173.865	179.967	188.751	197.144	205.194	212.940	220.414	227.643	234.649	241.452
0.90	165.634	172.398	178.906	185.185	194.224	202.860	211.143	219.114	226.804	234.243	241.452	248.452
0.95	170.173	177.122	183.808	190.259	199.546	208.419	216.929	225.118	233.019	240.661	248.068	255.260
1.00	174.594	181.723	188.583	195.202	204.730	213.833	222.565	230.966	239.073	246.913	254.512	261.891
1.05	178.906	186.211	193.240	200.023	209.786	219.114	228.061	236.670	244.977	253.011	260.798	268.359
1.10	183.116	190.593	197.788	204.730	214.722	224.270	233.428	242.239	250.742	258.965	266.935	274.674
1.15	187.231	194.877	202.233	209.331	219.548	229.311	238.674	247.684	256.377	264.785	272.934	280.847
1.20	191.258	199.068	206.583	213.833	224.270	234.243	243.807	253.011	261.891	270.480	278.804	286.887
1.25	195.202	203.173	210.842	218.243	228.895	239.073	248.835	258.228	267.292	276.057	284.554	292.803
1.30	199.068	207.196	215.018	222.565	233.428	243.807	253.763	263.342	272.585	281.524	290.189	298.602

Coefficient of Friction (f)	Radius (meters)									
	570	600	650	700	750	800	850	900	950	1000
0.05	60.165	61.728	64.249	66.674	69.014	71.278	73.471	75.601	77.673	79.691
0.10	85.087	87.297	90.862	94.292	97.601	100.802	103.904	106.917	109.846	112.700
0.15	104.209	106.917	111.282	115.483	119.536	123.457	127.256	130.946	134.534	138.029
0.20	120.331	123.457	128.498	133.348	138.029	142.555	146.943	151.203	155.346	159.382
0.25	134.534	138.029	143.665	149.088	154.321	159.382	164.287	169.050	173.682	178.194
0.30	147.374	151.203	157.377	163.318	169.050	174.594	179.967	185.185	190.259	195.202
0.35	159.183	163.318	169.987	176.403	182.595	188.583	194.387	200.023	205.504	210.842
0.40	170.173	174.594	181.723	188.583	195.202	201.604	207.809	213.833	219.693	225.400
0.45	180.496	185.185	192.747	200.023	207.043	213.833	220.414	226.804	233.019	239.073
0.50	190.259	195.202	203.173	210.842	218.243	225.400	232.337	239.073	245.624	252.005
0.55	199.546	204.730	213.089	221.133	228.895	236.402	243.677	250.742	257.613	264.305
0.60	208.419	213.833	222.565	230.966	239.073	246.913	254.512	261.891	269.068	276.057
0.65	216.929	222.565	231.653	240.397	248.835	256.996	264.905	272.585	280.054	287.330
0.70	225.118	230.966	240.397	249.472	258.228	266.697	274.905	282.875	290.626	298.176
0.75	233.019	239.073	248.835	258.228	267.292	276.057	284.554	292.803	300.827	308.642
0.80	240.661	246.913	256.996	266.697	276.057	285.111	293.886	302.406	310.692	318.764
0.85	248.068	254.512	264.905	274.905	284.554	293.886	302.930	311.713	320.254	328.574
0.90	255.260	261.891	272.585	282.875	292.803	302.406	311.713	320.750	329.539	338.100
0.95	262.255	269.068	280.054	290.626	300.827	310.692	320.254	329.539	338.569	347.365
1.00	269.068	276.057	287.330	298.176	308.642	318.764	328.574	338.100	347.365	356.389
1.05	275.712	282.875	294.425	305.540	316.264	326.636	336.688	346.449	355.943	365.190
1.10	282.200	289.532	301.354	312.730	323.706	334.322	344.611	354.602	364.319	373.784
1.15	288.543	296.039	308.127	319.758	330.981	341.836	352.357	362.572	372.507	382.184
1.20	294.749	302.406	314.754	326.636	338.100	349.188	359.935	370.370	380.519	390.404
1.25	300.827	308.642	321.244	333.371	345.072	356.389	367.357	378.007	388.366	398.455
1.30	306.784	314.754	327.606	339.973	351.906	363.447	374.632	385.493	396.057	406.346

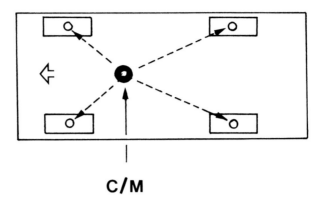

C/M

Figure 5-20. The center of mass must be measured to the contact area of each tire, which in turn must be related to tire marks on the roadway when using the center of mass to determine the speed of a vehicle in yaw.

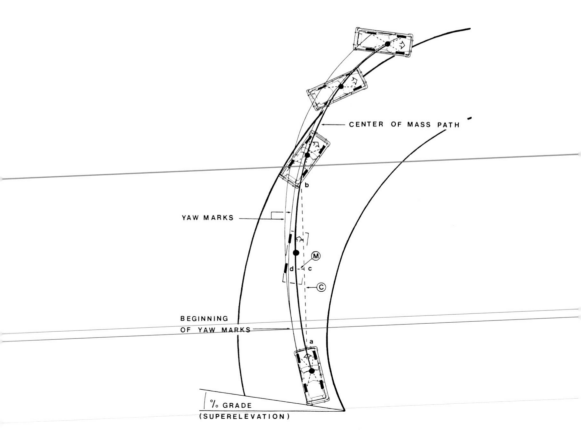

Figure 5-21. Method of plotting the radius of the center of mass path.

5.071 When calculating the speed of a vehicle in yaw or sideslip using the center of mass path, use Formula 5-12. (Formula 5-10 may also be used; the results are similar.)

United States	*Metric*
$S = 3.87 \sqrt{(f \pm e) \ R}$	$S = 11.27 \sqrt{(f \pm e) \ R}$

where S = speed
 f = coefficient of friction
 e = superelevation or bank
 R = radius

The numbers 3.87 and 11.27 are constants in calculating speed of vehicle in yaw using the center of mass path.

Example

A vehicle travelled into a curve at a high rate of speed and skidded sideways, leaving a sideslip or yaw mark of 300 ft (91.44 m). The location of the center of mass of the vehicle was determined and related to the roadway contact areas of all tires. Using the yaw marks as a guide, the path followed by the *center of mass* was then plotted. Using approximately the first one-third of the center of mass path, a chord was measured 75 ft (22.86 m) in length, having a middle ordinate of 3 ft (.914 m). The radius was calculated at 236 ft (72 m). The roadway superelevation was measured at +05 percent. Test skids revealed that the coefficient of friction was .70. The minimum speed of the vehicle as it started into yaw may be calculated using Formula 5-12:

United States	*Metric*
$S = 3.87 \sqrt{(.70 + .05) \ R}$	$S = 11.27 \sqrt{(.70 + .05) \ 72}$
$S = 3.87 \sqrt{.75 \times 236}$	$S = 11.27 \sqrt{.75 \times 72}$
$S = 3.87 \sqrt{177}$	$S = 11.27 \sqrt{54}$
$S = 3.87 \times 13.3$	$S = 11.27 \times 7.35$
$S = 51.47$	$S = 82.83$
$S = 51$ mph	$S = 83$ km/h

ACCELERATION AND DECELERATION

5.072 In reconstructing an accident, the investigator must be in a position to show relative positions of vehicles, pedestrians and other objects. This can be best done by preparing a scale diagram of the scene. In order to prepare a meaningful diagram, it is necessary to determine the speeds of the vehicles, including their acceleration and deceleration rates, if these are factors.

5.073 *Acceleration* and *deceleration* are the rates of speed or velocity change with time. Acceleration is an increase (+) and deceleration is a decrease (−) in speed or velocity.

5.074   The investigator must determine a driver's point of possible perception of another traffic unit or object. The brake application or any other evasive action such as steering should be determined and related to the point of possible perception and all other applicable on-scene series of events.

5.075   To place vehicles and pedestrians at certain locations, it is necessary to obtain vehicle, highway and roadway measurements including:

    a. vehicle dimensions
    b. roadway surface markings
    c. locations of traffic-control devices
    d. locations of view of other obstructions
    e. coefficient of friction

Constant Speed

5.076   A vehicle travelling at a *constant speed,* that is no acceleration or deceleration, covers a certain distance in a given time because there is a direct relationship between distance, speed and time. If any two of these three factors are known, the third may be calculated.

5.077   Speed or velocity may be calculated by using Formula 5-13:

United States	*Metric*
$S = \dfrac{D}{t}$	$S = \dfrac{D}{t}$

where S = speed or velocity
       D = distance traveled
       t = time

Example
   A vehicle travelled 500 ft (152 m) in 10 seconds. Its speed was:

United States	*Metric*
$S = \dfrac{500}{10}$	$S = \dfrac{152}{10}$
$S = 50$ ft/sec	$S = 15.2$ m/s

The numbers 1.467 and .278 are ft/sec and m/s conversion factors to convert ft/sec to mph and m/s to km/h. For conversion purposes use Formula 5-14

United States	*Metric*
$S = \dfrac{\text{ft/sec}}{1.467}$	$S = \dfrac{\text{m/sec}}{.278}$
$S = 34.08$	$S = 54.676$
$S = 34$ mph	$S = 55$ km/h

5.078   When time and speed are known, the distance a vehicle travelled may be calculated by using Formula 5-15:

	United States	
	D = tS	

	Metric
	D = tS

where D = distance travelled
         t = time
         S = speed in ft/sec (m/sec)

Example 1

A vehicle travelled for 10 seconds at a constant speed of 34 mph or 50 ft/sec (55 km/h or 15.2 m/s). The distance it travelled was:

United States	Metric
D = 10 × 50	D = 10 × 15.2
D = 500 ft	D = 152 m

Example 2 (see **Fig. 5-22**)

Vehicle 1 was travelling east on 1st Street at a constant speed of 30.5 mph or 44.744 ft/sec (49 km/h or 13.6 m/s). The driver did not see vehicle 2 until the time of collision. The driver's point of possible perception was at point *A*, a distance of 62.6 ft (19 m) before the point of impact. Knowing the constant speed of vehicle 1, it is possible to plot its position at any time from the point of impact back to the point of possible perception or to any other point along the path of travel using Formula 5-15:

United States			Metric		
Sec	Speed (ft/sec)	Distance (feet)	Sec	Speed (m/s)	Distance (m)
(t)	(S)	(D)	(t)	(S)	(D)
	0 at point of impact			0 at point of impact	
.1	44.744	4.474	.1	13.6	1.36
.2	44.744	8.949	.2	13.6	2.72
.4	44.744	17.898	.4	13.6	5.44
.6	44.744	26.846	.6	13.6	8.16
.8	44.744	35.795	.8	13.6	10.88
1.0	44.744	44.744	1.0	13.6	13.61
1.2	44.744	53.693	1.2	13.6	16.32
1.4	44.744	62.642	1.4	13.6	19.04
1.6	44.744	71.590	1.6	13.6	21.76
1.8	44.744	80.539	1.8	13.6	24.48

5.079   The time required to cover a given distance at a constant speed may be calculated using Formula 5-16:

	United States		Metric
	$t = \dfrac{D}{S}$		$t = \dfrac{D}{S}$

where t = time
         D = distance travelled
         S = speed in ft/sec (m/s)

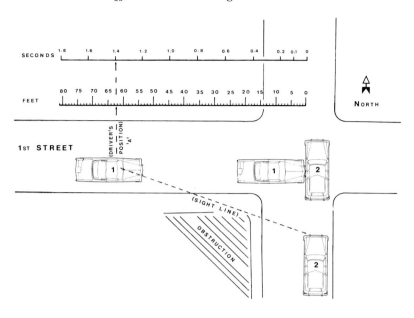

Figure 5-22. Formula 5-15: D = tS.

Example

A vehicle travelled 500 ft (152 m) at 34 mph or 50 ft/sec (55 km/h or 15.2 m/s). The time it took to travel the 500 ft (152 m) was:

United States	Metric
$t = \dfrac{500}{50}$	$t = \dfrac{152}{15.2}$
t = 10 seconds	t = 10 seconds

Acceleration

5.080 Gravity acts independently of outside forces. In Figure 5-23, for example, if vehicle 1 left the highway at a speed of 80 mph (128.72 km/h) and was catapulted horizontally out over a 100 ft (30.48 m) cliff at the same time vehicle 2 was pushed over the cliff, they would both strike level ground at the same time. This would occur because as vehicle 1 leaves the edge of the cliff, it would have the same vertical (downward) acceleration as vehicle 2, namely 32.2 ft/sec/sec (9.81 m/s/s) caused by the gravitational pull of the earth. What this means simply is that for each second the vehicles are falling, they gain 32.2 ft (9.81 m) over the previous second. In this case, at the end of the first second both vehicles would have fallen a distance of 16.1 ft (4.90 m), and at the end of the second second they both would have fallen 64.4 ft (19.62 m), and so on. To calculate the distance a vehicle falls in each second, use Formula 5-17:

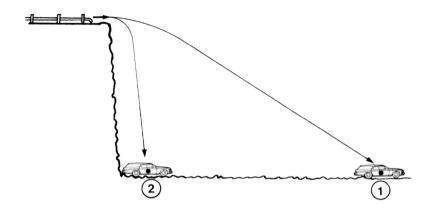

Figure 5-23

United States

$$D = \frac{at^2}{2}$$

where D = distance
     a = rate of acceleration
     t = time in seconds

$$D = \frac{32.2 \times 1^2}{2}$$

D = 16.1 ft at end of
     1st second

$$D = \frac{32.2 \times 2^2}{2}$$

D = 64.4 ft at end of
     2nd second

etc.

Metric

$$D = \frac{at^2}{2}$$

$$D = \frac{9.81 \times 1^2}{2}$$

D = 4.91 m at end
     of 1st second

$$D = \frac{9.81 \times 2^2}{2}$$

D = 19.62 m at end
     of 2nd second

etc.

Acceleration From a Stop or Known Speed

5.081 When the acceleration rate of a vehicle is known, the distance covered each second during acceleration from a stop or known speed may be calculated using Formula 5-18:

United States

$$D = (S_0 t) + (.5\ at^2)$$

Metric

$$D = (S_0 t) + (.5\ at^2)$$

where D = distance
     S_0 = initial speed in ft/sec(m/s)
     a = acceleration rate
     t = time in seconds

5.082 Motor vehicle acceleration rates may be obtained from car manufacturers' specification data sheets and from various automotive and traffic engineering publications. Normal acceleration rates may be determined by timing the travel of a vehicle from a stop sign over a measured distance. Witnesses can also sometimes give an estimate of the speed of a vehicle at a given distance from where the vehicle accelerated from a stop. The investigator may use a vehicle similar to the one involved in the accident and test the acceleration capabilities over a measured distance.

5.083 Acceleration rates vary with the size, weight and engine capability of vehicles. Heavy vehicles such as trucks and buses may have a low acceleration rate from a stop of approximately 3 ft/sec/sec (1 m/s/s). Late-model passenger cars have an acceleration rate as high as 10 ft/sec/sec (3 m/s/s). High-performance and modified vehicles often exceed this acceleration rate. Therefore, it is important in accidents involving acceleration that the investigator determine as closely as possible the acceleration rate of the vehicle involved.

5.084 For routine investigation purposes, the normal acceleration rate for modern passenger cars from a stop to 20 mph (32.18 km/h) may be considered to be 4 ft/sec/sec (1.219 m/s/s). As an example, a vehicle accelerating from a stop sign at an acceleration rate of 4 ft/sec/sec (1.219 m/s/s) covers the following distances during, for example, the first 3 seconds of acceleration (Formula 5-18):

United States	*Metric*
1st Second	
$D = (0 \times 0) + (.5 \times 4 \times 1^2)$	$D = (0 \times 0) + (.5 \times 1.219 \times 1^2)$
$D = 2$ ft (total)	$D = .61$ m (total)
2nd Second	
$D = (0 \times 0) + (.5 \times 4 \times 2^2)$	$D = (0 \times 0) + (.5 \times 1.219 \times 2^2)$
$D = 8$ ft (total)	$D = 2.438$ m (total)
$D = 8 - 2$	$D = 2.438 - .61$
$D = 6$ ft travelled in 2nd second	$D = 1.828$ m travelled in 2nd second
3rd Second	
$D = (0 \times 0) + (.5 \times 4 \times 3^2)$	$D = (0 \times 0) + (.5 \times 1.219 \times 3^2)$
$D = 18$ ft (total)	$D = 5.486$ m (total)
$D = 18 - 8$	$D = 5.486 - 2.438$
$D = 10$ ft travelled in 3rd second	$D = 3.048$ m travelled in 3rd second

5.085 When a vehicle accelerates from a stop at a known acceleration rate, its speed at any time during its acceleration may be calculated using Formula 5-19:

United States	*Metric*
$S = at \times .682$	$S = at \times 3.6$

where S = speed in mph or km/h
a = acceleration rate
t = time in seconds (1st second, 2nd second, etc.)

The numbers .682 and 3.6 are conversion factors for converting ft/sec to mph and m/s to km/h (Table 5-V).

Example

A vehicle accelerated from a stop at a rate of 4 ft/sec/sec (1.219 m/s/s) for 3 seconds. The speed at the end of each second was:

United States	*Metric*
1st Second	
S = 4 × 1 × .682	S = 1.219 × 1 × 3.6
S = 2.728 mph	S = 4.388 km/h
2nd Second	
S = 4 × 2 × .682	S = 1.219 × 2 × 3.6
S = 5.456 mph	S = 8.777 km/h
3rd Second	
S = 4 × 3 × .682	S = 1.219 × 3 × 3.6
S = 8.184	S = 13.165
S = 8 mph	S = 13 km/h

5.086 When a vehicle accelerates from a stop at a known acceleration rate over a known distance, the speed after acceleration may be calculated by using Formula 5-20:

United States	*Metric*
$S = \sqrt{2aD}$	$S = \sqrt{2aD}$

where S = speed after acceleration
     a = acceleration rate
     D = distance of acceleration

The numbers 1.467 and .278 are conversion factors for converting ft/sec to mph and m/s to km/h (*see* Table 5-V).

Example

A vehicle accelerated from a stop sign at a rate of 10 ft/sec/sec (3 m/s/s) over a distance of 40 ft (12.19 m). The speed attained was:

$S = \sqrt{2 \times 10 \times 40}$	$S = \sqrt{2 \times 3 \times 12.19}$
$S = \sqrt{800}$	$S = \sqrt{73.14}$
S = 28.28 ft/sec	S = 8.55 m/s
$S = \dfrac{28.28}{1.467}$	$S = \dfrac{8.55}{.278}$
S = 19.28	S = 30.76
S = 19 mph	S = 31 km/h

5.087 The total time it takes a vehicle to accelerate from a stop to a given speed may be calculated by using Formula 5-21:

United States	*Metric*
$t = \dfrac{S}{a}$	$t = \dfrac{S}{a}$

where t = time in seconds
     S = speed in ft/sec (m/s)
     a = acceleration rate

Example
  Using the circumstances in the foregoing example, the total time it would have taken the vehicle to accelerate from a stop to 28.28 ft/sec (8.55 m/s) would have been:

$$t = \frac{28.28}{10}$$ $$t = \frac{8.55}{3}$$

$$t = 3 \text{ seconds}$$ $$t = 3 \text{ seconds}$$

Acceleration from a Known Speed

5.088   When a vehicle travels at a known speed and then accelerates over a certain distance at a known acceleration rate, the speed at the end of the distance may be calculated by using Formula 5-22:

United States	*Metric*
$S_2 = \sqrt{S_1{}^2 + (2aD)}$	$S_2 = \sqrt{S_1{}^2 + (2aD)}$

where S_2 = speed after acceleration
       S_1 = initial speed in ft/sec (m/s)
       a = acceleration rate
       D = distance travelled

The numbers 1.467 and .278 are conversion factors for converting ft/sec to mph and m/s to km/h.

Example
  Vehicles A and B were travelling side-by-side at 23 mph or 33.741 ft/sec (37 km/h or 10.278 m/s). After passing a traffic light, vehicle B accelerated at 10 ft/sec/sec (3 m/s/s). At the end of the block, a distance of 300 ft (91.44 m), the vehicle struck a pedestrian in a crosswalk.

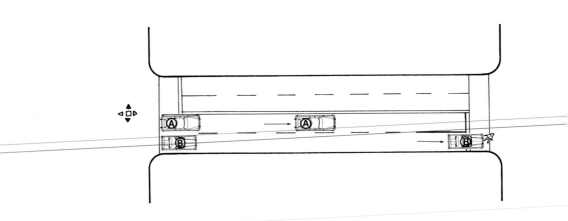

Figure 5-24

The speed of vehicle B when it struck the pedestrian was:

United States	Metric

$$S_2 = \sqrt{33.74^2 + (2 \times 10 \times 300)}$$

$$S_2 = \sqrt{1138.39 + 6000}$$

$$S_2 = \sqrt{7138.39}$$

$$S_2 = 84.49 \text{ ft/sec}$$

$$S_2 = \frac{84.49}{1.467}$$

$$S_2 = 57.59$$

$$S_2 = 58 \text{ mph}$$

$$S_2 = \sqrt{10.28^2 + (2 \times 3 \times 91.44)}$$

$$S_2 = \sqrt{105.68 + 548.64}$$

$$S_2 = \sqrt{654.32}$$

$$S_2 = 25.58 \text{ m/s}$$

$$S_2 = \frac{25.58}{.278}$$

$$S_2 = 92.01$$

$$S_2 = 92 \text{ km/h}$$

Time for Acceleration from a Known Speed

The time it took vehicle B in this example to travel the 300 ft (91.44 m) under acceleration may be calculated using Formula 5-23:

United States	Metric

$$t = \frac{S_2 - S_1}{a} \qquad\qquad t = \frac{S_2 - S_1}{a}$$

where t = time in seconds
$\quad$ S_1 = initial speed in ft/sec (m/s)
$\quad$ S_2 = speed after acceleration
$\quad$ a = acceleration rate

$$t = \frac{84.49 - 33.74}{10} \qquad\qquad t = \frac{25.58 - 10.28}{3}$$

$$t = \frac{50.75}{10} \qquad\qquad t = \frac{15.3}{3}$$

$$t = 5 \text{ seconds} \qquad\qquad t = 5 \text{ seconds}$$

Deceleration

5.089   The deceleration rate, as related to friction between a skidding or sliding tire and the roadway surface due to the force of gravity, is expressed as a decimal fraction or multiple of gravity. This fraction or multiple is known as the coefficient of friction or f value. The coefficient of friction of 1.00 is equal to the acceleration rate of gravity or 32.2 ft/sec/sec (9.81 m/s/s), which is actual gravitational force (g).

5.090   When the coefficient of friction is known, the acceleration or deceleration rate may be calculated (Table 5-VI) using Formula 5-24:

United States	Metric

$$a = fg \qquad\qquad\qquad\qquad a = fg$$

where a = acceleration or deceleration rate
$\quad$ f = coefficient of friction
$\quad$ g = acceleration of gravity (32.2 ft/sec/sec) (9.81 m/s/s)

TABLE 5-V-A
MILES-PER-HOUR TO FEET-PER-SECOND CONVERSION TABLE

mph	ft/sec	mph	ft/sec	mph	ft/sec	mph	ft/sec
1.0	1.467	31.0	45.477	61.0	89.487	91.0	133.497
1.5	2.201	31.5	46.211	61.5	90.221	91.5	134.231
2.0	2.934	32.0	46.944	62.0	90.954	92.0	134.964
2.5	3.668	32.5	47.678	62.5	91.688	92.5	135.698
3.0	4.401	33.0	48.411	63.0	92.421	93.0	136.431
3.5	5.135	33.5	49.145	63.5	93.155	93.5	137.165
4.0	5.868	34.0	49.878	64.0	93.888	94.0	137.898
4.5	6.602	34.5	50.612	64.5	94.622	94.5	138.632
5.0	7.335	35.0	51.345	65.0	95.355	95.0	139.365
5.5	8.069	35.5	52.079	65.5	96.089	95.5	140.099
6.0	8.802	36.0	52.812	66.0	96.822	96.0	140.832
6.5	9.536	36.5	53.546	66.5	97.556	96.5	141.566
7.0	10.269	37.0	54.279	67.0	98.289	97.0	142.299
7.5	11.003	37.5	55.013	67.5	99.023	97.5	143.033
8.0	11.736	38.0	55.746	68.0	99.756	98.0	143.766
8.5	12.470	38.5	56.480	68.5	100.490	98.5	144.500
9.0	13.203	39.0	57.213	69.0	101.223	99.0	145.233
9.5	13.937	39.5	57.947	69.5	101.957	99.5	145.967
10.0	14.670	40.0	58.680	70.0	102.690	100.0	146.700
10.5	15.404	40.5	59.414	70.5	103.424	100.5	147.434
11.0	16.137	41.0	60.147	71.0	104.157	101.0	148.167
11.5	16.871	41.5	60.881	71.5	104.891	101.5	148.901
12.0	17.604	42.0	61.614	72.0	105.624	102.0	149.634
12.5	18.338	42.5	62.348	72.5	106.358	102.5	150.368
13.0	19.071	43.0	62.081	73.0	107.091	103.0	151.101
13.5	19.805	43.5	68.815	73.5	107.825	103.5	151.835
14.0	20.538	44.0	64.548	74.0	108.558	104.0	152.568
14.5	21.272	44.5	65.282	74.5	109.292	104.5	153.302
15.0	22.005	45.0	66.015	75.0	110.025	105.0	154.035
15.5	22.739	45.5	66.749	75.5	110.759	105.5	154.769
16.0	23.472	46.0	67.482	76.0	111.492	106.0	155.502
16.5	24.206	46.5	68.216	76.5	112.226	106.5	156.236
17.0	24.939	47.0	68.949	77.0	112.959	107.0	156.969
17.5	25.673	47.5	69.683	77.5	113.693	107.5	157.703
18.0	26.406	48.0	70.416	78.0	114.426	108.0	158.436
18.5	27.140	48.5	71.150	78.5	115.160	108.5	159.170
19.0	27.873	49.0	71.883	79.0	115.893	109.0	159.903
19.5	28.607	49.5	72.617	79.5	116.627	109.5	160.637
20.0	29.340	50.0	73.350	80.0	117.360	110.0	161.370
20.5	30.074	50.5	74.084	80.5	118.094	110.5	162.104
21.0	30.807	51.0	74.817	81.0	118.827	111.0	162.837
21.5	31.541	51.5	75.551	81.5	119.561	111.5	163.571
22.0	32.274	52.0	76.284	82.0	120.294	112.0	164.304
22.5	33.008	52.5	77.018	82.5	121.028	112.5	165.038
23.0	33.741	53.0	77.751	83.0	121.761	113.0	165.771
23.5	34.475	53.5	78.485	83.5	122.495	113.5	166.505
24.0	35.208	54.0	79.218	84.0	123.228	114.0	167.238
24.5	35.942	54.5	79.952	84.5	123.962	114.5	167.972
25.0	36.675	55.0	80.685	85.0	124.695	115.0	168.705
25.5	37.409	55.5	81.419	85.5	125.429	115.5	169.439
26.0	38.142	56.0	82.152	86.0	126.162	116.0	170.172
26.5	38.876	56.5	82.886	86.5	126.896	116.5	170.906
27.0	39.609	57.0	83.619	87.0	127.629	117.0	171.639
27.5	40.343	57.5	84.353	87.5	128.363	117.5	172.373
28.0	41.076	58.0	85.086	88.0	129.096	118.0	173.106
28.5	41.810	58.5	85.820	88.5	129.830	118.5	173.840
29.0	42.543	59.0	86.553	89.0	130.563	119.0	174.573
29.5	43.277	59.5	87.287	89.5	131.297	119.5	175.307
30.0	44.010	60.0	88.020	90.0	132.030	120.0	176.040
30.5	44.744	60.5	88.754	90.5	132.764		

TABLE 5-V-B
KILOMETERS-PER-HOUR TO METERS-PER-SECOND CONVERSION TABLE

km/h	m/s	km/h	m/s	km/h	m/s	km/h	m/s
1.0	0.278	26.0	7.228	51.0	14.178	76.0	21.128
1.5	0.417	26.5	7.367	51.5	14.317	76.5	21.267
2.0	0.556	27.0	7.506	52.0	14.456	77.0	21.406
2.5	0.695	27.5	7.645	52.5	14.595	77.5	21.545
3.0	0.834	28.0	7.784	53.0	14.734	78.0	21.684
3.5	0.973	28.5	7.923	53.5	14.873	78.5	21.823
4.0	1.112	29.0	8.062	54.0	15.012	79.0	21.962
4.5	1.251	29.5	8.201	54.5	15.151	79.5	22.101
5.0	1.390	30.0	8.340	55.0	15.290	80.0	22.240
5.5	1.529	30.5	8.479	55.5	15.429	80.5	22.379
6.0	1.668	31.0	8.618	56.0	15.568	81.0	22.518
6.5	1.807	31.5	8.757	56.5	15.707	81.5	22.657
7.0	1.946	32.0	8.896	57.0	15.846	82.0	22.796
7.5	2.085	32.5	9.035	57.5	15.985	82.5	22.935
8.0	2.224	33.0	9.174	58.0	16.124	83.0	23.074
8.5	2.363	33.5	9.313	58.5	16.263	83.5	23.213
9.0	2.502	34.0	9.452	59.0	16.402	84.0	23.352
9.5	2.641	34.5	9.591	59.5	16.541	84.5	23.491
10.0	2.780	35.0	9.730	60.0	16.680	85.0	23.630
10.5	2.919	35.5	9.869	60.5	16.819	85.5	23.769
11.0	3.058	36.0	10.008	61.0	16.958	86.0	23.908
11.5	3.197	36.5	10.147	61.5	17.097	86.5	24.047
12.0	3.336	37.0	10.286	62.0	17.236	87.0	24.186
12.5	3.475	37.5	10.425	62.5	17.375	87.5	24.325
13.0	3.614	38.0	10.564	63.0	17.514	88.0	24.464
13.5	3.753	38.5	10.703	63.5	17.653	88.5	24.603
14.0	3.892	39.0	10.842	64.0	17.792	89.0	24.742
14.5	4.031	39.5	10.981	64.5	17.931	89.5	24.881
15.0	4.170	40.0	11.120	65.0	18.070	90.0	25.020
15.5	4.309	40.5	11.259	65.5	18.209	90.5	25.159
16.0	4.448	41.0	11.398	66.0	18.348	91.0	25.298
16.5	4.587	41.5	11.537	66.5	18.487	91.5	25.437
17.0	4.726	42.0	11.676	67.0	18.626	92.0	25.576
17.5	4.865	42.5	11.815	67.5	18.765	92.5	25.715
18.0	5.004	43.0	11.954	68.0	18.904	93.0	25.854
18.5	5.143	43.5	12.093	68.5	19.043	93.5	25.993
19.0	5.282	44.0	12.232	69.0	19.182	94.0	26.132
19.5	5.421	44.5	12.371	69.5	19.321	94.5	26.271
20.0	5.560	45.0	12.510	70.0	19.460	95.0	26.410
20.5	5.699	45.5	12.649	70.5	19.599	95.5	26.549
21.0	5.838	46.0	12.788	71.0	19.738	96.0	26.688
21.5	5.977	46.5	12.927	71.5	19.877	96.5	26.827
22.0	6.116	47.0	13.066	72.0	20.016	97.0	26.966
22.5	6.255	47.5	13.205	72.5	20.155	97.5	27.105
23.0	6.394	48.0	13.344	73.0	20.294	98.0	27.244
23.5	6.533	48.5	13.483	73.5	20.433	98.5	27.383
24.0	6.672	49.0	13.622	74.0	20.572	99.0	27.522
24.5	6.811	49.5	13.761	74.5	20.711	99.5	27.661
25.0	6.950	50.0	13.900	75.0	20.850	100.0	27.800
25.5	7.089	50.5	14.039	75.5	20.989	100.5	27.939

Traffic Accident Investigators' Handbook

TABLE 5-V-B *(Continued)*
KILOMETERS-PER-HOUR TO METERS-PER-SECOND CONVERSION TABLE

km/h	m/s	km/h	m/s	km/h	m/s	km/h	m/s
101.0	28.078	126.0	35.028	151.0	41.978	176.0	48.928
101.5	28.217	126.5	35.167	151.5	42.117	176.5	49.067
102.0	28.356	127.0	35.306	152.0	42.256	177.0	49.206
102.5	28.495	127.5	35.445	152.5	42.395	177.5	49.345
103.0	28.634	128.0	35.584	153.0	42.534	178.0	49.484
103.5	28.773	128.5	35.723	153.5	42.673	178.5	49.623
104.0	28.912	129.0	35.862	154.0	42.812	179.0	49.762
104.5	29.051	129.5	36.001	154.5	42.951	179.5	49.901
105.0	29.190	130.0	36.140	155.0	43.090	180.0	50.040
105.5	29.329	130.5	36.279	155.5	43.229	180.5	50.179
106.0	29.468	131.0	36.418	156.0	43.368	181.0	50.318
106.5	29.607	131.5	36.557	156.5	43.507	181.5	50.457
107.0	29.746	132.0	36.696	157.0	43.646	182.0	50.596
107.5	29.885	132.5	36.835	157.5	43.785	182.5	50.735
108.0	30.024	133.0	36.974	158.0	43.924	183.0	50.874
108.5	30.163	133.5	37.113	158.5	44.063	183.5	51.013
109.0	30.302	134.0	37.252	159.0	44.202	184.0	51.152
109.5	30.441	134.5	37.391	159.5	44.341	184.5	51.291
110.0	30.580	135.0	37.530	160.0	44.480	185.0	51.430
110.5	30.719	135.5	37.669	160.5	44.619	185.5	51.569
111.0	30.858	136.0	37.808	161.0	44.758	186.0	51.708
111.5	30.997	136.5	37.947	161.5	44.897	186.5	51.847
112.0	31.136	137.0	38.086	162.0	45.036	187.0	51.986
112.5	31.275	137.5	38.225	162.5	45.175	187.5	52.125
113.0	31.414	138.0	38.364	163.0	45.314	188.0	52.264
113.5	31.553	138.5	38.503	163.5	45.453	188.5	52.403
114.0	31.692	139.0	38.642	164.0	45.592	189.0	52.542
114.5	31.831	139.5	38.781	164.5	45.731	189.5	52.681
115.0	31.970	140.0	38.920	165.0	45.870	190.0	52.820
115.5	32.109	140.5	39.059	165.5	46.009	190.5	52.959
116.0	32.248	141.0	39.198	166.0	46.148	191.0	53.098
116.5	32.387	141.5	39.337	166.5	46.287	191.5	53.237
117.0	32.526	142.0	39.476	167.0	46.426	192.0	53.376
117.5	32.665	142.5	39.615	167.5	46.565	192.5	53.515
118.0	32.804	143.0	39.754	168.0	46.704	193.0	53.654
118.5	32.943	143.5	39.893	168.5	46.843	193.5	53.793
119.0	33.082	144.0	40.032	169.0	46.982	194.0	53.932
119.5	33.221	144.5	40.171	169.5	47.121	194.5	54.071
120.0	33.360	145.0	40.310	170.0	47.260	195.0	54.210
120.5	33.499	145.5	40.449	170.5	47.399	195.5	54.349
121.0	33.638	146.0	40.588	171.0	47.538	196.0	54.488
121.5	33.777	146.5	40.727	171.5	47.677	196.5	54.627
122.0	33.916	147.0	40.866	172.0	47.816	197.0	54.766
122.5	34.055	147.5	41.005	172.5	47.955	197.5	54.905
123.0	34.194	148.0	41.144	173.0	48.094	198.0	55.044
123.5	34.333	148.5	41.283	173.5	48.233	198.5	55.183
124.0	34.472	149.0	41.422	174.0	48.372	199.0	55.322
124.5	34.611	149.5	41.561	174.5	48.511	199.5	55.461
125.0	34.750	150.0	41.700	175.0	48.650	200.0	55.600
125.5	34.889	150.5	41.839	175.5	48.789		

TABLE 5-VI-A
COEFFICIENT OF FRICTION TO DECELERATION RATE IN
FEET-PER-SECOND-PER-SECOND CONVERSION TABLE
(g = 32.2 ft/sec/sec)

Deceleration Rate (a) (ft/sec/sec)	Coefficient of Friction (f)	Deceleration Rate (a) (ft/sec/sec)	Coefficient of Friction (f)
32.20	1.00	16.10	.50
31.88	.99	15.78	.49
31.56	.98	15.46	.48
31.23	.97	15.13	.47
30.91	.96	14.81	.46
30.59	.95	14.49	.45
30.27	.94	14.17	.44
29.95	.93	13.85	.43
29.62	.92	13.52	.42
29.30	.91	13.20	.41
28.98	.90	12.88	.40
28.66	.89	12.56	.39
28.34	.88	12.24	.38
28.01	.87	11.91	.37
27.69	.86	11.59	.36
27.37	.85	11.27	.35
27.05	.84	10.95	.34
26.73	.83	10.63	.33
26.40	.82	10.30	.32
26.08	.81	9.98	.31
25.76	.80	9.66	.30
25.44	.79	9.34	.29
25.12	.78	9.02	.28
24.79	.77	8.69	.27
24.47	.76	8.37	.26
24.15	.75	8.05	.25
23.83	.74	7.73	.24
23.51	.73	7.41	.23
23.18	.72	7.08	.22
22.86	.71	6.76	.21
22.54	.70	6.44	.20
22.22	.69	6.12	.19
21.90	.68	5.80	.18
21.57	.67	5.47	.17
21.25	.66	5.15	.16
20.93	.65	4.83	.15
20.61	.64	4.51	.14
20.29	.63	4.19	.13
19.96	.62	3.86	.12
19.64	.61	3.54	.11
19.32	.60	3.22	.10
19.00	.59	2.90	.09
18.68	.58	2.58	.08
18.35	.57	2.25	.07
18.03	.56	1.93	.06
17.71	.55	1.61	.05
17.39	.54	1.29	.04
17.07	.53	.97	.03
16.74	.52	.64	.02
16.42	.51	.32	.01
		.00	.00

TABLE 5-VI-B

COEFFICIENT OF FRICTION TO DECELERATION RATE IN METERS-PER-SECOND-PER SECOND CONVERSION TABLE

(g = 9.81 m/s/s)

Deceleration Rate (a) (m/s/s)	Coefficient of Friction (f)	Deceleration Rate (a) (m/s/s)	Coefficient of Friction (f)
9.81	1.00	4.91	.50
9.71	.99	4.81	.49
9.61	.98	4.71	.48
9.52	.97	4.61	.47
9.42	.96	4.51	.46
9.32	.95	4.41	.45
9.22	.94	4.32	.44
9.12	.93	4.22	.43
9.03	.92	4.12	.42
8.93	.91	4.02	.41
8.83	.90	3.92	.40
8.73	.89	3.83	.39
8.63	.88	3.73	.38
8.53	.87	3.63	.37
8.44	.86	3.53	.36
8.34	.85	3.43	.35
8.24	.84	3.34	.34
8.14	.83	3.24	.33
8.04	.82	3.14	.32
7.95	.81	3.04	.31
7.85	.80	2.94	.30
7.75	.79	2.84	.29
7.65	.78	2.75	.28
7.55	.77	2.65	.27
7.46	.76	2.55	.26
7.36	.75	2.45	.25
7.26	.74	2.35	.24
7.16	.73	2.26	.23
7.06	.72	2.16	.22
6.97	.71	2.06	.21
6.87	.70	1.96	.20
6.77	.69	1.86	.19
6.67	.68	1.77	.18
6.57	.67	1.67	.17
6.47	.66	1.57	.16
6.38	.65	1.47	.15
6.28	.64	1.37	.14
6.18	.63	1.28	.13
6.08	.62	1.18	.12
5.98	.61	1.08	.11
5.89	.60	0.98	.10
5.79	.59	0.88	.09
5.69	.58	0.78	.08
5.59	.57	0.69	.07
5.49	.56	0.59	.06
5.40	.55	0.49	.05
5.30	.54	0.39	.04
5.20	.53	0.29	.03
5.10	.52	0.20	.02
5.00	.51	0.10	.01

Example

A vehicle left skid marks on a roadway. Tests revealed that the coefficient of friction was .75. The *deceleration rate* of the vehicle during the skid was:

$$a = .75 \times 32.2 \qquad\qquad a = .75 \times 9.81$$
$$a = 24.15 \text{ ft/sec/sec} \qquad\qquad a = 7.36 \text{ m/s/s}$$

5.091 When the initial speed and skid distance of a vehicle and the coefficient of friction of the roadway (or deceleration rate) are known, the speed at any given point during deceleration may be calculated using Formula 5-25:

United States   *Metric*

$$S_2 = \sqrt{S_1{}^2 - (2aD)} \qquad\qquad S_2 = \sqrt{S_1{}^2 - (2aD)}$$

where S_2 = speed after deceleration in ft/sec (m/s)
     S_1 = initial speed in ft/sec (m/s)
     a = deceleration rate (*see* Table 5-VI).
     D = distance or length of skid mark to point being measured

The numbers 1.467 and .278 are conversion factors for converting ft/sec to mph and m/s to km/h.

Example 1

A vehicle was travelling at 45 mph or 66.015 ft/sec (72.405 km/h or 20.129 m/s) and skidded 80 ft (24.384 m) to a stop in an attempt to avoid striking a pedestrian who had walked onto the roadway as the vehicle approached. After skidding 45 ft (13.716 m), the vehicle struck the pedestrian. The roadway coefficient of friction was .85 or a deceleration rate of 27.37 ft/sec/sec (8.3 m/s/s). The speed of the vehicle at the time it struck the pedestrian was:

United States

$$S_2 = \sqrt{66.015^2 - (2 \times 27.37 \times 45)}$$
$$S_2 = \sqrt{4357.980 - 2463.30}$$
$$S_2 = \sqrt{1894.68}$$
$$S_2 = 43.528 \text{ ft/sec}$$
$$S_2 = \frac{43.528}{1.467}$$
$$S_2 = 29.67$$
$$S_2 = 30 \text{ mph}$$

Metric

$$S_2 = \sqrt{20.129^2 - (2 \times 8.3 \times 13.716)}$$
$$S_2 = \sqrt{405.177 - 227.69}$$
$$S_2 = \sqrt{177.49}$$
$$S_2 = 13.32 \text{ m/s}$$
$$S_2 = \frac{13.32}{.278}$$
$$S_2 = 47.9$$
$$S_2 = 48 \text{ km/h}$$

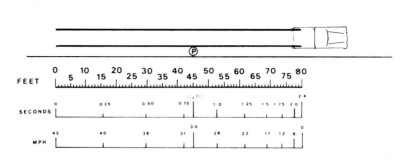

Figure 5-25. Formula 5-26: t = (S₁ − S₂)/a. Formula 5-25: S₂ = √‾S₁² − (2aD)‾

5.092   The time it takes a vehicle to decelerate from its initial speed to any point along its path before it stops may be calculated using Formula 5-26:

United States	*Metric*
$t = \dfrac{S_1 - S_2}{a}$	$t = \dfrac{S_1 - S_2}{a}$

where t = time in seconds
     S₁ = initial speed in ft/sec (m/s)
     S₂ = speed in ft/sec (m/s) at predetermined point
     a = deceleration rate

Example 2

   Using the circumstances outlined in Example 1, the time it took the vehicle to travel from the commencement of the skid to where it struck the pedestrian was:

United States	*Metric*
$t = \dfrac{66 - 43.528}{27.37}$	$t = \dfrac{20.129 - 13.32}{8.3}$
$t = \dfrac{22.472}{27.37}$	$t = \dfrac{6.81}{8.3}$
t = 0.8 second	t = 0.8 second

5.093   When the skid distance and roadway coefficient of friction are known, the time it takes a vehicle to stop may be calculated by using Formula 5-27:

United States	*Metric*
$t = 0.25 \sqrt{\dfrac{D}{f}}$	$t = 0.45 \sqrt{\dfrac{D}{f}}$

where t = time in seconds
    D = distance
    f = coefficient of friction

Example

A vehicle travelling at 45 mph (72.4 km/h), skidded a distance of 80 ft (24.38 m) to a stop on a roadway having a coefficient of friction of .85. The total time it took the vehicle to skid the 80 ft (24.38 m) was:

$$t = 0.25 \sqrt{\frac{80}{.85}} \qquad\qquad t = 0.45 \sqrt{\frac{24.38}{.85}}$$

$$t = 0.25 \sqrt{94} \qquad\qquad t = 0.45 \sqrt{28.68}$$

$$t = 0.25 \times 9.7 \qquad\qquad t = 0.45 \times 5.36$$

$$t = 2.4 \text{ seconds} \qquad\qquad t = 2.4 \text{ seconds}$$

5.094   When the initial speed and deceleration rate of a vehicle are known, the time required for the vehicle to stop may be calculated by using Formula 5-28:

United States   *Metric*

$$t = \frac{S_1}{a} \qquad\qquad\qquad t = \frac{S_1}{a}$$

where t = time in seconds
        S_1 = initial speed — in ft/sec(m/s)
        a = deceleration rate

Example

Same circumstances as outlined in Example 1 in paragraph 5.091.

$$t = \frac{66}{27.37} \qquad\qquad t = \frac{20.129}{8.3}$$

$$t = 2.4 \text{ seconds} \qquad\qquad t = 2.4 \text{ seconds}$$

5.095   When the skid distance and roadway coefficient of friction are known, the distance travelled during each consecutive second of deceleration may be calculated using Formula 5-29:

United States   *Metric*

$$D = (S_0 t) - (.5 a t^2) \qquad\qquad D = (S_0 t) - (.5 a t^2)$$

where D = distance
        S_0 = initial speed in ft/sec (m/s)
        a = deceleration rate
        t = time in seconds

Example

Using the circumstances outlined in Example 1 (5.091) and knowing that it took the vehicle 2.4 seconds to decelerate to a stop, the distance travelled during each second of deceleration was:

United States   *Metric*

1st Second

$D = (66 \times 1) - (.5 \times 27.37 \times 1^2)$ $D = (20.129 \times 1) - (.5 \times 8.3 \times 1^2)$

$D = 66 - 13.69$ $D = 20.129 - 4.15$

$D = 52.3$ ft travelled in 1st second $D = 15.98$ m travelled in 1st second

2nd Second
D = (66 × 2) − (.5 × 27.37 × 2²)   D = (20.129 × 2) − (.5 × 8.3 × 2²)
D = 132 − 54.74   D = 40.26 − 16.6
D = 77.26 ft (total)   D = 23.66 m (total)
D = 77.26 − 52.3   D = 23.66 − 15.98
D = 24.96 ft travelled in 2nd second   D = 7.68 m travelled in 2nd second

3rd Second (.4 sec)

D = 80 − 77.26   D = 24.38 − 23.66
D = 2.74 ft travelled in .4 second   D = 0.72 m travelled in .4 second

FALLS, FLIPS AND VAULTS

Falls

5.096   When a vehicle leaves a highway, such as in the case of failing to negotiate a curve, the area leading to the point of takeoff is level, and the vehicle travels through the air striking the ground some considerable distance away, then the speed at the time it left the highway can be calculated by using Formula 5-30:

United States   *Metric*

$$S = \frac{2.74\ D}{\sqrt{H}} \qquad\qquad S = \frac{7.97\ D}{\sqrt{H}}$$

where S = speed
       D = horizontal distance
       H = vertical fall

The numbers 2.74 and 7.97 are constants in calculating speed involving a vehicle or other object travelling through the air and falling.

It is important that the horizontal and vertical distances are measured from the point where vehicle left the highway to where it *first* struck the ground. All measurements should be taken as closely as possible from the center of mass of the vehicle at takeoff to center of mass at the point where it *first* struck the ground. The distance that a vehicle slides or rolls after first striking the ground need not be considered in calculating the speed at the time it left the highway.

Example 1
    A vehicle left the highway on a curve. The area leading up to the point of takeoff was level or zero grade. The vehicle *first* struck the ground at a

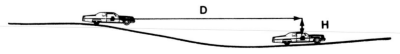

Figure 5-26

horizontal distance *(D)* of 40 ft (12 m) and a vertical distance *(H)* of 10 ft (3 m) below the takeoff point. Measurements were taken to centers of mass.

United States	*Metric*
$S = \dfrac{2.74 \times 40}{\sqrt{10}}$	$S = \dfrac{7.97 \times 12}{\sqrt{3}}$
$S = \dfrac{109.6}{3.16}$	$S = \dfrac{95.64}{1.732}$
$S = 34.68$	$S = 55.22$
$S = 35$ mph	$S = 55$ km/h

Completed speed calculations for falls from level takeoff surfaces will be found in Table 5-VII.

Example 2

Same circumstances as in Example 1 except the vehicle travelled on a grade *(e)* of −8 percent leading to the point where it left the highway. This grade is not necessarily the roadway grade but rather the path followed by the vehicle before leaving the highway. The speed in this situation can be calculated using Formula 5-31:

United States	*Metric*
$S = \dfrac{2.74\ D}{\sqrt{H \pm (De)}}$	$S = \dfrac{7.97\ D}{\sqrt{H \pm (De)}}$

where S = speed
      D = horizontal distance
      H = vertical fall or rise
      e = grade or elevation

$S = \dfrac{2.74 \times 40}{\sqrt{10 - (40 \times .08)}}$	$S = \dfrac{7.97 \times 12}{\sqrt{3 - (12 \times .08)}}$
$S = \dfrac{109.6}{\sqrt{10 - 3.2}}$	$S = \dfrac{95.64}{\sqrt{3 - .96}}$
$S = \dfrac{109.6}{\sqrt{6.8}}$	$S = \dfrac{95.64}{\sqrt{2.04}}$
$S = \dfrac{109.6}{2.6}$	$S = \dfrac{95.64}{1.428}$
$S = 42.15$	$S = 66.97$
$S = 42$ mph	$S = 67$ km/h

Figure 5-27

TABLE 5-VII-A
SPEED IN MILES PER HOUR BASED ON LEVEL HORIZONTAL TAKEOFF AND FALL

Vertical Distance (feet)	Horizontal Distance (feet)										
	2	4	6	8	10	12	14	16	18	20	22
1	5.480	10.960	16.440	21.920	27.400	32.880	38.360	43.840	49.320	54.800	60.280
2	3.875	7.750	11.625	15.500	19.375	23.250	27.125	31.000	34.875	38.749	42.624
3	3.164	6.328	9.492	12.656	15.819	18.983	22.147	25.311	28.475	31.639	34.803
4	2.740	5.480	8.220	10.960	13.700	16.440	19.180	21.920	24.660	27.400	30.140
5	2.451	4.901	7.352	9.803	12.254	14.704	17.155	19.606	22.057	24.507	26.958
6	2.237	4.474	6.712	8.949	11.186	13.423	15.660	17.898	20.135	22.372	24.609
7	2.071	4.142	6.214	8.285	10.356	12.427	14.499	16.570	18.641	20.712	22.784
8	1.937	3.875	5.812	7.750	9.687	11.625	13.562	15.500	17.437	19.375	21.312
9	1.827	3.653	5.480	7.307	9.133	10.960	12.787	14.613	16.440	18.267	20.093
10	1.733	3.466	5.199	6.932	8.665	10.398	12.130	13.863	15.596	17.329	19.062
11	1.652	3.305	4.957	6.609	8.261	9.914	11.566	13.218	14.871	16.523	18.175
12	1.582	3.164	4.746	6.328	7.910	9.492	11.074	12.656	14.237	15.819	17.401
13	1.520	3.040	4.560	6.080	7.599	9.119	10.639	12.159	13.679	15.199	16.719
14	1.465	2.929	4.394	5.858	7.323	8.788	10.252	11.717	13.181	14.646	16.111
15	1.415	2.830	4.245	5.660	7.075	8.490	9.905	11.319	12.734	14.149	15.564
16	1.370	2.740	4.110	5.480	6.850	8.220	9.590	10.960	12.330	13.700	15.070
17	1.329	2.658	3.987	5.316	6.645	7.975	9.304	10.633	11.962	13.291	14.620
18	1.292	2.583	3.875	5.167	6.458	7.750	9.042	10.333	11.625	12.916	14.208
19	1.257	2.514	3.772	5.029	6.286	7.543	8.800	10.058	11.315	12.572	13.829
20	1.225	2.451	3.676	4.901	6.127	7.352	8.578	9.803	11.028	12.254	13.479
21	1.196	2.392	3.588	4.783	5.979	7.175	8.371	9.567	10.763	11.958	13.154

22	1.168	2.337	3.505	4.673	5.842	7.010	8.178	9.347	10.515	11.683	12.852
23	1.143	2.285	3.428	4.571	5.713	6.856	7.999	9.141	10.284	11.427	12.569
24	1.119	2.237	3.356	4.474	5.593	6.712	7.830	8.949	10.067	11.186	12.305
25	1.096	2.192	3.288	4.384	5.480	6.576	7.672	8.768	9.864	10.960	12.056
26	1.075	2.149	3.224	4.299	5.374	6.448	7.523	8.598	9.672	10.747	11.822
27	1.055	2.109	3.164	4.219	5.273	6.328	7.382	8.437	9.492	10.546	11.601
28	1.036	2.071	3.107	4.142	5.178	6.214	7.249	8.285	9.321	10.356	11.392
29	1.018	2.035	3.053	4.070	5.088	6.106	7.123	8.141	9.158	10.176	11.194
30	1.001	2.001	3.002	4.002	5.003	6.003	7.004	8.004	9.005	10.005	11.006
31	0.984	1.968	2.953	3.937	4.921	5.905	6.890	7.874	8.858	9.842	10.827
32	0.969	1.937	2.906	3.875	4.844	5.812	6.781	7.750	8.719	9.687	10.656
33	0.954	1.908	2.862	3.816	4.770	5.724	6.678	7.632	8.586	9.539	10.493
34	0.940	1.880	2.819	3.759	4.699	5.639	6.579	7.518	8.458	9.398	10.338
35	0.926	1.853	2.779	3.705	4.631	5.558	6.484	7.410	8.337	9.263	10.189
36	0.913	1.827	2.740	3.653	4.567	5.480	6.393	7.307	8.220	9.133	10.047
37	0.901	1.802	2.703	3.604	4.505	5.405	6.306	7.207	8.108	9.009	9.910
38	0.889	1.778	2.667	3.556	4.445	5.334	6.223	7.112	8.001	8.890	9.779
39	0.878	1.755	2.633	3.510	4.388	5.265	6.143	7.020	7.898	8.775	9.653
40	0.866	1.733	2.599	3.466	4.332	5.199	6.065	6.932	7.798	8.665	9.531
41	0.856	1.712	2.567	3.423	4.279	5.135	5.991	6.847	7.702	8.558	9.414
42	0.846	1.691	2.537	3.382	4.228	5.073	5.919	6.765	7.610	8.456	9.301
43	0.837	1.671	2.507	3.343	4.178	5.014	5.850	6.686	7.521	8.357	9.193
44	0.826	1.652	2.478	3.305	4.131	4.957	5.783	6.609	7.435	8.261	9.088
45	0.817	1.634	2.451	3.268	4.085	4.901	5.718	6.535	7.352	8.169	8.986
46	0.808	1.616	2.424	3.232	4.040	4.848	5.656	6.464	7.272	8.080	8.888
47	0.799	1.599	2.398	3.197	3.997	4.796	5.595	6.395	7.194	7.993	8.793
48	0.791	1.582	2.373	3.164	3.955	4.746	5.537	6.328	7.119	7.910	8.701
49	0.783	1.566	2.349	3.131	3.914	4.697	5.480	6.263	7.046	7.829	8.611
50	0.775	1.550	2.325	3.100	3.875	4.650	5.425	6.200	6.975	7.750	8.525

TABLE 5-VII-A (Continued)

SPEED IN MILES PER HOUR BASED ON LEVEL HORIZONTAL TAKEOFF AND FALL

Horizontal Distance (feet)

Vertical Distance (feet)	24	26	28	30	32	34	36	38	40	42	44
1	65.760	71.240	76.720	82.200	87.680	93.160	98.640	104.120	109.600	115.080	120.560
2	46.499	50.374	54.249	58.124	61.999	65.874	69.749	73.624	77.499	81.374	85.249
3	37.967	41.130	44.294	47.458	50.622	53.786	56.950	60.114	63.278	66.441	69.605
4	32.880	35.620	38.360	41.100	43.840	46.580	49.320	52.060	54.800	57.540	60.280
5	29.409	31.859	34.310	36.761	39.212	41.662	44.113	46.564	49.015	51.465	53.916
6	26.846	29.084	31.321	33.558	35.795	38.032	40.270	42.507	44.744	46.981	49.218
7	24.855	26.926	28.997	31.069	33.140	35.211	37.282	39.354	41.425	43.496	45.567
8	23.250	25.187	27.125	29.062	31.000	32.937	34.875	36.812	38.749	40.687	42.624
9	21.920	23.747	25.573	27.400	29.227	31.053	32.880	34.707	36.533	38.360	40.187
10	20.795	22.528	24.261	25.994	27.727	29.460	31.193	32.926	34.659	36.391	38.124
11	19.827	21.480	23.132	24.784	26.437	28.089	29.741	31.393	33.046	34.698	36.350
12	18.983	20.565	22.147	23.729	25.311	26.893	28.475	30.057	31.639	33.221	34.803
13	18.239	19.758	21.278	22.798	24.318	25.838	27.358	28.878	30.398	31.917	33.437
14	17.575	19.040	20.504	21.969	23.433	24.898	26.363	27.827	29.292	30.756	32.221
15	16.979	18.394	19.809	21.224	22.639	24.054	25.469	26.884	28.299	29.714	31.128
16	16.440	17.810	19.180	20.550	21.920	23.290	24.660	26.030	27.400	28.770	30.140
17	15.949	17.278	18.607	19.936	21.266	22.595	23.924	25.253	26.582	27.911	29.240
18	15.500	16.791	18.083	19.375	20.666	21.958	23.250	24.541	25.833	27.125	28.416
19	15.086	16.344	17.601	18.858	20.115	21.372	22.630	23.887	25.144	26.401	27.658
20	14.704	15.930	17.155	18.380	19.606	20.831	22.057	23.282	24.507	25.733	26.958
21	14.350	15.546	16.742	17.938	19.133	20.329	21.525	22.721	23.917	25.113	26.308
22	14.020	15.188	16.357	17.525	18.693	19.862	21.030	22.198	23.367	24.535	25.703

23	13.712	14.855	15.997	17.140	18.283	19.425	20.568	21.711	22.853	23.996	25.138
24	13.423	14.542	15.660	16.779	17.898	19.016	20.135	21.253	22.372	23.491	24.609
25	13.152	14.248	15.344	16.440	17.536	18.632	19.728	20.824	21.920	23.016	24.112
26	12.897	13.971	15.046	16.121	17.195	18.270	19.345	20.420	21.494	22.569	23.644
27	12.656	13.710	14.765	15.819	16.874	17.929	18.983	20.038	21.093	22.147	23.202
28	12.427	13.463	14.499	15.534	16.570	17.606	18.641	19.677	20.712	21.748	22.784
29	12.211	13.229	14.247	15.264	16.282	17.299	18.317	19.335	20.352	21.370	22.387
30	12.006	13.007	14.007	15.008	16.008	17.009	18.009	19.010	20.010	21.011	22.011
31	11.811	12.795	13.779	14.764	15.748	16.732	17.716	18.701	19.685	20.669	21.653
32	11.625	12.594	13.562	14.531	15.500	16.469	17.437	18.406	19.375	20.343	21.312
33	11.447	12.401	13.355	14.309	15.263	16.217	17.171	18.125	19.079	20.033	20.987
34	11.278	12.218	13.157	14.097	15.037	15.977	16.917	17.856	18.796	19.736	20.676
35	11.115	12.042	12.968	13.894	14.821	15.747	16.673	17.599	18.526	19.452	20.378
36	10.960	11.873	12.787	13.700	14.613	15.527	16.440	17.353	18.267	19.180	20.093
37	10.811	11.712	12.613	13.514	14.415	15.315	16.216	17.117	18.018	18.919	19.820
38	10.668	11.557	12.446	13.335	14.224	15.113	16.002	16.890	17.779	18.668	19.557
39	10.530	11.408	12.285	13.163	14.040	14.918	15.795	16.673	17.550	18.428	19.305
40	10.398	11.264	12.130	12.997	13.863	14.730	15.596	16.463	17.329	18.196	19.062
41	10.270	11.126	11.982	12.837	13.693	14.549	15.405	16.261	17.117	17.972	18.828
42	10.147	10.993	11.838	12.684	13.529	14.375	15.220	16.066	16.912	17.757	18.603
43	10.028	10.864	11.700	12.535	13.371	14.207	15.042	15.878	16.714	17.550	18.385
44	9.914	10.739	11.566	12.392	13.218	14.044	14.871	15.697	16.523	17.349	18.175
45	9.803	10.620	11.437	12.254	13.071	13.887	14.704	15.521	16.338	17.155	17.972
46	9.696	10.504	11.312	12.120	12.928	13.736	14.544	15.352	16.160	16.968	17.776
47	9.592	10.391	11.191	11.990	12.789	13.589	14.388	15.187	15.987	16.786	17.585
48	9.492	10.283	11.074	11.865	12.656	13.446	14.237	15.028	15.819	16.610	17.401
49	9.394	10.177	10.960	11.743	12.526	13.309	14.091	14.874	15.657	16.440	17.223
50	9.300	10.075	10.850	11.625	12.400	13.175	13.950	14.725	15.500	16.275	17.050

TABLE 5-VII-A (Continued)
SPEED IN MILES PER HOUR BASED ON LEVEL HORIZONTAL TAKEOFF AND FALL

Vertical Distance (feet)	Horizontal Distance (feet)										
	46	48	50	52	54	56	58	60	62	64	66
1	89.124	92.999	96.874	100.749	104.624	108.498	112.373	116.248	120.123		
2	72.769	75.933	79.097	82.261	85.425	88.589	91.753	94.916	98.080	101.244	104.408
3	63.020	65.760	68.500	71.240	73.980	76.720	79.460	82.200	84.940	87.680	90.420
4	56.367	58.818	61.268	63.719	66.170	68.620	71.071	73.522	75.973	78.423	80.874
5	51.456	53.693	55.930	58.167	60.404	62.642	64.879	67.116	69.353	71.590	73.828
6	47.639	49.710	51.781	53.852	55.924	57.995	60.066	62.137	64.209	66.280	68.351
7	44.562	46.499	48.437	50.374	52.312	54.249	56.187	58.124	60.062	61.999	63.937
8	42.013	43.840	45.667	47.493	49.320	51.147	52.973	54.800	56.627	58.453	60.280
9	39.857	41.590	43.323	45.056	46.789	48.522	50.255	51.988	53.721	55.454	57.187
10	38.002	39.655	41.307	42.959	44.612	46.264	47.916	49.568	51.221	52.873	54.525
11	36.385	37.967	39.548	41.130	42.712	44.294	45.876	47.458	49.040	50.622	52.204
12	34.957	36.477	37.997	39.517	41.037	42.557	44.076	45.596	47.116	48.636	50.156
13	33.686	35.150	36.615	38.079	39.544	41.009	42.473	43.938	45.402	46.867	48.332
14	32.543	33.958	35.373	36.788	38.203	39.618	41.033	42.448	43.863	45.278	46.693
15	31.510	32.880	34.250	35.620	36.990	38.360	39.730	41.100	42.470	43.840	45.210
16	30.569	31.898	33.227	34.556	35.886	37.215	38.544	39.873	41.202	42.531	43.860
17	29.708	31.000	32.291	33.583	34.875	36.166	37.458	38.749	40.041	41.333	42.624
18	28.916	30.173	31.430	32.687	33.944	35.202	36.459	37.716	38.973	40.230	41.488
19	28.183	29.409	30.634	31.859	33.085	34.310	35.536	36.761	37.986	39.212	40.437
20	27.504	28.700	29.896	31.092	32.288	33.483	34.679	35.875	37.071	38.267	39.463

22	26.872	28.040	29.208	30.377	31.545	32.714	33.882	35.050	36.219	37.387	38.555
23	26.281	27.424	28.566	29.709	30.852	31.995	33.137	34.280	35.422	36.565	37.708
24	25.728	26.846	27.965	29.084	30.202	31.321	32.439	33.558	34.677	35.795	36.914
25	25.208	26.304	27.400	28.496	29.592	30.688	31.784	32.880	33.976	35.072	36.168
26	24.718	25.793	26.868	27.943	29.017	30.092	31.167	32.241	33.316	34.391	35.466
27	24.256	25.311	26.366	27.420	28.475	29.530	30.584	31.639	32.693	33.748	34.803
28	23.819	24.855	25.891	26.926	27.962	28.997	30.033	31.069	32.104	33.140	34.176
29	23.405	24.423	25.440	26.458	27.475	28.493	29.511	30.528	31.546	32.564	33.581
30	23.012	24.012	25.013	26.013	27.014	28.014	29.015	30.015	31.016	32.016	33.017
31	22.637	23.622	24.606	25.590	26.574	27.559	28.543	29.527	30.511	31.496	32.480
32	22.281	23.250	24.218	25.187	26.156	27.125	28.093	29.062	30.031	31.000	31.968
33	21.941	22.895	23.849	24.803	25.757	26.710	27.664	28.618	29.572	30.526	31.480
34	21.616	22.555	23.495	24.435	25.375	26.315	27.255	28.194	29.134	30.074	31.014
35	21.305	22.231	23.157	24.084	25.010	25.936	26.862	27.789	28.715	29.641	30.567
36	21.007	21.920	22.833	23.747	24.660	25.573	26.487	27.400	28.313	29.227	30.140
37	20.721	21.622	22.523	23.424	24.324	25.225	26.126	27.027	27.928	28.829	29.730
38	20.446	21.335	22.224	23.113	24.002	24.891	25.780	26.669	27.558	28.447	29.336
39	20.183	21.060	21.938	22.815	23.693	24.570	25.448	26.325	27.203	28.080	28.958
40	19.929	20.795	21.662	22.528	23.395	24.261	25.127	25.994	26.860	27.727	28.593
41	19.684	20.540	21.396	22.252	23.107	23.963	24.819	25.675	26.531	27.387	28.242
42	19.448	20.294	21.140	21.985	22.831	23.676	24.522	25.367	26.213	27.059	27.904
43	19.221	20.057	20.892	21.728	22.564	23.399	24.235	25.071	25.906	26.742	27.578
44	19.001	19.827	20.654	21.480	22.306	23.132	23.958	24.784	25.610	26.437	27.263
45	18.789	19.606	20.423	21.240	22.057	22.873	23.690	24.507	25.324	26.141	26.958
46	18.584	19.392	20.200	21.008	21.816	22.623	23.431	24.239	25.047	25.855	26.663
47	18.385	19.184	19.984	20.783	21.582	22.382	23.181	23.980	24.780	25.579	26.378
48	18.192	18.983	19.774	20.565	21.356	22.147	22.938	23.729	24.520	25.311	26.102
49	18.006	18.789	19.571	20.354	21.137	21.920	22.703	23.486	24.269	25.051	25.834
50	17.825	18.600	19.375	20.150	20.925	21.700	22.475	23.250	24.025	24.800	25.575

TABLE 5-VII-A (Continued)
SPEED IN MILES PER HOUR BASED ON LEVEL HORIZONTAL TAKEOFF AND FALL

Vertical Distance (feet)	Horizontal Distance (feet)										
	68	70	72	74	76	78	80	82	84	86	88
1											
2											
3	107.572	110.736	113.900	117.063	120.227						
4	93.160	95.900	98.640	101.380	104.120	106.860	109.600	112.340	115.080	117.820	120.560
5	83.325	85.776	88.226	90.677	93.128	95.578	98.029	100.480	102.931	105.381	107.832
6	76.065	78.302	80.539	82.776	85.014	87.251	89.488	91.725	93.962	96.200	98.437
7	70.422	72.494	74.565	76.636	78.707	80.779	82.850	84.921	86.992	89.064	91.135
8	65.874	67.812	69.749	71.686	73.624	75.561	77.499	79.436	81.374	83.311	85.249
9	62.107	63.933	65.760	67.587	69.413	71.240	73.067	74.893	76.720	78.547	80.373
10	58.920	60.652	62.385	64.118	65.851	67.584	69.317	71.050	72.783	74.516	76.249
11	56.178	57.830	59.482	61.134	62.787	64.439	66.091	67.744	69.396	71.048	72.700
12	53.786	55.368	56.950	58.532	60.114	61.696	63.278	64.860	66.441	68.023	69.605
13	51.676	53.196	54.716	56.236	57.755	59.275	60.795	62.315	63.835	65.355	66.875
14	49.796	51.261	52.725	54.190	55.654	57.119	58.584	60.048	61.513	62.977	64.442
15	48.108	49.523	50.937	52.352	53.767	55.182	56.597	58.012	59.427	60.842	62.257
16	46.580	47.950	49.320	50.690	52.060	53.430	54.800	56.170	57.540	58.910	60.280
17	45.189	46.518	47.847	49.177	50.506	51.835	53.164	54.493	55.822	57.151	58.480
18	43.916	45.208	46.499	47.791	49.083	50.374	51.666	52.958	54.249	55.541	56.833
19	42.745	44.002	45.259	46.516	47.774	49.031	50.288	51.545	52.802	54.060	55.317
20	41.662	42.888	44.113	45.339	46.564	47.789	49.015	50.240	51.465	52.691	53.916
21	40.658	41.854	43.050	44.246	45.442	46.638	47.833	49.029	50.225	51.421	52.617

22	39.724	40.892	42.060	43.229	44.397	45.565	46.734	47.902	49.070	50.239	51.407
23	38.850	39.993	41.136	42.278	43.421	44.564	45.706	46.849	47.992	49.134	50.277
24	38.032	39.151	40.270	41.388	42.507	43.625	44.744	45.863	46.981	48.100	49.218
25	37.264	38.360	39.456	40.552	41.648	42.744	43.840	44.936	46.032	47.128	48.224
26	36.540	37.615	38.690	39.765	40.839	41.914	42.987	44.063	45.138	46.213	47.288
27	35.857	36.912	37.967	39.021	40.076	41.130	42.185	43.240	44.294	45.349	46.404
28	35.211	36.247	37.282	38.318	39.354	40.389	41.425	42.461	43.496	44.532	45.567
29	34.598	35.616	36.634	37.652	38.669	39.687	40.704	41.722	42.740	43.757	44.775
30	34.017	35.018	36.018	37.019	38.019	39.020	40.020	41.021	42.021	43.022	44.022
31	33.464	34.448	35.433	36.417	37.401	38.385	39.369	40.354	41.338	42.322	43.306
32	32.937	33.906	34.875	35.843	36.812	37.781	38.749	39.718	40.687	41.656	42.624
33	32.434	33.388	34.342	35.296	36.250	37.204	38.158	39.112	40.066	41.020	41.974
34	31.954	32.893	33.833	34.773	35.713	36.653	37.592	38.532	39.472	40.412	41.352
35	31.494	32.420	33.346	34.273	35.199	36.125	37.052	37.978	38.904	39.830	40.757
36	31.053	31.967	32.880	33.793	34.707	35.620	36.533	37.447	38.360	39.273	40.187
37	30.631	31.532	32.433	33.334	34.234	35.135	36.036	36.937	37.838	38.739	39.640
38	30.225	31.114	32.003	32.892	33.781	34.670	35.559	36.448	37.337	38.226	39.115
39	29.835	30.713	31.590	32.468	33.345	34.223	35.100	35.978	36.855	37.733	38.610
40	29.460	30.326	31.193	32.059	32.926	33.792	34.659	35.525	36.391	37.258	38.124
41	29.098	29.954	30.810	31.666	32.522	33.377	34.233	35.089	35.945	36.801	37.657
42	28.750	29.595	30.441	31.287	32.132	32.978	33.823	34.669	35.514	36.360	37.206
43	28.414	29.249	30.085	30.921	31.756	32.592	33.428	34.263	35.099	35.935	36.770
44	28.089	28.915	29.741	30.567	31.393	32.220	33.046	33.872	34.698	35.524	36.350
45	27.775	28.592	29.409	30.226	31.043	31.859	32.676	33.493	34.310	35.127	35.944
46	27.471	28.279	29.087	29.895	30.703	31.511	32.319	33.127	33.935	34.743	35.551
47	27.178	27.977	28.776	29.576	30.375	31.174	31.974	32.773	33.572	34.372	35.171
48	26.893	27.684	28.475	29.266	30.057	30.848	31.639	32.430	33.221	34.012	34.803
49	26.617	27.400	28.183	28.966	29.749	30.531	31.314	32.097	32.880	33.663	34.446
50	26.350	27.125	27.900	28.675	29.450	30.225	31.000	31.775	32.550	33.325	34.100

TABLE 5-VII-A (*Continued*)

SPEED IN MILES PER HOUR BASED ON LEVEL HORIZONTAL TAKEOFF AND FALL

Horizontal Distance (feet)

Vertical Distance (feet)	90	92	94	96	98	100	102	104	106	108	110
1											
2											
3											
4											
5	110.283	112.734	115.184	117.635	120.086						
6	100.674	102.911	105.148	107.386	109.623	111.860	114.097	116.334	118.572	120.809	
7	93.206	95.277	97.349	99.420	101.491	103.562	105.634	107.705	109.776	111.847	113.918
8	87.186	89.124	91.061	92.999	94.936	96.874	98.811	100.749	102.686	104.624	106.561
9	82.200	84.027	85.853	87.680	89.507	91.333	93.160	94.987	96.813	98.640	100.467
10	77.982	79.715	81.448	83.181	84.913	86.646	88.379	90.112	91.845	93.578	95.311
11	74.353	76.005	77.657	79.310	80.962	82.614	84.266	85.919	87.571	89.223	90.876
12	71.187	72.769	74.351	75.933	77.515	79.097	80.679	82.261	83.843	85.425	87.007
13	68.395	69.914	71.434	72.954	74.474	75.994	77.514	79.034	80.554	82.073	83.593
14	65.907	67.371	68.836	70.300	71.765	73.230	74.694	76.159	77.623	79.088	80.553
15	63.672	65.087	66.502	67.917	69.332	70.746	72.161	73.576	74.991	76.406	77.821
16	61.650	63.020	64.390	65.760	67.130	68.500	69.870	71.240	72.610	73.980	75.350
17	59.809	61.138	62.467	63.797	65.126	66.455	67.784	69.113	70.442	71.771	73.100
18	58.124	59.416	60.707	61.999	63.291	64.582	65.874	67.166	68.457	69.749	71.041
19	56.574	57.831	59.088	60.346	61.603	62.860	64.117	65.374	66.632	67.889	69.146
20	55.141	56.367	57.592	58.818	60.043	61.268	62.494	63.719	64.944	66.170	67.395
21	53.813	55.008	56.204	57.400	58.596	59.792	60.988	62.183	63.379	64.575	65.771

22	52.575	53.744	54.912	56.080	57.249	58.417	59.585	60.754	61.922	63.090	64.259
23	51.420	52.562	53.705	54.848	55.990	57.133	58.276	59.418	60.561	61.704	62.846
24	50.337	51.456	52.574	53.693	54.811	55.930	57.049	58.167	59.286	60.404	61.523
25	49.320	50.416	51.512	52.608	53.704	54.800	55.896	56.992	58.088	59.184	60.280
26	48.362	49.437	50.512	51.586	52.661	53.736	54.811	55.885	56.960	58.035	59.109
27	47.458	48.513	49.567	50.622	51.677	52.731	53.786	54.841	55.895	56.950	58.004
28	46.603	47.639	48.674	49.710	50.746	51.781	52.817	53.852	54.888	55.924	56.959
29	45.792	46.810	47.828	48.845	49.863	50.881	51.898	52.916	53.933	54.951	55.969
30	45.023	46.023	47.024	48.024	49.025	50.025	51.026	52.026	53.027	54.027	55.028
31	44.291	45.275	46.259	47.243	48.228	49.212	50.196	51.180	52.165	53.149	54.133
32	43.593	44.562	45.531	46.499	47.468	48.437	49.406	50.374	51.343	52.312	53.280
33	42.928	43.881	44.835	45.789	46.743	47.697	48.651	49.605	50.559	51.513	52.467
34	42.292	43.231	44.171	45.111	46.051	46.991	47.930	48.870	49.810	50.750	51.690
35	41.683	42.609	43.536	44.462	45.388	46.314	47.241	48.167	49.093	50.020	50.946
36	41.100	42.013	42.927	43.840	44.753	45.667	46.580	47.493	48.407	49.320	50.233
37	40.541	41.442	42.343	43.244	44.144	45.045	45.946	46.847	47.748	48.649	49.550
38	40.004	40.893	41.782	42.671	43.560	44.449	45.338	46.227	47.116	48.005	48.894
39	39.488	40.365	41.243	42.120	42.998	43.875	44.753	45.630	46.508	47.385	48.263
40	38.991	39.857	40.724	41.590	42.457	43.323	44.190	45.056	45.923	46.789	47.656
41	38.512	39.368	40.224	41.080	41.936	42.792	43.647	44.503	45.359	46.215	47.071
42	38.051	38.897	39.742	40.588	41.434	42.279	43.125	43.970	44.816	45.661	46.507
43	37.606	38.442	39.278	40.113	40.949	41.785	42.620	43.456	44.292	45.127	45.963
44	37.176	38.002	38.829	39.655	40.481	41.307	42.133	42.959	43.785	44.612	45.438
45	36.761	37.578	38.395	39.212	40.029	40.846	41.662	42.479	43.296	44.113	44.930
46	36.359	37.167	37.975	38.783	39.591	40.399	41.207	42.015	42.823	43.631	44.439
47	35.970	36.770	37.569	38.368	39.168	39.967	40.766	41.566	42.365	43.164	43.964
48	35.594	36.385	37.176	37.967	38.758	39.548	40.339	41.130	41.921	42.712	43.503
49	35.229	36.011	36.794	37.577	38.360	39.143	39.926	40.709	41.491	42.274	43.057
50	34.875	35.649	36.424	37.199	37.974	38.749	39.524	40.299	41.074	41.849	42.624

TABLE 5-VII-A (Continued)

SPEED IN MILES PER HOUR BASED ON LEVEL HORIZONTAL TAKEOFF AND FALL

Vertical Distance (feet)	Horizontal Distance (feet)										
	112	114	116	118	120	122	124	126	128	130	132
1											
2											
3											
4											
5											
6											
7	115.990	118.061	120.132								
8	108.498	110.436	112.373	114.311	116.248	118.186	120.123				
9	102.293	104.120	105.947	107.773	109.600	111.427	113.253	115.080	116.907	118.733	120.560
10	97.044	98.777	100.510	102.243	103.976	105.709	107.442	109.174	110.907	112.640	114.373
11	92.528	94.180	95.832	97.485	99.137	100.789	102.441	104.094	105.746	107.398	109.051
12	88.589	90.171	91.753	93.334	94.916	96.498	98.080	99.662	101.244	102.826	104.408
13	85.113	86.633	88.153	89.673	91.193	92.713	94.232	95.752	97.272	98.792	100.312
14	82.017	83.482	84.946	86.411	87.875	89.340	90.805	92.269	93.734	95.198	96.663
15	79.236	80.651	82.066	83.481	84.896	86.311	87.726	89.141	90.556	91.970	93.385
16	76.720	78.090	79.460	80.830	82.200	83.570	84.940	86.310	87.680	89.050	90.420
17	74.429	75.758	77.088	78.417	79.746	81.075	82.404	83.733	85.062	86.391	87.720
18	72.332	73.624	74.916	76.207	77.499	78.791	80.082	81.374	82.665	83.957	85.249
19	70.403	71.660	72.917	74.175	75.432	76.689	77.946	79.203	80.461	81.718	82.975
20	68.620	69.846	71.071	72.297	73.522	74.747	75.973	77.198	78.423	79.649	80.874
21	66.967	68.163	69.358	70.554	71.750	72.946	74.142	75.338	76.533	77.729	78.925

22	65.427	66.595	67.764	68.932	70.100	71.269	72.437	73.605	74.774	75.942	77.110
23	63.989	65.132	66.274	67.417	68.560	69.702	70.845	71.988	73.130	74.273	75.415
24	62.642	63.760	64.879	65.997	67.116	68.235	69.353	70.472	71.590	72.709	73.828
25	61.376	62.472	63.568	64.664	65.760	66.856	67.952	69.048	70.144	71.240	72.336
26	60.184	61.259	62.334	63.408	64.483	65.558	66.632	67.707	68.782	69.857	70.931
27	59.059	60.114	61.168	62.223	63.278	64.332	65.387	66.441	67.496	68.551	69.605
28	57.995	59.030	60.066	61.102	62.137	63.173	64.209	65.244	66.280	67.315	68.351
29	56.986	58.004	59.021	60.039	61.057	62.074	63.092	64.109	65.127	66.145	67.162
30	56.028	57.029	58.029	59.030	60.030	61.031	62.031	63.032	64.032	65.033	66.033
31	55.117	56.102	57.086	58.070	59.054	60.038	61.023	62.007	62.991	63.975	64.960
32	54.249	55.218	56.187	57.155	58.124	59.093	60.062	61.030	61.999	62.968	63.937
33	53.421	54.375	55.329	56.283	57.237	58.191	59.145	60.099	61.053	62.006	62.960
34	52.629	53.569	54.509	55.449	56.389	57.329	58.268	59.208	60.148	61.088	62.028
35	51.872	52.798	53.725	54.651	55.577	56.504	57.430	58.356	59.283	60.209	61.135
36	51.147	52.060	52.973	53.887	54.800	55.713	56.627	57.540	58.453	59.367	60.280
37	50.451	51.352	52.253	53.153	54.054	54.955	55.856	56.757	57.658	58.559	59.460
38	49.783	50.671	51.560	52.449	53.338	54.227	55.116	56.005	56.894	57.783	58.672
39	49.140	50.018	50.895	51.773	52.650	53.528	54.405	55.283	56.160	57.038	57.915
40	48.522	49.388	50.255	51.121	51.988	52.854	53.721	54.587	55.454	56.320	57.187
41	47.927	48.782	49.638	50.494	51.350	52.206	53.062	53.917	54.773	55.629	56.485
42	47.353	48.198	49.044	49.889	50.735	51.581	52.426	43.272	54.117	54.963	55.808
43	46.799	47.634	48.470	49.306	50.142	50.977	51.813	52.649	53.484	54.320	55.156
44	46.264	47.090	47.916	48.742	49.568	50.395	51.221	52.047	52.873	53.699	54.525
45	45.747	46.564	47.381	48.198	49.015	49.832	50.648	51.465	52.282	53.099	53.916
46	45.247	46.055	46.863	47.671	48.479	49.287	50.095	50.903	51.711	52.519	53.327
47	44.763	45.562	46.362	47.161	47.960	48.760	49.559	50.358	51.158	51.957	52.756
48	44.294	45.085	45.876	46.667	47.458	48.249	49.040	49.831	50.622	51.413	52.204
49	43.840	44.623	45.406	46.189	46.971	47.754	48.537	49.320	50.103	50.886	51.669
50	43.399	44.174	44.949	45.724	46.499	47.274	48.049	48.824	49.599	50.374	51.149

TABLE 5-VII-A (Continued)

SPEED IN MILES PER HOUR BASED ON LEVEL HORIZONTAL TAKEOFF AND FALL

Vertical Distance (feet)	Horizontal Distance (feet)								
	134	136	138	140	142	144	146	148	150
1									
2									
3									
4									
5									
6									
7									
8									
8									
9									
10	116.106	117.839	119.572	121.305					
11	110.703	112.355	114.007	115.660	117.312	118.964	120.617		
12	105.990	107.572	109.154	110.736	112.318	113.900	115.482	117.064	118.645
13	101.832	103.352	104.872	106.391	107.911	109.431	110.951	112.471	113.991
14	98.128	99.592	101.057	102.521	103.986	105.451	106.915	108.380	109.844
15	94.800	96.215	97.630	99.045	100.460	101.875	103.290	104.705	106.120
16	91.790	93.160	94.530	95.900	97.270	98.640	100.010	101.380	102.750
17	89.049	90.378	91.708	93.037	94.366	95.695	97.024	98.353	99.682
18	86.540	87.832	89.124	90.415	91.707	92.999	94.290	95.582	96.874
19	84.232	85.489	86.747	88.004	89.261	90.518	91.775	93.033	94.290
20	82.099	83.325	84.550	85.776	87.001	88.226	89.452	90.677	91.902
21	80.121	81.317	82.513	83.708	84.904	86.100	87.296	88.492	89.688

22	78.279	79.447	80.615	81.784	82.952	84.120	85.289	86.457	87.625
23	76.558	77.701	78.843	79.986	81.129	82.271	83.414	84.557	85.699
24	74.946	76.065	77.183	78.302	79.421	80.539	81.658	82.776	83.895
25	73.432	74.528	75.624	76.720	77.816	78.912	80.008	81.104	82.200
26	72.006	73.081	74.155	75.230	76.305	77.380	78.454	79.529	80.604
27	70.660	71.715	72.769	73.824	74.878	75.933	76.988	78.042	79.097
28	69.387	70.422	71.458	72.494	73.529	74.565	75.600	76.636	77.672
29	68.180	69.198	70.215	71.233	72.250	73.268	74.286	75.303	76.321
30	67.034	68.034	69.035	70.035	71.036	72.036	73.037	74.037	75.038
31	65.944	66.928	67.912	68.897	69.881	70.865	71.849	72.834	73.818
32	64.905	65.874	66.843	67.812	68.780	69.749	70.718	71.686	72.655
33	63.914	64.868	65.822	66.776	67.730	68.684	69.638	70.592	71.546
34	62.967	63.907	64.847	65.787	66.727	67.666	68.606	69.546	70.486
35	62.061	62.988	63.914	64.840	65.767	66.693	67.619	68.545	69.472
36	61.193	62.107	63.020	63.933	64.847	65.760	66.673	67.587	68.500
37	60.361	61.262	62.163	63.063	63.964	64.865	65.766	66.667	67.568
38	59.561	60.450	61.339	62.228	63.117	64.006	64.895	65.784	66.673
39	58.793	59.670	60.548	61.425	62.303	63.180	64.058	64.935	65.813
40	58.053	58.920	59.786	60.652	61.519	62.385	63.252	64.118	64.985
41	57.341	58.197	59.052	59.908	60.764	61.620	62.476	63.332	64.187
42	56.654	57.500	58.346	59.191	60.036	60.882	61.728	62.573	63.419
43	55.991	56.827	57.663	58.498	59.334	60.170	61.006	61.841	62.677
44	55.351	56.178	57.004	57.830	58.656	59.482	60.308	61.134	61.961
45	54.733	55.550	56.367	57.184	58.001	58.818	59.634	60.451	61.268
46	54.135	54.943	55.751	56.559	57.367	58.175	58.983	59.791	60.599
47	53.556	54.355	55.154	55.954	56.753	57.552	58.352	59.151	59.951
48	52.995	53.786	54.577	55.368	56.159	56.950	57.741	58.532	59.323
49	52.451	53.234	54.017	54.800	55.583	56.366	57.149	57.931	58.714
50	51.924	52.699	53.474	54.249	55.024	55.799	56.574	57.349	58.124

TABLE 5-VII-B

SPEED IN KILOMETERS PER HOUR BASED ON LEVEL TAKEOFF AND FALL

Vertical Distance (meters)	Horizontal Distance (meters)										
	2	3	4	5	6	7	8	9	10	11	12
0.5	22.543	33.814	45.085	56.356	67.628	78.899	90.170	101.442	112.713	123.984	135.255
1.0	15.940	23.910	31.880	39.850	47.820	55.790	63.760	71.730	79.700	87.670	95.640
1.5	13.015	19.522	26.030	32.537	39.045	45.552	52.060	58.567	65.075	71.582	78.090
2.0	11.271	16.907	22.543	28.178	33.814	39.449	45.085	50.721	56.356	61.992	67.628
2.5	10.081	15.122	20.163	25.203	30.244	35.285	40.325	45.366	50.407	55.447	60.488
3.0	9.203	13.804	18.406	23.077	27.609	32.210	36.812	41.413	46.015	50.616	55.218
3.5	8.520	12.780	17.041	21.301	25.561	29.821	34.081	38.341	42.601	46.862	51.122
4.0	7.970	11.955	15.940	19.925	23.910	27.895	31.880	35.865	39.850	43.835	47.820
4.5	7.514	11.271	15.028	18.785	22.543	26.300	30.057	33.814	37.571	41.328	45.085
5.0	7.129	10.693	14.257	17.821	21.386	24.950	28.514	32.079	35.643	39.207	42.772
5.5	6.797	10.195	13.594	16.992	20.391	23.789	27.187	30.586	33.984	37.383	40.781
6.0	6.507	9.761	13.015	16.269	19.522	22.776	26.030	29.284	32.537	35.791	39.045
6.5	6.252	9.378	12.504	15.630	18.757	21.883	25.009	28.135	31.261	34.387	37.513
7.0	6.025	9.037	12.050	15.062	18.074	21.087	24.099	27.111	30.124	33.136	36.149
7.5	5.820	8.731	11.641	14.551	17.461	20.372	23.282	26.192	29.102	32.013	34.923
8.0	5.636	8.453	11.271	14.089	16.907	19.725	22.543	25.360	28.178	30.996	33.814

8.5	5.467	8.201	10.935	13.668	16.402	19.136	21.869	24.603	27.337	30.071	32.804
9.0	5.313	7.970	10.627	13.283	15.940	18.597	21.253	23.910	26.567	29.223	31.880
9.5	5.172	7.757	10.343	12.929	15.515	18.101	20.686	23.272	25.858	28.444	31.030
10.0	5.041	7.561	10.081	12.602	15.122	17.642	20.163	22.683	25.203	27.724	30.244
10.5	4.919	7.379	9.838	12.298	14.758	17.217	19.677	22.136	24.596	27.056	29.515
11.0	4.806	7.209	9.612	12.016	14.418	16.821	19.224	21.627	24.030	26.434	28.837
11.5	4.700	7.051	9.401	11.751	14.101	16.452	18.802	21.152	23.502	25.852	28.203
12.0	4.601	6.902	9.203	11.504	13.804	16.105	18.406	20.707	23.007	25.308	27.609
12.5	4.509	6.763	9.017	11.271	13.526	15.780	18.034	20.288	22.543	24.797	27.051
13.0	4.421	6.631	8.842	11.052	13.263	15.473	17.684	19.894	22.105	24.315	26.526
13.5	4.338	6.507	8.677	10.846	13.015	15.184	17.353	19.522	21.692	23.861	26.030
14.0	4.260	6.390	8.520	10.650	12.780	14.911	17.041	19.171	21.301	23.431	25.561
14.5	4.186	6.279	8.372	10.465	12.558	14.651	16.744	18.837	20.930	23.023	25.116
15.0	4.116	6.174	8.231	10.289	12.347	14.405	16.463	18.521	20.578	22.636	24.694
15.5	4.049	6.073	8.098	10.122	12.146	14.171	16.195	18.219	20.244	22.268	24.293
16.0	3.985	5.978	7.970	9.963	11.955	13.948	15.940	17.933	19.925	21.918	23.910
16.5	3.924	5.886	7.848	9.810	11.772	13.735	15.697	17.659	19.621	21.583	23.545
17.0	3.866	5.799	7.732	9.665	11.598	13.531	15.464	17.397	19.330	21.263	23.196
17.5	3.810	5.716	7.621	9.526	11.431	13.336	15.242	17.147	19.052	20.957	22.862
18.0	3.757	5.636	7.514	9.393	11.271	13.150	15.028	16.907	18.785	20.664	22.543
18.5	3.706	5.559	7.412	9.265	11.118	12.971	14.824	16.677	18.530	20.383	22.236
19.0	3.657	5.485	7.314	9.142	10.971	12.799	14.628	16.456	18.284	20.113	21.941
19.5	3.610	5.415	7.219	9.024	10.829	12.634	14.439	16.244	18.048	19.853	21.658
20.0	3.564	5.346	7.129	8.911	10.693	12.475	14.257	16.039	17.821	19.604	21.386

TABLE 5-VII-B (Continued)

SPEED IN KILOMETERS PER HOUR BASED ON LEVEL TAKEOFF AND FALL

Vertical Distance (meters)	Horizontal Distance (meters)										
	13	14	15	16	17	18	19	20	21	22	23
0.5	146.527	157.798	169.069	180.341	191.612	202.883					
1.0	103.610	111.580	119.550	127.520	135.490	143.460	151.430	159.400	167.370	175.340	183.310
1.5	84.597	91.105	97.612	104.120	110.627	117.135	123.642	130.150	136.657	143.165	149.672
2.0	73.263	78.899	84.535	90.170	95.806	101.442	107.077	112.713	118.348	123.984	129.620
2.5	65.529	70.569	75.610	80.651	85.691	90.732	95.773	100.813	105.854	110.895	115.935
3.0	59.819	64.421	69.022	73.624	78.225	82.827	87.428	92.030	96.631	101.233	105.834
3.5	55.382	59.642	63.902	68.162	72.422	76.683	80.943	85.203	89.463	93.723	97.983
4.0	51.805	55.790	59.775	63.760	67.745	71.730	75.715	79.700	83.685	87.670	91.655
4.5	48.842	52.599	56.356	60.114	63.871	67.628	71.385	75.142	78.899	82.656	86.413
5.0	46.336	49.900	53.464	57.029	60.593	64.157	67.722	71.286	74.850	78.414	81.979
5.5	44.179	47.578	50.976	54.375	57.773	61.172	64.570	67.968	71.367	74.765	78.164
6.0	42.299	45.552	48.806	52.060	55.314	58.567	61.821	65.075	68.329	71.582	74.836
6.5	40.639	43.765	46.891	50.017	53.144	56.270	59.396	62.522	65.648	68.774	71.900
7.0	39.161	42.173	45.186	48.198	51.210	54.223	57.235	60.248	63.260	66.272	69.285
7.5	37.833	40.743	43.653	46.564	49.474	52.384	55.294	58.205	61.115	64.025	66.935
8.0	36.632	39.449	42.267	45.085	47.903	50.721	53.539	56.356	59.174	61.992	64.810

8.5	35.538	38.272	41.005	43.739	46.473	49.206	51.940	54.674	57.407	60.141	62.875
9.0	34.537	37.193	39.850	42.507	45.163	47.820	50.477	53.133	55.790	58.447	61.103
9.5	33.616	36.201	38.787	41.373	43.959	46.545	49.130	51.716	54.302	56.888	59.474
10.0	32.764	35.285	37.805	40.325	42.846	45.366	47.886	50.407	52.927	55.447	57.968
10.5	31.975	34.434	36.894	39.354	41.813	44.273	46.732	49.192	51.652	54.111	56.571
11.0	31.240	33.643	36.046	38.449	40.852	43.255	45.658	48.061	50.464	52.867	55.270
11.5	30.553	32.903	35.253	37.604	39.954	42.304	44.654	47.004	49.355	51.705	54.055
12.0	29.910	32.210	34.511	36.812	39.113	41.413	43.714	46.015	48.316	50.616	52.917
12.5	29.305	31.560	33.814	36.068	38.322	40.577	42.831	45.085	47.339	49.594	51.848
13.0	28.736	30.947	33.157	35.368	37.578	39.789	41.999	44.210	46.420	48.631	50.841
13.5	28.199	30.368	32.537	34.707	36.876	39.045	41.214	43.383	45.552	47.722	49.891
14.0	27.691	29.821	31.951	34.081	36.211	38.341	40.471	42.601	44.732	46.862	48.992
14.5	27.209	29.302	31.395	33.488	35.581	37.674	39.767	41.860	43.954	46.047	48.140
15.0	26.752	28.810	30.868	32.926	34.983	37.041	39.099	41.157	43.215	45.273	47.330
15.5	26.317	28.341	30.366	32.390	34.414	36.439	38.463	40.488	42.512	44.536	46.561
16.0	25.903	27.895	29.888	31.880	33.873	35.865	37.858	39.850	41.843	43.835	45.828
16.5	25.507	27.469	29.431	31.393	33.355	35.317	37.279	39.242	41.204	43.166	45.128
17.0	25.129	27.062	28.995	30.928	32.861	34.794	36.727	38.660	40.593	42.526	44.459
17.5	24.768	26.673	28.578	30.483	32.388	34.293	36.199	38.104	40.009	41.914	43.819
18.0	24.421	26.300	28.178	30.057	31.935	33.814	35.692	37.571	39.449	41.328	43.207
18.5	24.089	25.942	27.795	29.648	31.501	33.354	35.207	37.060	38.913	40.766	42.619
19.0	23.770	25.598	27.427	29.255	31.084	32.912	34.740	36.569	38.397	40.226	42.054
19.5	23.463	25.268	27.073	28.878	30.682	32.487	34.292	36.097	37.902	39.707	41.512
20.0	23.168	24.950	26.732	28.514	30.296	32.079	33.861	35.643	37.425	39.207	40.989

TABLE 5-VII-B (Continued)

SPEED IN KILOMETERS PER HOUR BASED ON LEVEL TAKEOFF AND FALL

Vertical Distance (meters)	Horizontal Distance (meters)										
	24	25	26	27	28	29	30	31	32	33	34
0.5											
1.0	191.280	199.250	207.220								
1.5	156.179	162.687	169.194	175.702	182.209	188.717	195.224	201.732			
2.0	135.255	140.891	146.527	152.162	157.798	163.434	169.069	174.705	180.341	185.976	191.612
2.5	120.976	126.017	131.057	136.098	141.139	146.179	151.220	156.261	161.301	166.342	171.383
3.0	110.436	115.037	119.639	124.240	128.841	133.443	138.044	142.646	147.247	151.849	156.450
3.5	102.243	106.504	110.764	115.024	119.284	123.544	127.804	132.064	136.325	140.585	144.845
4.0	95.640	99.625	103.610	107.595	111.580	115.565	119.550	123.535	127.520	131.505	135.490
4.5	90.170	93.927	97.684	101.442	105.199	108.956	112.713	116.470	120.227	123.984	127.741
5.0	85.543	89.107	92.672	96.236	99.800	103.364	106.929	110.493	114.057	117.622	121.186
5.5	81.562	84.960	88.359	91.757	95.156	98.554	101.953	105.351	108.749	112.148	115.546
6.0	78.090	81.343	84.597	87.851	91.105	94.358	97.612	100.866	104.120	107.373	110.627
6.5	75.026	78.152	81.278	84.404	87.531	90.657	93.783	96.909	100.035	103.161	106.287
7.0	72.297	75.309	78.322	81.334	84.347	87.359	90.371	93.384	96.396	99.408	102.421
7.5	69.846	72.756	75.666	78.576	81.487	84.397	87.307	90.217	93.127	96.038	98.948
8.0	67.628	70.446	73.263	76.081	78.899	81.717	84.535	87.352	90.170	92.988	95.806

8.5	65.608	68.342	71.076	73.810	76.543	79.277	82.011	84.744	87.478	90.212	92.945
9.0	63.760	66.417	69.073	71.730	74.387	77.043	79.700	82.357	85.013	87.670	90.327
9.5	62.059	64.645	67.231	69.817	72.403	74.988	77.574	80.160	82.746	85.332	87.918
10.0	60.488	63.008	65.529	68.049	70.569	73.090	75.610	78.130	80.651	83.171	85.691
10.5	59.030	61.490	63.949	66.409	68.869	71.328	73.788	76.247	78.707	81.167	83.626
11.0	57.673	60.076	62.479	64.882	67.285	69.688	72.091	74.494	76.897	79.301	81.704
11.5	56.405	58.756	61.106	63.456	65.806	68.157	70.507	72.857	75.207	77.557	79.908
12.0	55.218	57.519	59.819	62.120	64.421	66.721	69.022	71.323	73.624	75.924	78.225
12.5	54.102	56.356	58.611	60.865	63.119	65.373	67.628	69.882	72.136	74.390	76.645
13.0	53.052	55.262	57.472	59.683	61.893	64.104	66.314	68.525	70.735	72.946	75.156
13.5	52.060	54.229	56.398	58.567	60.736	62.906	65.075	67.244	69.413	71.582	73.751
14.0	51.122	53.252	55.382	57.512	59.642	61.772	63.902	66.032	68.162	70.292	72.422
14.5	50.233	52.326	54.418	56.512	58.605	60.698	62.791	64.884	66.977	69.070	71.163
15.0	49.388	51.446	53.504	55.562	57.620	59.678	61.735	63.793	65.851	67.909	69.967
15.5	48.585	50.610	52.634	54.658	56.683	58.707	60.731	62.756	64.780	66.805	68.829
16.0	47.820	49.813	51.805	53.798	55.790	57.783	59.775	61.768	63.760	65.753	67.745
16.5	47.090	49.052	51.014	52.976	54.938	56.900	58.862	60.824	62.787	64.749	66.711
17.0	46.392	48.325	50.258	52.191	54.124	56.057	57.990	59.923	61.856	63.789	65.722
17.5	45.725	47.630	49.535	51.440	53.345	55.251	57.156	59.061	60.966	62.871	64.777
18.0	45.085	46.964	48.842	50.721	52.599	54.478	56.356	58.235	60.114	61.992	63.871
18.5	44.472	46.325	48.178	50.031	51.884	53.737	55.590	57.443	59.296	61.149	63.002
19.0	43.883	45.711	47.540	49.368	51.196	53.025	54.853	56.682	58.510	60.339	62.167
19.5	43.316	45.121	46.926	48.731	50.536	52.341	54.145	55.950	57.755	59.560	61.365
20.0	42.772	44.554	46.336	48.118	49.900	51.682	53.464	55.247	57.029	58.811	60.593

TABLE 5-VII-B (*Continued*)

SPEED IN KILOMETERS PER HOUR BASED ON LEVEL TAKEOFF AND FALL

Vertical Distance (meters)	Horizontal Distance (meters)										
	35	36	37	38	39	40	41	42	43	44	45
0.5											
1.0											
1.5											
2.0	197.247	202.883									
2.5	176.423	181.464	186.505	191.545	196.586	201.627					
3.0	161.052	165.653	170.255	174.856	179.458	184.059	188.661	193.262	197.864	202.465	
3.5	149.105	153.365	157.625	161.885	166.146	170.406	174.666	178.926	183.186	187.446	191.706
4.0	139.475	143.460	147.445	151.430	155.415	159.400	163.385	167.370	171.355	175.340	179.325
4.5	131.498	135.255	139.012	142.770	146.527	150.284	154.041	157.798	161.555	165.312	169.069
5.0	124.750	128.315	131.879	135.443	139.007	142.572	146.136	149.700	153.265	156.829	160.393
5.5	118.945	122.343	125.742	129.140	132.538	135.937	139.335	142.734	146.132	149.530	152.929
6.0	113.881	117.135	120.388	123.642	126.896	130.150	133.403	136.657	139.911	143.165	146.418
6.5	109.413	112.539	115.665	118.791	121.918	125.044	128.170	131.296	134.422	137.548	140.674
7.0	105.433	108.446	111.458	114.470	117.483	120.495	123.507	126.520	129.532	132.545	135.557
7.5	101.858	104.768	107.679	110.589	113.499	116.409	119.320	122.230	125.140	128.050	130.960
8.0	98.624	101.442	104.259	107.077	109.895	112.713	115.531	118.348	121.166	123.984	126.802

8.5	95.679	98.413	101.146	103.880	106.614	109.347	112.081	114.815	117.549	120.282	123.016
9.0	92.983	95.640	98.297	100.953	103.610	106.267	108.923	111.580	114.237	116.893	119.550
9.5	90.503	93.089	95.675	98.261	100.847	103.432	106.018	108.604	111.190	113.776	116.361
10.0	88.212	90.732	93.252	95.773	98.293	100.813	103.334	105.854	108.375	110.895	113.415
10.5	86.086	88.545	91.005	93.465	95.924	98.384	100.843	103.303	105.763	108.222	110.682
11.0	84.107	86.510	88.913	91.316	93.719	96.122	98.525	100.928	103.331	105.734	108.137
11.5	82.258	84.608	86.958	89.309	91.659	94.009	96.359	98.709	101.060	103.410	105.760
12.0	80.526	82.827	85.127	87.428	89.729	92.030	94.330	96.631	98.932	101.233	103.533
12.5	78.899	81.153	83.407	85.662	87.916	90.170	92.425	94.679	96.933	99.187	101.442
13.0	77.367	79.577	81.788	83.998	86.209	88.419	90.630	92.840	95.051	97.261	99.472
13.5	75.921	78.090	80.259	82.428	84.597	86.766	88.936	91.105	93.274	95.443	97.612
14.0	74.553	76.683	78.813	80.943	83.073	85.203	87.333	89.463	91.593	93.723	95.853
14.5	73.256	75.349	77.442	79.535	81.628	83.721	85.814	87.907	90.000	92.093	94.186
15.0	72.025	74.082	76.140	78.198	80.256	82.314	84.372	86.429	88.487	90.545	92.603
15.5	70.853	72.878	74.902	76.927	78.951	80.975	83.000	85.024	87.048	89.073	91.097
16.0	69.738	71.730	73.723	75.715	77.708	79.700	81.693	83.685	85.678	87.670	89.663
16.5	68.673	70.635	72.597	74.559	76.521	78.483	80.445	82.407	84.369	86.331	88.294
17.0	67.655	69.588	71.521	73.454	75.387	77.320	79.253	81.186	83.119	85.052	86.985
17.5	66.682	68.587	70.492	72.397	74.303	76.208	78.113	80.018	81.923	83.829	85.734
18.0	65.749	67.628	69.506	71.385	73.263	75.142	77.020	78.899	80.778	82.656	84.535
18.5	64.855	66.708	68.561	70.414	72.267	74.119	75.972	77.825	79.678	81.531	83.384
19.0	63.996	65.824	67.652	69.481	71.309	73.138	74.966	76.795	78.623	80.452	82.280
19.5	63.170	64.975	66.779	68.584	70.389	72.194	73.999	75.804	77.609	79.413	81.218
20.0	62.375	64.157	65.939	67.722	69.504	71.286	73.068	74.850	76.632	78.414	80.197

TABLE 5-VII-B *(Continued)*

SPEED IN KILOMETERS PER HOUR BASED ON LEVEL TAKEOFF AND FALL

Vertical Distance (meters)	46	47	48	49	*Horizontal Distance (meters)* 50
0.5					
1.0					
1.5					
2.0					
2.5					
3.0					
3.5	195.967	200.227			
4.0	183.310	187.295	191.280	195.265	199.250
4.5	172.826	176.583	180.341	184.098	187.855
5.0	163.957	167.522	171.086	174.650	178.215
5.5	156.327	159.726	163.124	166.523	169.921
6.0	149.672	152.926	156.179	159.433	162.687
6.5	143.800	146.926	150.052	153.178	156.305
7.0	138.569	141.582	144.594	147.606	150.619
7.5	133.871	136.781	139.691	142.601	145.512
8.0	129.620	132.438	135.255	138.073	140.891

8.5	125.750	128.483	131.217	133.951	136.684
9.0	122.207	124.863	127.520	130.177	132.833
9.5	118.947	121.533	124.119	126.705	129.290
10.0	115.935	118.456	120.976	123.496	126.017
10.5	113.141	115.601	118.061	120.520	122.980
11.0	110.540	112.943	115.346	117.749	120.152
11.5	108.110	110.461	112.811	115.161	117.511
12.0	105.834	108.135	110.436	112.736	115.037
12.5	103.696	105.950	108.204	110.459	112.713
13.0	101.682	103.893	106.103	108.314	110.524
13.5	99.781	101.950	104.120	106.289	108.458
14.0	97.983	100.113	102.243	104.374	106.504
14.5	96.279	98.372	100.465	102.558	104.651
15.0	94.661	96.719	98.777	100.834	102.892
15.5	93.122	95.146	97.170	99.195	101.219
16.0	91.655	93.648	95.640	97.633	99.625
16.5	90.256	92.218	94.180	96.142	98.104
17.0	88.918	90.851	92.784	94.717	96.650
17.5	87.639	89.544	91.449	93.355	95.260
18.0	86.413	88.292	90.170	92.049	93.927
18.5	85.237	87.090	88.943	90.796	92.649
19.0	84.108	85.937	87.765	89.594	91.422
19.5	83.023	84.828	86.633	88.438	90.242
20.0	81.979	83.761	85.543	87.325	89.107

Example 3

Same circumstances as in Example 1 except the vehicle travelled on a grade *(e)* of +8 per cent leading to the point where it left the highway:

United States

$$S = \frac{2.74 \times 40}{\sqrt{10 + (40 \times .08)}}$$

$$S = \frac{109.6}{\sqrt{10 + 3.2}}$$

$$S = \frac{109.6}{\sqrt{13.2}}$$

$$S = \frac{109.6}{3.63}$$

$$S = 30.19$$

$$S = 30 \text{ mph}$$

Metric

$$S = \frac{7.97 \times 12}{\sqrt{3 + (12 \times .08)}}$$

$$S = \frac{95.64}{\sqrt{3 + .96}}$$

$$S = \frac{95.64}{\sqrt{3.96}}$$

$$S = \frac{95.64}{1.99}$$

$$S = 48.06$$

$$S = 48 \text{ km/h}$$

Example 4

A vehicle struck a utility pole head-on and stopped abruptly. Debris that had been situated on the vehicle 3 ft (1 m) from the roadway level was catapaulted 23 ft (7 m) forward, where it struck the ground. The approximate speed of the vehicle at the time it struck the pole may be calculated by using Formula 5-30:

United States

$$S = \frac{2.74 \times 23}{\sqrt{3}}$$

$$S = \frac{63.02}{1.73}$$

$$S = 36.43$$

$$S = 36 \text{ mph}$$

Metric

$$S = \frac{7.97 \times 7}{\sqrt{1}}$$

$$S = \frac{55.79}{1}$$

$$S = 55.79$$

$$S = 56 \text{ km/h}$$

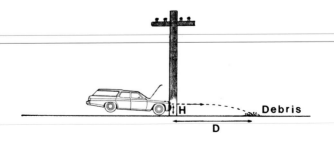

Figure 5-28

Flips and Vaults

5.097   If the speed is great enough when a vehicle strikes a substantial object such as a curb and the height of the object is less than the height of the center of gravity of the vehicle, the vehicle will pivot at the point of impact and flip or vault through the air, usually landing on its top or side. Such flips or vaults can occur when the vehicle strikes the object head-on or slides sideways into it. By determining the positions of the centers of mass in relation to the roadway at the time of impact and time the vehicle first strikes the ground after the flip or vault and measuring the horizontal distance between these two points, the speed of the vehicle at the time it struck the object may be calculated. Formulae 5-32 and 5-33 are intended for an assumed takeoff of 45 degrees. Speed estimates for a lesser or greater degree takeoff will be conservative.

Example 1

A vehicle travelled into an intersection, struck a curb with its front, flipped and vaulted through the air, landing on its roof on a lawn. The position of the centers of mass at takeoff and landing were level and measured a horizontal distance of 46 ft (14 m). In calculating the speed where takeoff and landing are level, use Formula 5-32:

United States	*Metric*
$S = 3.87 \sqrt{D}$	$S = 11.27 \sqrt{D}$

where S = speed at takeoff
       D = horizontal distance between centres of mass

$S = 3.87 \sqrt{46}$	$S = 11.27 \sqrt{14}$
$S = 3.87 \times 6.782$	$S = 11.27 \times 3.742$
$S = 26.25$	$S = 42.17$
$S = 26$ mph	$S = 42$ km/h

Example 2

In this example, the circumstances are the same as in Example 1 except the vehicle landed 10 ft (3 m) below the level at takeoff, measured to centers of mass positions. When vault or flip landings are below the level

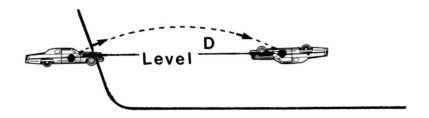

Figure 5-29

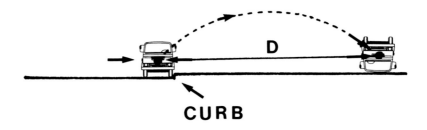

CURB

Figure 5-30

of takeoff, the vertical distance *(H)* is added (+) in the square root formula. In these cases use Formula 5-33:

<table>
<tr><td align="center">United States</td><td align="center">Metric</td></tr>
</table>

$$S = \frac{3.87\ D}{\sqrt{D \pm H}} \qquad\qquad S = \frac{11.27\ D}{\sqrt{D \pm H}}$$

where S = speed
    D = horizontal distance
    H = Vertical fall or rise

$$S = \frac{3.87 \times 46}{\sqrt{46 + 10}} \qquad\qquad S = \frac{11.27 \times 14}{\sqrt{14 + 3}}$$

$$S = \frac{178.02}{\sqrt{56}} \qquad\qquad S = \frac{157.78}{\sqrt{17}}$$

$$S = \frac{178.02}{7.483} \qquad\qquad S = \frac{157.78}{4.123}$$

$$S = 23.79 \qquad\qquad S = 38.27$$
$$S = 24\ \text{mph} \qquad\qquad S = 38\ \text{km/h}$$

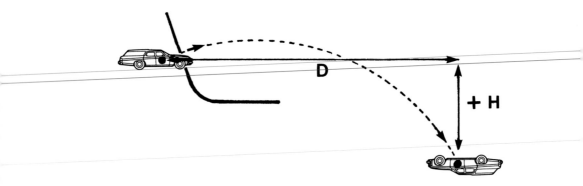

Figure 5-31

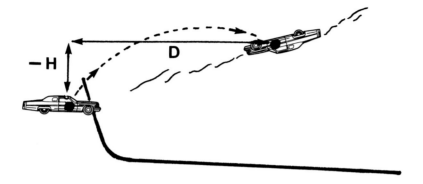

Figure 5-32

Example 3

The circumstances are the same as in example 1 except that the vehicle landed 10 ft (3 m) above the level of takeoff, measured from centers of mass positions. When vault landing is above the level of takeoff, the vertical distance *(H)* is subtracted (−) in the square root formula. In these cases use Formula 5-33:

United States

$$S = \frac{3.87 \ D}{\sqrt{D \pm H}}$$

$$S = \frac{3.87 \times 46}{\sqrt{46 - 10}}$$

$$S = \frac{178.02}{\sqrt{36}}$$

$$S = \frac{178.02}{6}$$

$$S = 29.67$$
$$S = 30 \ \text{mph}$$

Metric

$$S = \frac{11.27 \ D}{\sqrt{D \pm H}}$$

$$S = \frac{11.27 \times 14}{\sqrt{14 - 3}}$$

$$S = \frac{157.78}{\sqrt{11}}$$

$$S = \frac{157.78}{3.317}$$

$$S = 47.57$$
$$S = 48 \ \text{km/h}$$

Combined Speeds

5.098   Skid marks sometimes lead to the point from where a vehicle vaults or takes off and falls from the highway. The skid marks and the vault or fall do not by themselves allow for a calculation of the total speed. In these situations, the two speeds should be calculated separately and placed in the *combined speed formula,* Formula 5-9:

United States

$$S_c = \sqrt{S_1^2 + S_2^2}$$

Metric

$$S_c = \sqrt{S_1^2 + S_2^2}$$

Example

Circumstances in this case are the same as in Example 1 in paragraph 5.096 and Figure 5-26, except that the vehicle left 33 ft (10 m) skid marks before it left the highway. By using Formula 5-4, we know that skid marks 33 ft (10 m) in length on a roadway having a coefficient of friction of .70 indicate a speed of 26 mph (42 km/h). We will call this S_1. We know from Example 1 (Fig. 5-26) that the speed of the vehicle at the time it left the highway was 35 mph (55 km/h). We will call this S_2. To find the speed of the vehicle at the time of the commencement of the skid marks, we put both speeds, S_1 and S_2, into Formula 5-9:

<table>
<tr><td colspan="2" align="center">United States</td><td colspan="2" align="center">Metric</td></tr>
<tr><td>S_c</td><td>$= \sqrt{26^2 + 35^2}$</td><td>S_c</td><td>$= \sqrt{42^2 + 55^2}$</td></tr>
<tr><td>S_c</td><td>$= \sqrt{676 + 1225}$</td><td>S_c</td><td>$= \sqrt{1764 + 3025}$</td></tr>
<tr><td>S_c</td><td>$= \sqrt{1901}$</td><td>S_c</td><td>$= \sqrt{4789}$</td></tr>
<tr><td>S_c</td><td>$= 43.6$</td><td>S_c</td><td>$= 69.2$</td></tr>
<tr><td>S_c</td><td>$= 44$ mph</td><td>S_c</td><td>$= 69$ km/h</td></tr>
</table>

MOMENTUM

5.099   *Momentum,* as expressed in Newton's Law 3 (paragraph 3.001), is the product of the mass or weight times the velocity *(MV)* or the amount of motion a vehicle or other object has. Heavier vehicles have more momentum than lighter vehicles. Similarly, a vehicle travelling at a high rate of speed has more momentum than a vehicle of equal weight travelling at a lesser speed.

5.100   Momentum is not related to damage. Therefore, momentum equations may be used without considering the physical damages caused to vehicles during collision.

5.101   The conservation of momentum equation states that the total amount of momentum at any time remains fixed or constant. Applying this to vehicle collisions, we can say that the momentum of a vehicle remains constant before and after a collision or, in other terms, that the weight times the velocity *(WV)* does not change during collision.

5.102   The conservation of momentum equation applied to vehicle collisions is the same for both United States and metric calculations (Formula 5-34):

$$W_1S_1 + W_2S_2 = W_1S_3 + W_2S_4$$

where W_1 = weight of vehicle 1
          W_2 = weight of vehicle 2
          S_1 = speed (velocity) of vehicle 1 prior to impact
          S_2 = speed (velocity) of vehicle 2 prior to impact
          S_3 = speed (velocity) of vehicle 1 after impact
          S_4 = speed (velocity) of vehicle 2 after impact

Example 1
    Vehicle 1 stopped in an intersection and was struck broadside by vehicle 2. Both vehicles remained engaged and skidded to a stop. The speed of

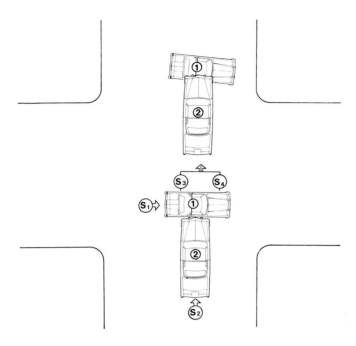

Figure 5-33

both vehicles immediately *after* impact may be calculated using the conservation of momentum equation. In this example:

W_1 = 3,500 lb (1588 kg)
W_2 = 6,000 lb (2722 kg)
S_1 = zero speed (velocity) at impact
S_2 = 30 mph (48 km/h) at impact according to witnesses' statements
S_3 = speed (velocity) of vehicle 1 immediately after impact
S_4 = speed (velocity) of vehicle 2 immediately after impact

United States

Momentum Before Impact

$$W_1S_1 + W_2S_2 = (3.500 \times 0) + (6,000 \times 30)$$
$$= 180,000 \text{ momentum units}$$

Momentum After Impact (S_3)

$$S_3(W_1 + W_2) = 180,000 \text{ momentum units}$$
$$S_3(3,500 + 6,000) = 180,000$$
$$S_3 \times 9,500 = 180,000$$
$$S_3 = \frac{180,000}{9,500}$$
$$S_3 = 18.9 \text{ mph}$$
$$S_3 = 19 \text{ mph}$$
$$\therefore \ S_4 = 19 \text{ mph}$$

Metric

Momentum Before Impact

$$W_1S_1 + W_2S_2 = (1,588 \times 0) + (2,722 \times 48)$$
$$= 130,656 \text{ momentum units}$$

Momentum After Impact (S_3)

$$S_3(W_1 + W_2) = 130,656 \text{ momentum units}$$
$$S_3(1,588 + 2,722) = 130,656$$
$$S_3 \times 4,310 = 130,656$$
$$S_3 = \frac{130,656}{4,310}$$
$$S_3 = 30.3$$
$$S_3 = 30 \text{ km/h}$$
$$\therefore S_4 = 30 \text{ km/h}$$

Example 2

Vehicle 1 skidded 50 ft (15.2 m), D_3, and struck vehicle 2, which was stopped, in the rear. After impact, both vehicles remained engaged and skidded another 40 ft (12.2 m), D_1 and D_2, before coming to rest. The coefficient of friction was .70. The weight of vehicle 1 was 4,000 lb (1814.4 kg). Weight of vehicle 2 was 3,000 lb (1360.8 kg). The problem is to calculate the speed of vehicle 1 at the commencement of its 50 ft (15.2 m) skid.

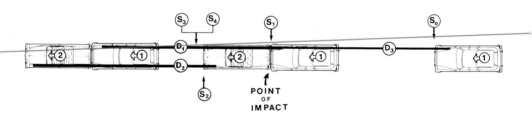

Figure 5-34

Step 1

Determine the speeds of both vehicles just after impact (S_3 and S_4) using the speed from skid mark formula, Formula 5-4. In this example, both vehicles skidded 40 ft (12.2 m); therefore, their speeds are the same:

United States	*Metric*
$S_3 = 5.5 \sqrt{D_1f}$	$S_3 = 15.9 \sqrt{D_1f}$
$S_3 = 5.5 \sqrt{40 \times .70}$	$S_3 = 15.9 \sqrt{12.2 \times .70}$
$S_3 = 5.5 \sqrt{28}$	$S_3 = 15.9 \sqrt{8.54}$
$S_3 = 5.5 \times 5.29$	$S_3 = 15.9 \times 2.92$
$S_3 = 29.09$	$S_3 = 46.43$
$S_3 = 29 \text{ mph after impact}$	$S_3 = 46 \text{ km/h after impact}$
$\therefore S_4 = 29 \text{ mph after impact}$	$\therefore S_4 = 46 \text{ km/h after impact}$

Step 2

Determine speed of vehicle 1 at impact (S_1). We know that the speed of vehicle 2, S_2, was zero. Therefore, in the conservation of momentum equation we need to concern ourselves only with the weight and speed of vehicle 1 at impact which, according to conservation of energy equation, is equal to the momentum of both vehicles after impact.

United States

$$W_1S_1 = W_1S_3 + W_2S_4$$
$$W_1S_1 = (4,000 \times 29) + (3,000 \times 29)$$
$$W_1S_1 = 116,000 + 87,000$$
$$4,000 \times S_1 = 203,000 \text{ momentum units}$$
$$S_1 = \frac{203,000}{4,000}$$
$$S_1 = 50.75$$
$$S_1 = 51 \text{ mph at impact}$$

Metric

$$W_1S_1 = W_1S_3 + W_2S_4$$
$$W_1S_1 = (1814.4 \times 46.47) + (1360.8 \times 46.47)$$
$$W_1S_1 = 84,315.17 + 63,236.38$$
$$1814.4 \times S_1 = 147,551.55 \text{ momentum units}$$
$$S_1 = \frac{147,551.55}{1,814.40}$$
$$S_1 = 81.32$$
$$S_1 = 81 \text{ km/h at impact}$$

Step 3

Determine the speed of vehicle 1 at the commencement of the skid using Formula 5-35:

United States

$$S_0 = \sqrt{30 \ D_3f + S_1{}^2}$$
$$S_0 = \sqrt{30 \times 50 \times .70 + 50.75^2}$$
$$S_0 = \sqrt{30 \times 50 \times .70 + 2575.56}$$
$$S_0 = \sqrt{3625.56}$$
$$S_0 = 60.21$$
$$S_0 = 60 \text{ mph at commencement of skid}$$

Metric

$$S_0 = \sqrt{254 \ D_3f + S_1{}^2}$$
$$S_0 = \sqrt{254 \times 15.2 \times .70 + 81.32^2}$$
$$S_0 = \sqrt{254 \times 15.2 \times .70 + 6612.94}$$
$$S_0 = \sqrt{9315.5}$$
$$S_0 = 96.5$$
$$S_0 = 96 \text{ km/h at commencement of skid}$$

where S_0 = initial speed of vehicle
D_3 = skid distance
f = coefficient of friction
S_1 = impact speed

The numbers 30 and 254 represent squares of the numbers 5.5 and 15.9 respectively, which are constants in calculating speed.

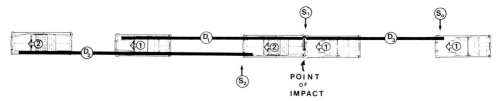

Figure 5-35

Example 3

Vehicles 1 and 2 were travelling in the same direction. Vehicle 1 struck the rear of vehicle 2. If the speed of one of the vehicles at the time of impact can be established, the speed of the other may be calculated. In most instances, it is necessary to rely on driver 2's estimate or knowledge of his own speed or evidence given by other witnesses. If the speed is given as approximate, the calculated speed for the other vehicle will likewise be approximate. In these situations, we may determine the speed of vehicle 1 (S_1) at the time of impact using Formula 5-36:

United States

$$W_1S_1 + W_2S_2 = W_1 \sqrt{30D_1f} + W_2 \sqrt{30D_2f}$$

Metric

$$W_1S_1 + W_2S_2 = W_1 \sqrt{254D_1f} + W_2 \sqrt{254D_2f}$$

In this case, we will assume that the investigation revealed the following information:

$$
\begin{aligned}
W_1 &= 2{,}000 \text{ lb } (907.2 \text{ kg}) \\
W_2 &= 2{,}500 \text{ lb } (1134 \text{ kg}) \\
S_2 &= 20 \text{ mph } (32 \text{ km/h}) \text{ (driver's statement)} \\
D_1 &= 25 \text{ ft } (7.6 \text{ m}) \text{ after impact} \\
D_2 &= 35 \text{ ft } (10.67 \text{ m}) \text{ after impact} \\
f &= .60
\end{aligned}
$$

United States

$$
\begin{aligned}
W_1S_1 + W_2S_2 &= 2{,}000 \sqrt{30 \times 25 \times .60} \\
&+ 2{,}500 \sqrt{30 \times 35 \times .60} \\
&= 2{,}000 \sqrt{450} + 2{,}500 \sqrt{630} \\
&= 2{,}000 \times 21.21 + 2{,}500 \times 25.10 \\
&= 42{,}420 + 62{,}750 \\
&= 105{,}170 \text{ momentum units}
\end{aligned}
$$

$$
\begin{aligned}
2{,}000 \times S_1 + (2{,}500 \times 20) &= 105{,}170 \\
2{,}000 \times S_1 + 50{,}000 &= 105{,}170 \\
2{,}000 \times S_1 &= 105{,}170 - 50{,}000 \\
2{,}000 \times S_1 &= 55{,}170 \\
S_1 &= \frac{55{,}170}{2{,}000} \\
S_1 &= 27.59 \\
S_1 &= 28 \text{ mph at impact}
\end{aligned}
$$

Metric

$$W_1 S_1 + W_2 S_2 = 907.2 \sqrt{254 \times 7.6 \times .60}$$
$$+ 11.34 \sqrt{254 \times 10.67 \times .60}$$
$$= 907.2 \sqrt{1,158.24} + 1,134 \sqrt{1626.11}$$
$$= 907.2 \times 34 + 1,134 \times 40.33$$
$$= 30,844.8 + 45,734.22$$
$$= 76,579.02 \text{ momentum units}$$

$$907.2 \times S_1 + (1,134 \times 32) = 76,579.02$$
$$907.2 \times S_1 + 36,288 = 76,579.02$$
$$907.2 \times S_1 = 76,579.02 - 36,288$$
$$907.2 \times S_1 = 40,291.02$$
$$S_1 = \frac{40,291.02}{907.2}$$
$$S_1 = 44.41$$
$$S_1 = 44 \text{ km/h at impact}$$

If, in this case, vehicle 1 skidded before striking vehicle 2, the speed at the commencement of its skid, S_0, may be calculated using Formula 5-35.

Example 4

Vehicle 1 was travelling east on A Street and collided at right angles with vehicle 2, which was travelling north on B Street. When two vehicles collide at right angles, which is common in intersection accidents, their speeds at the time of impact may be calculated using Formula 5-37 for vehicle 1:

$$S'_1 = S_1 \cos \theta + \frac{W_2}{W_1} S_2 \cos \phi$$

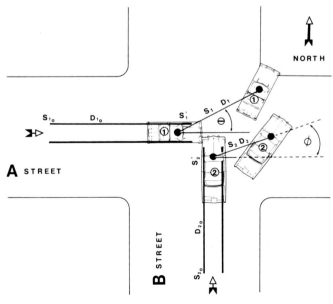

Figure 5-36

And Formula 5-38 for vehicle 2:

$$S'_2 = \frac{W_1}{W_2} S_1 \sin \theta + S_2 \sin \phi$$

where S'_1 = speed of vehicle 1 at time of impact
S_1 = speed of vehicle 1 immediately after impact
S'_2 = speed of vehicle 2 at time of impact
S_2 = speed of vehicle 2 immediately after impact
W_1 = weight of vehicle 1
W_2 = weight of vehicle 2
$\cos \theta$ = cosine of angle θ (theta) or the angle at which vehicle 1 departed the point of impact, measured from mass centers
$\sin \theta$ = sine of angle θ
$\sin \phi$ = sine of angle ϕ (phi) or the angle at which vehicle 2 departed the point of impact, measured from mass centers
$\cos \phi$ = cosine of angle ϕ

In this example, both drivers applied their brakes and skidded into the intersection, where they collided, then separated and skidded to rest in the intersection. Investigation at the scene revealed the following information:

D_{1o} = 35 ft (10.67 m)   The skid distance of vehicle 1 before impact
D_{2o} = 25 ft (7.62 m)   Skid distance of vehicle 2 before impact
D_1 = 30 ft (9.14 m)   Skid or slide distance between centers of mass of vehicle 1 from point of impact to point of rest
D_2 = 20 ft (6 m)   Skid or slide distance between centers of mass of vehicle 2 from point of impact to point of rest
W_1 = 3,500 lb (1587.6 kg)   Weight of vehicle 1
W_2 = 4,500 lb (2041.2 kg)   Weight of vehicle 2
f = .75   Coefficient of friction
θ = 28°   Angle for vehicle 1
ϕ = 20°   Angle for vehicle 2

Step 1. Determine speeds of both vehicles after impact (S_1 and S_2). Remember, the skid distance is considered to be the distance a vehicle moves from point of impact to point of rest, measured from mass center to mass center. To calculate vehicle speeds based on skid distances D_1 and D_2, use Formula 5-4 or Table 5-III:

$$S_1 = 26 \text{ mph (41.8 km/h)}$$
$$S_2 = 21 \text{ mph (33.8 km/h)}$$

Step 2. Determine speeds of vehicles at point of impact (S'_1 and S'_2):

United States

Vehicle 1

$$S'_1 = S_1 \cos \theta + \frac{W_2}{W_1} S_2 \cos \phi$$

$$S'_1 = (26)(.883) + \left(\frac{4500}{3500}\right) (21)(.94)$$

$$S'_1 = 22.96 + 1.29 \times 19.74$$
$$S'_1 = 22.96 + 25.46$$

$$S'_1 = 48.42$$
$$S'_1 = 48 \text{ mph}$$

Vehicle 2

$$S'_2 = \frac{W_1}{W_2} S_1 \sin \phi + S_2 \sin \theta$$

$$S'_2 = \left(\frac{3500}{4500}\right) (26)(.342) + (21)(.47)$$

$$S'_2 = (.778)(8.89) + 9.87$$
$$S'_2 = 6.916 + 9.87$$
$$S'_2 = 16.79$$
$$S'_2 = 17 \text{ mph}$$

Metric

Vehicle 1

$$S'_1 = S_1 \cos \theta + \frac{W_2}{W_1} S_2 \cos \phi$$

$$S'_1 = (41.8)(.883) + \left(\frac{2041.2}{1587.6}\right) (33.8)(.94)$$

$$S'_1 = 36.91 + 1.29 \times 31.772$$
$$S'_1 = 36.9 + 40.986$$
$$S'_1 = 77.886$$
$$S'_1 = 78 \text{ km/h}$$

Vehicle 2

$$S'_2 = \frac{W_1}{W_2} S_1 \sin \phi + S_2 \sin \theta$$

$$S'_2 = \left(\frac{1587.6}{2041.2}\right) (41.8)(.342) + (33.8)(.47)$$

$$S'_2 = .778 \times 14.30 + 15.886$$
$$S'_2 = 11 + 15.886$$
$$S'_2 = 26.886$$
$$S'_2 = 27 \text{ km/h}$$

To calculate the speeds of vehicles 1 and 2 at the commencement of their skid marks, use Formula 5-35:

United States

$$S_0 = \sqrt{30D_0f + (S'^2)}$$

Metric

$$S_0 = \sqrt{254D_0f + (S'^2)}$$

where S_0 = initial speed of vehicle
D_0 = skid distance
f = coefficient of friction
S' = speed at point of impact

Vehicle 1

$$S_{1_0} = \sqrt{30D_{1_0}f + (S'_1{}^2)}$$
$$S_{1_0} = \sqrt{(30)(35)(.75) + (48^2)}$$
$$S_{1_0} = \sqrt{787.5 + 2304}$$
$$S_{1_0} = \sqrt{3091.5}$$
$$S_{1_0} = 55.6$$
$$S_{1_0} = 56 \text{ mph}$$

$$S_{1_0} = \sqrt{254D_{1_0}f + (S'_1{}^2)}$$
$$S_{1_0} = \sqrt{(254)(10.67)(.75) + (78^2)}$$
$$S_{1_0} = \sqrt{2032.64 + 6084}$$
$$S_{1_0} = \sqrt{8116.64}$$
$$S_{1_0} = 90 \text{ km/h}$$

Vehicle 2

$$S_{2_0} = \sqrt{30D_2 f + (S'_2{}^2)}$$
$$S_{2_0} = \sqrt{(30)(25)(.75) + (17^2)}$$
$$S_{2_0} = \sqrt{562.5 + 289}$$
$$S_{2_0} = \sqrt{8515}$$
$$S_{2_0} = 29.18$$
$$S_{2_0} = 29 \text{ mph}$$

$$S_{2_0} = \sqrt{254D_2 f + (S'_2{}^2)}$$
$$S_{2_0} = \sqrt{(254)(7.62)(.75) + (27^2)}$$
$$S_{2_0} = \sqrt{1451.61 + 729}$$
$$S_{2_0} = \sqrt{2180.61}$$
$$S_{2_0} = 46.7$$
$$S_{2_0} = 47 \text{ km/h}$$

Chapter 6

FAILURE TO REMAIN AT SCENE OF ACCIDENT

6.001 The failure of a driver to remain at the scene of an accident involving another vehicle or a pedestrian is a serious and, in most jurisdictions, a criminal offence. This type of accident involves the same accident investigation procedures as other serious motor vehicle accidents except that the investigation must be enlarged to locate a driver and vehicle involved.

6.002 Initial hit-and-run investigations should try to determine as many facts about the offending vehicle, the driver and passengers as possible.

Vehicle
1. Licence number and jurisdiction
2. Make and model
3. Color
4. Odd or noticeable noises, e.g., loud muffler, loose fenders or bumper, dragging tailpipe, horn
5. Descriptive items
   a. Windshield or window stickers
   b. Dented or damaged body, particularly fenders
   c. Headlamps, e.g. one or two on each side and whether they were all working
   e. Taillamps, e.g., number on each side, their size, shape and color and whether they were all working
   f. Parking lights, e.g., size, shape and color and whether they were all working
   g. Ornaments, e.g., ornaments on hood, fenders, aerial, steering wheel and wheels or hanging from windshield or windows
   h. Broken or cracked windshield or windows
   i. Distinctive color or color combinations
6. Physical evidence at scene
   a. Broken headlamp, window or windshield glass
   b. Body parts, e.g., metal fragments from fenders, headlamp rims, door handles, hubcaps
   c. Paint chips or scrapings

    d. Mud or dirt fallen from vehicles, particularly underbody dirt and other debris

    e. Objects such as part of vehicle load that may have fallen off of or out of vehicle

    f. Tire prints

7. Direction of travel before and after accident

Driver and Passengers

1. Male or female, age
2. Physical features, e.g., height, weight, color of complexion, eyes, hair, deformities
3. Color and type of clothing
4. Footprints left at scene
5. Fingerprints on articles thrown from vehicle such as liquor bottles

6.003   There are many reasons a driver flees the scene when involved in an accident with another vehicle or a pedestrian. Some of these are:

    a. Driving while under the influence of alcohol or a drug.
    b. Driving without a driver's licence.
    c. Driving without insurance coverage.
    d. Married person accompanied by other than his or her spouse.
    e. Having stolen goods in vehicle.
    f. Fleeing another previous accident.
    g. Fleeing scene of criminal offence such as armed robbery.
    h. Driver "wanted" for a crime.
    i. Panic struck. When a suspect driver is located and the only reason he has to offer for leaving the accident scene is that he panicked, his background, associates and activities just prior to the accident should be investigated.

6.004   Upon arrival at the accident scene, the investigator should check and make notes of persons and license plate numbers of vehicles found at or near the scene. Question victims and witnesses and examine the scene in an attempt to gain sufficient evidence and information to commence a deeper investigation and to alert other investigative units for assistance. The investigator should bear in mind that the hit-and-run driver may return to the scene through curiosity or to try to discover what evidence the investigator is able to uncover.

6.005   An attempt to locate witnesses should be made not only at the scene, but also in the immediate neighborhood. Someone working or driving in the area may have been attracted by an erratic driver or for some other reason observed a suspect vehicle.

6.006   It may be necessary to rope off the area in order that short-lived or delicate evidence not be lost or destroyed. In serious cases, a systematic search of the scene for evidence and clues should be made using several investigators in such a way as to ensure that a most minute examination is conducted. The path taken by the hit-and-run vehicle away from the scene should be examined in the event evidence was carried and dropped from the vehicle or thrown out of vehicle as it departed. Similarly, depending on the speed of the vehicle and force of impact, vehicle parts and other evidence might be thrown for a considerable distance from the place of impact in the direction of the force.

6.007   Stolen car files for recently stolen vehicles resembling the hit-and-run vehicle must be checked. An immediate patrol should be made along the departure path of the vehicle in the event it was abandoned. In a hit-and-run investigation, the investigator must give careful consideration to a complaint of a stolen vehicle. Drivers involved in this type of accident sometimes report their vehicles stolen and by various devious means attempt to establish that the vehicle was stolen prior to the time of the accident. Such reports should be reviewed in relation to evidence gathered at the accident scene.

6.008   Garages, body shops, used car lots, parking lots and other places where a vehicle may be repaired or stored should be checked as soon as possible. In most cases, if a vehicle is not located in a reasonable time after an accident, it may be assumed that the driver has placed it in a private garage or destroyed it. A destroyed vehicle, for example, burned or driven over an embankment should be examined closely for evidence that might match it up with evidence found at the accident scene.

6.009   Assistance of the news media such as radio, TV and newspapers should be solicited. They are usually cooperative in these cases, and their coverage is greater than what could be done by police investigation alone.

6.010   A broken part found at the scene may establish the make, model and year of the hit-and-run vehicle by simple comparison of that part with the same part of another vehicle. Parts men in garages are often able to offer advice in this regard to establish the make, model and type of vehicle that the part came from or at least to narrow the field of possibilities to assist in further investigation.

6.011   When a suspect vehicle is located, it should be examined for damaged parts and traces of blood, paint, hair and fibers. Special attention should be given to all protruding parts such as door handles, grille, radiator or hood ornaments and bumper guards where foreign objects might be caught. This type of evidence can be matched scientifically to similar evidence obtained from a victim. Evidence of recent damages, repairs, new paint jobs or wash jobs should be carefully noted and recorded. If new parts have replaced damaged parts, the old or damaged parts should be recovered for matching purposes. If a suspect vehicle has been washed, blood stains or flesh may still be found in such places as openings in the auto body, the undercarriage and the frame, in various crevices, behind the grille, lodged in the radiator, and so on. Soil samples found on the vehicle or that have been washed off should be collected for matching with soil at the scene.

6.012   The undercarriage of a suspect vehicle should be examined for areas that have recently been rubbed clean, scraped or damaged. Protruding parts, for example, bolts, frame or steering parts, should also be examined for hairs, fibers and blood spots.

6.013   Scientific examination and analysis is one of the investigator's most valuable and effective weapons in the investigation of hit-and-run accidents. Some of the most common types of evidence found in hit-and-run investigations are amenable to scientific analysis. Many police departments have crime detection laboratories with chemists, metallurgists and engineers on staff. If they are not available as part of the police laboratory, it may be necessary to obtain their services either from the public or private sector. Scientific examinations can in many instances determine the make and year of a vehicle from paint residues or determine whether the vehicle had been painted with paint other than its original color. Clothing of a pedestrian accident victim should be submitted for laboratory examination to determine whether paint or dirt residue is imbedded in the clothing material. Such residue might be matched to similar material found on a suspect vehicle. Examinations can also determine whether lights were on or off at time of collision, match broken or damaged parts, and match and determine blood, hair and fiber types (see Fig. 4-11).

6.014   All pieces of glass found at the accident scene should be collected and carefully preserved. Motor vehicle headlamp, windshield and side window glass fragments and glass fragments found in or on the clothing of an accident victim can yield valuable information pertaining to the hit-and-run vehicle when submitted to laboratory examination. Examinations can physically match two or more pieces of glass and reconstruct glass items such as a headlamp or window. In many cases a positive identification can be made between pieces found at the accident scene and pieces found on a suspect vehicle. Additionally, laboratory examinations are able to determine whether glass pieces have similar properties and whether they have a common origin.

6.015   When seeking the assistance or expertise of professionals or specialists in a particular field, it is very important that the investigator tell him precisely what is required of him for the investigation. Failure to do this often results in considerable work being done that is not required and that possibly has no bearing on the matter under investigation.

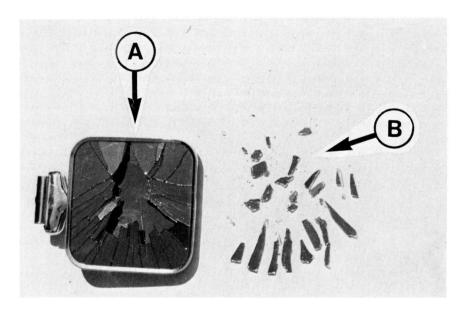

Figure 6-1. Broken mirror, *A*, found on vehicle should be matched up with glass fragments, *B*, found at accident scene.

6.016 Regular patrols to the scene should be made at the same time of day and on the same day of the week subsequent to the accident. A suspicious vehicle or a vehicle answering the description of the suspect vehicle or driver may be seen because many drivers, of course, travel a route as the result of habit or because of employment. Such a driver may have been involved or he might have seen the suspect vehicle. Spot traffic checks in the vicinity at this time may result in contacting a witness to the accident.

Chapter 7

PHOTOGRAPHY

7.001 An investigator must be familiar with the operation of his camera under various conditions. Camera operation is not a subject of this text; however, it should be a part of an investigator's training. There are various sources for this training, including many texts for self-study and improvement.

Photography serves to:

a. Provide a permanent and accurate record of observable accident information that may be used for many purposes, including court evidence.
b. Support or verify other evidence such as verbal and written statements.
c. Match up two or more pieces of evidence, e.g., contact damages, prints on shoe soles with brake pedal or accelerator pedal tread patterns.
d. Enable an investigator or witnesses to more accurately describe an accident scene or some aspect of evidence and to refresh their memories at a later time.
e. Permit a subsequent examination of the scene, objects or other evidence, e.g., tire marks, liquid spills or paths. Skillful use of a camera often brings out evidence during subsequent examination of pictures that would otherwise possibly be unobserved.
f. Assist a prosecutor in deciding whether a prosecution should be entered.
g. Assist in settling civil claims for damages.
h. Assist a professional accident reconstructionist in reconstructing an accident.

7.002 Probably one of an investigator's greatest concerns is deciding which photographs to take. Experience can possibly solve this problem for him. Certainly, photographs are not required in all accidents. If there is any doubt about whether they are required, however, the investigator should take photographs. As a general rule, as many meaningful photographs as possible or, depending upon the circumstances, are warranted, should be taken. An investigator should not be criticized unfavorably for

Figure 7-1. Photograph showing the position of vehicle on roadway at the commencement of the skid, *A*. The skid marks are tied to the vehicle that made them, *B*, and the positions of traffic lights are indicated at *C*.

taking too many photographs, providing that amongst them are pictures sufficient to satisfy the requirements of that investigation.

7.003 Upon arrival at an accident scene, an investigator should take several photographs from various angles as soon as possible so that vital or short-lived evidence such as blood, water spatters or trails, light skid marks is not lost or altered. When more than one investigator arrives at the scene, one should be assigned to take photographs immediately. When it is not possible to photograph evidence before it is moved from the original location, its position should be outlined with chalk so that the location can be photographed later.

7.004 The investigator should be careful to keep the camera on a level plane. If it is tilted up, down or sideways, the picture may suggest a grade or superelevation that does not exist.

7.005 Photographs should be taken from various angles and distances in such a way as to clearly depict the distances and relationships of all things. Particular attention should be given to the relationships of vehicles and pedestrians to the edges of the roadway, lane and center roadway markings and crosswalks. Photographs should be taken parallel to the roadway

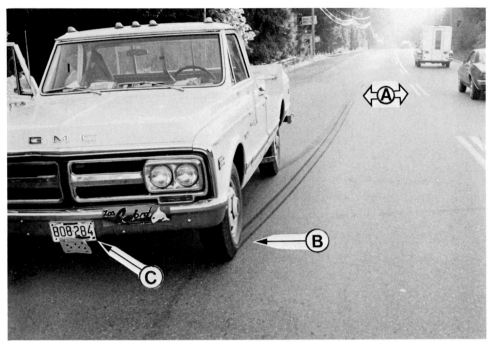

Figure 7-2. Photograph showing vehicle placement on roadway during braking action, *A* and *B*, and vehicle identification, *C*.

at various locations and at right angles to the roadway to properly record these positions.

7.006 Pictures should include vehicle licence plate numbers, vehicle damages, roadway conditions, roadway markings, roadway damages, view obstructions, traffic-control devices, surrounding terrain if applicable, skid and tire marks and all other matter of evidence that relates to the accident.

7.007 Photographs should be taken not only to show visible evidence but also to show that certain evidence did not exist, for example, lack of skid marks, vehicle damages, view obstructions and others.

7.008 The investigator should record the location, date, time, weather conditions, position of camera from which each photograph is taken and measurements from camera to objects in the picture.

7.009 Photographs should be taken from eye level in a sequence or series of events as a party to the accident would have viewed the area. The investigator should consider simulating vehicle and pedestrian positions as indicated by the series of events and taking a sequence of photographs to show their visibility at various locations.

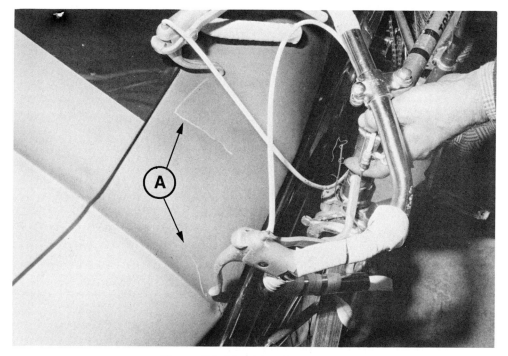

Figure 7-3. Matching damages, *A*.

7.010 Photographs do not replace the need to take and properly record measurements, descriptions of vehicles, damages and other data. Rather, they should supplement the many notes and records an investigator must make during his investigation.

7.011 Matching damages should be photographed (Fig. 7-3). Photograph vehicle parts that cause roadway damage and the roadway damage itself. Similarly, matching broken vehicle parts should be photographed.

7.012 If there are sufficient points of comparison, vehicle damages may show points and position and direction of thrust during primary and secondary contacts. Overhead pictures often help in showing matching damages to vehicles. This type of evidence is very important and helpful in giving testimony as well as reconstructing accidents.

7.013 When photographing skid marks, the relationship to the vehicle that made them and the position in relation to the roadway center line and lane markings and roadway edge should be shown. Skid marks should also be photographed from each end and from a right angle, ensuring that each end of the skid mark is included. In this way, direction of travel,

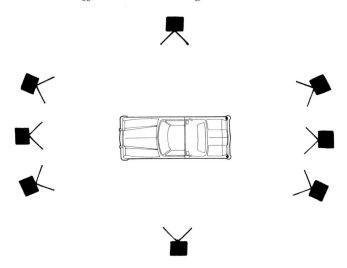

Figure 7-4. Camera positions.

impending skid marks, deviation from a straight skid, action at the end of the skid mark and the skid mark length are recorded.

7.014 Photographs should be taken of both sides, front end and rear end of a vehicle to show damage or lack of damage and damage location on the vehicle itself. Additional photographs, including close-ups, should be taken to show damage detail.

7.015 Corner photographs are generally necessary only to show damage and should be taken to supplement other photographs. Normally, they do not give adequate detail from which to reconstruct an accident.

7.016 Close-up photographs should be taken of tire marks so as to show tread grooves, roadway grooves, chips, gouges and marks that do not permit proper evaluation with distance photography. All close-up photographs should, however, be supported with distant photographs to show relationships of that evidence to other evidence at the scene.

7.017 Color photography should be used when paint colors, new and old damages and hair fibers are a part of evidence.

7.018 Night photographs should be supplemented with daytime photographs of the same scene or location for record purposes.

7.019 When a driver, passenger or pedestrian is injured or killed as a result of having impact with a vehicle part, the part should be noted and photographed. This type of evidence can be useful to pathologists and coroners in determining cause of death and can be of assistance to vehicle administrators in setting construction standards.

Chapter 8

FIELD MEASUREMENTS AND SCALE DIAGRAMS

REASONS TO MEASURE

8.001   An investigator should take or ensure that sufficient and accurate measurements are taken at an accident scene in order to avoid conjecture in locating things later in the investigation, preparing a scale diagram or giving evidence in court.

8.002   Measurements are required to show distances between vehicles, bodies, objects and other things at an accident scene. These measurements, however, are not always the measurements required to prepare a scale diagram. In Figure 8-1, for example, the measurements are sufficient to fix the vehicle and body on a scale diagram or to reposition them at the accident scene. However, for court evidence purposes, additional measurements such as those in Figure 8-2 would also be required. It is important to remember that in taking field measurements, the measurements taken must be sufficient to satisfy both of these requirements.

8.003   In most cases, an investigator is able to adequately measure the accident scene. In serious or complicated cases, however, a surveyor or civil engineer may be used to take measurements at the scene and to prepare scale drawings. When this is done, it is important that the investigator accompany the surveyor or engineer at the scene and explain to him precisely what measurements are required. Measurements so taken must be in addition to and not in place of measurements taken by an investigator as part of his investigation.

MEASUREMENTS TO BE TAKEN

8.004   Upon arriving at an accident scene, the investigator must decide what to measure and how the measurements can best be completed along with the many other urgent requirements of him at the scene.

8.005   The positions of vehicles and other things that are not likely to be immediately moved from their final positions can be measured after the immediate concerns such as caring for the injured, ensuring the safety of the scene and short-lived evidence measurements are taken care of.

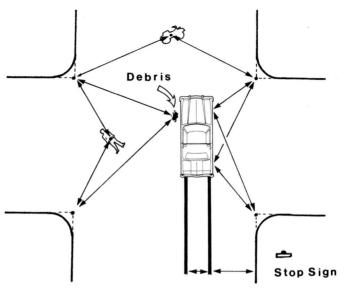

Figure 8-1. Measurements taken at scene using triangulation method to locate positions of things for use in preparing scale diagram.

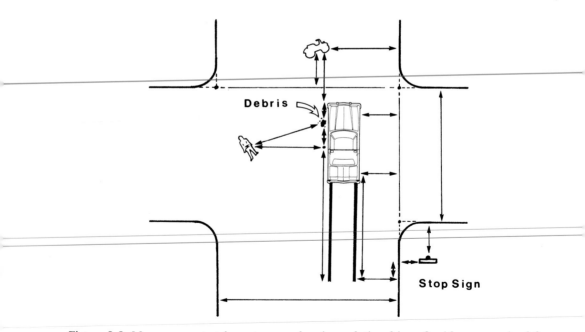

Figure 8-2. Measurements taken at scene showing relationships of evidence required for court purposes, such as relationship of stop sign to where vehicle began to skid, lengths of skid marks, distances motorcycle and operator were thrown after impact, and so on.

8.006 Some measurements, at least, should be taken at all accident scenes. The seriousness of the accident dictates the extent of measurements required. Generally, comprehensive measurements should be taken in all fatal and personal injury accidents. Measurements should also be taken in accidents where the driver may be prosecuted for a driving infraction.

8.007 Measurements are often taken that are not needed later. It is far better to have too many measurements than not enough. Because measurements may be made simply and quickly, many should be taken in the event they are required later.

8.008 An investigator is often required to appear as a witness years later; measurements properly taken will assist him in refreshing his memory of the accident. In all accident cases, the professional investigator gathers sufficient evidence so as to enable him to testify with precision and confidence about his observations of where things were regardless of when or where he might be called upon to give evidence.

8.009 For reasons of safety, measurements should be taken along the edge of the roadway whenever possible. The edge of the roadway often suffices as a baseline from which other measurements may be taken.

SCALE DIAGRAMS

8.010 Provided that proper and sufficient measurements are taken at an accident scene, it is quite easy to reconstruct the scene to scale on a diagram. The investigator must choose the scale he wishes to use for his scale diagram. For example, he may wish to choose an inch or any part thereof to represent one foot. In metric measurements, he may choose one millimeter or one centimeter to represent one meter or a greater number of meters. For example, ¼ in = 1 ft, 1 in = 10 ft, 1 in = 20 ft, or 1 mm = 1 m, 1 cm = 1 m, 1 cm = 10 m, 1 cm = 20 m, and so forth.

8.011 A sharp-pointed pencil or pen must be used to prepare a scale diagram. A broad point may otherwise represent several inches (centime-

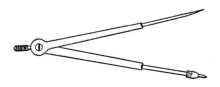

Figure 8-3. Compass.

Figure 8-4. Ruler.

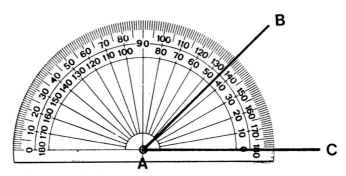

Figure 8-5. Protractor.

ters) or even feet (meters), depending upon the scale being used. Other items should include:

    a. Compass (Fig. 8-3)
    b. Ruler (United States or metric) (Fig. 8-4)
    c. Protractor (Fig. 8-5)

A traffic engineer's traffic template is also very beneficial to the investigator. Many such templates have cutouts for vehicles, traffic lights, traffic-control devices, scale curves and a protractor. A good template can save many hours' labor in calculations and scale drawings.

MEASURING AND RECORDING

8.012 It is often necessary to determine the distance a vehicle fell or rolled over an embankment, off a bridge, into a ditch, or flew through the air, striking an elevated object or landing on the ground at a different level than where it left the roadway. There are several different ways to measure these distances. They may be measured directly with a tape measure if the distances are not too great or if it is convenient to do so. However, there are many instances in which it is not possible to take measurements of the distances with a tape. In these cases, the investigator may wish to have the measurements taken by a surveyor or an engineer. If he can satisfy his investigation with an approximate distance, however, he may do so quite easily by applying a few simple rules of geometry or trigonometry, which will be explained later in this chapter.

8.013 For measurements required over extended distances, use an assistant. Have the assistant hold the *zero* end of the tape. Always keep the tape taut. The *investigator* must read the measurements from the tape or measuring device as well as record the measurements.

8.014 For measurements in excess of the tape length, make a crayon mark at the end of the tape, also marking the number of feet (meters) on the pavement beside the mark. Allow the assistant to come to this mark and observe him put the zero end of the tape at the mark. Then, continue on to complete additional measurements.

8.015 For measurements of less than 12 ft (3 m), use a pocket-type tape measure.

8.016 Measurements should be taken to the closest inch or even centimeter.

8.017 A rolling-wheel measuring device is quite suitable for measuring long distances. Caution must be used, however, when measurements are being made on slippery surfaces or surfaces covered by loose material such as coarse sand or gravel. Under these conditions, the wheel may skip or slide, and recorded measurements may be shorter than the actual distance.

8.018 Measurements may be made by pacing or heel-to-toe steps. When the investigator uses the pacing method, he should first determine what his pacing distance is, then multiply that distance by the number of paces made over the given distance. This method can be expected to have an error rate as much as ±10 percent. In the heel-to-toe step method, the investigator should record the length of the shoes worn and multiply this by the number of heel-to-toe movements made. These methods of measuring should be used only as a last resort, as they denote a lack of professionalism and can be strongly objected to in court.

8.019 In measuring great distances, the average lengths of broken center lines on the roadway and distances that separate them or the distances between utility poles may be measured and multiplied by their number over the distances being measured. In the case of broken center lines, measure the distance from the beginning of one center line to the beginning of the next center line. This distance represents the combined distances of a center line and the space separating it from the next line. To make the measurement over a given distance, simply multiply the number of center lines by the combined distances. In Figure 8-6, the distance from the beginning of one line to the beginning of the next line is 40 ft (12 m). The distance from *A* to *B* is 7 × 40 = 280 ft (7 × 12 = 84 m).

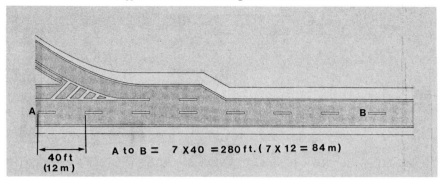

Figure 8-6. By knowing the distance from the beginning of one center line to the beginning of the next, it is possible to measure distances by simply multiplying the distance from one center line to the next by the number of center lines over the distance to be measured.

8.020 In writing measurements, the investigator should not use the apostrophe (') nor the quote mark (") to indicate feet and inches. These symbols can be easily mistaken for the numbers 1 and 11. Record feet and inches in the manner outlined in the following examples:[24]

  a. Record fifteen feet and three inches as $15^{\underline{3}}$.
  b. Record ten feet as $10^{\underline{0}}$.
  c. Record eighteen inches as $^{\underline{18}}$.

8.021 When using measuring devices marked in feet and tenths of a foot, use the decimal point to set out the tenths of a foot.

  a. Record nine feet as 9.0.
  b. Record nine and five-tenths feet as 9.5.

8.022 When using the metric system of measurement, indicate whether the measurements are in centimeters (cm), meters (m) or kilometers (km).

  a. Record 8.24 centimeters as 8.24 cm.
  b. Record 8.24 meters as 8.24 m.
  c. Record 8.24 kilometers as 8.24 km.

8.023 Most measurements at an accident scene are in meters or parts of a meter. It is acceptable to show all measurements in meters or parts of a meter without being followed by the meter designation provided that any other measurement such as centimeters also taken at the scene or otherwise recorded in the investigation is properly designated.

APPLICATION OF MATHEMATICS

8.024 It is essential that an investigator be knowledgeable in the basic mathematics involved in taking measurements at an accident scene, preparing a field sketch and drawing a scale diagram. Not only should the investigator have this knowledge for investigation purposes, but he should

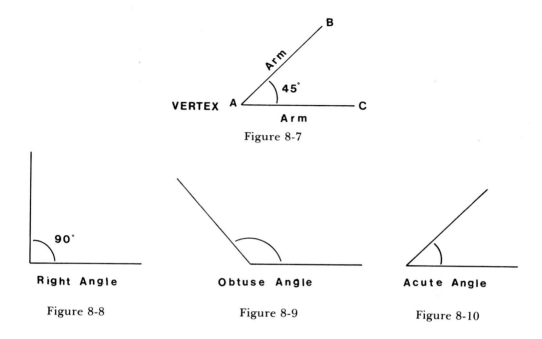

Figure 8-7

Right Angle

Figure 8-8

Obtuse Angle

Figure 8-9

Acute Angle

Figure 8-10

also have it for purposes of relating to other professionals in the accident investigation field and giving evidence in court.

Plane Geometry

A *plane* is a flat surface that has length and breadth but no thickness. A figure drawn on a plane is called *plane geometry*. A *plane figure* is the portion of a plane surface bounded by one line, in the case of a circle, or more lines, in the case of other figures such as triangles.

Angles

When two straight lines meet at a point, they are said to form an *angle*. In Figure 8-7, the straight lines *AB* and *AC* are called *arms* of the angle. The point at which they meet, *A*, is called the *vertex*. The angle does not depend on the length of the arms but only on the amount of their opening at the vertex. In an angle, the arms and vertex are designated by capital letters, and the middle letter in any reference to the angle represents the angle. For example, in Figure 8-7, the angle at *A* in *BAC* is 45°.

Angles are measured in degrees. An *acute* angle is one that is less than 90°. An *obtuse* angle is one greater than 90°. A *right* angle is 90°.

8.025 Figure 8-11 represents measurements taken at the scene of an accident on a field sketch. The angle drawn at the scene can be called angle

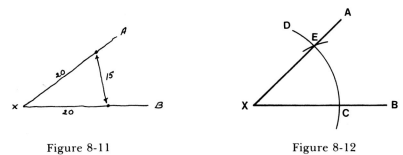

Figure 8-11   Figure 8-12

TRIANGLES

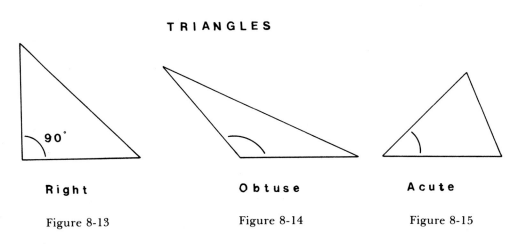

Right   **Obtuse**   **Acute**

Figure 8-13   Figure 8-14   Figure 8-15

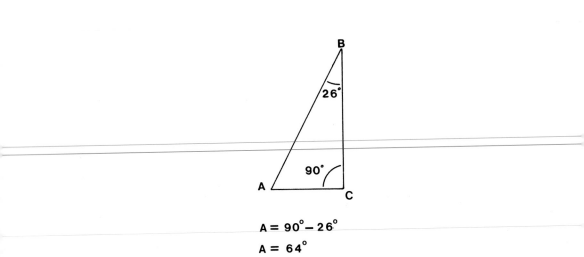

$$A = 90° - 26°$$
$$A = 64°$$

Figure 8-16

AXB. Using the compass and a ruler, this angle may be duplicated to scale in the following manner (Fig. 8-12):

   a. Draw a baseline *XB* at any convenient length.
   b. Open the compass to a distance of 20 (ft or m) at the required scale.
   c. Place the compass pinpoint at *X* and scribe an arc from *C* to *D*.
   d. Open the compass to 15 (ft or m) at the required scale.
   e. Place the pinpoint at *C* and scribe another arc bisecting arc *CD.* Mark this point *E*.
   f. Draw a line *XEA.* Arms *A* and *B* provide the required angle.

Triangle

8.026   A *triangle* is a three-sided figure. In the case of acute, obtuse and right triangles, they are actually acute, obtuse and right *angles* with their *arms* connected by another straight line. The sum of all angles in a triangle always equals 180°.

Right Triangle

8.027   In accident investigation, the right triangle is the one most commonly used. As mentioned previously, a right triangle has one angle that is a right angle at 90°. In a right triangle, the sum of the two acute angles is always 90°. Therefore, if the size of one acute angle is known, it is a simple matter of subtracting that measurement from 90° to obtain the angle of the remaining acute angle.

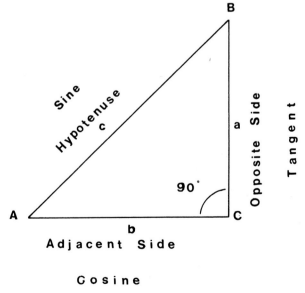

Figure 8-17

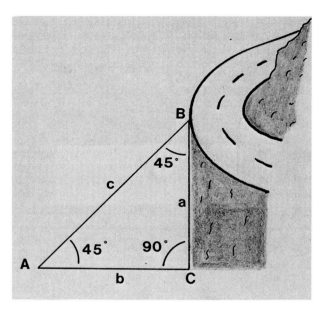

Figure 8-18

8.028 In Figure 8-17, the letters *A*, *B* and *C* denote the angles, and the small letters *a*, *b* and *c* denote the lengths of the sides, *a* being opposite *A*, *b* opposite *B* and *c* (the hypotenuse) opposite *C*.

8.029 If, in Figure 8-18, the investigator wished to determine the approximate height of the cliff (side *a* of the triangle), he should move out to a point where by sighting the hypotenuse to *B*, angle *A* is 45°. This would indicate that the angle at *B* is also 45°. The distance of side *b* could then be measured. Since sides *a* and *b* are equal, the measurement of side *b* would be all that would be necessary to determine the height of the cliff.

Pythagorean Theorem

8.030 If the lengths of two sides of a right triangle are known, the third side may be calculated by using the Pythagorean theorem, which may be stated as follows (Formula 8-1):

In a right triangle, the square of the side opposite the right angle is equal to the sum of the squares of the other two sides.

United States	*Metric*
$c = \sqrt{a^2 + b^2}$	$c = \sqrt{a^2 + b^2}$

where c = hypotenuse
    a = side
    b = side

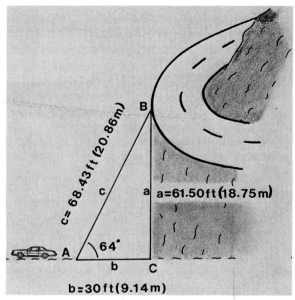

Figure 8-19

Example

8.031 In Figure 8-19, if it is known that side a = 61.5 ft (18.75 m) and side b = 30 ft (9.14 m), then the length of the hypotenuse, c, would be:

$$c = \sqrt{61.5^2 + 30^2}$$
$$c = \sqrt{3782.25 + 900}$$
$$c = \sqrt{4682.25}$$
$$c = 68.43 \text{ ft}$$

$$c = \sqrt{18.75^2 + 9.14^2}$$
$$c = \sqrt{351.56 + 83.54}$$
$$c = \sqrt{435.10}$$
$$c = 20.86 \text{ m}$$

8.032 When the length of one side of a right triangle is known and the length of the hypotenuse is also known, the length of the remaining side may be calculated by using the Pythagorean theorem (Formula 8-2):

United States

$$a = \sqrt{c^2 - b^2}$$

Metric

$$a = \sqrt{c^2 - b^2}$$

Example (using Fig. 8-19

$$a = \sqrt{68.43^2 - 30^2}$$
$$a = \sqrt{4682.66 - 900}$$
$$a = \sqrt{3782.66}$$
$$a = 61.5 \text{ ft}$$

$$a = \sqrt{20.86^2 - 9.14^2}$$
$$a = \sqrt{435.14 - 83.54}$$
$$a = \sqrt{351.60}$$
$$a = 18.75 \text{ m}$$

Trigonometry

8.033 The use of trigonometry provides the investigator with a method of calculating the length of a side of a right triangle if the angle at A is known (*see* Fig. 8-17). As indicated in this figure, a right triangle has an *adjacent* side, *b*, an *opposite* side, *a*, and a hypotenuse, *c*. In trigonometry, the angle at *A* and the ratio of one side to the other side or to the hypotenuse may be used to calculate the length of the remaining side. These ratios are known as the tangent, sine and cosine of the angle *A*.

Tangent

8.034   The value of tangent *A*, abbreviated as *tan A*, in Figure 8-17 is equal to the ratio of the opposite side, *a*, to the adjacent side, *b* (Formula 8-3):

United States

$$\tan A = \frac{a}{b}$$

Metric

$$\tan A = \frac{a}{b}$$

Example

In Figure 8-19, a vehicle left the highway and landed 30 ft (9.14 m), *b*, from the base of a cliff. The angle at *A* where the vehicle landed was 64°. The height of the cliff, *a*, may be calculated by using Formula 8-3:

United States

$$\tan° = \frac{a}{30}$$

Metric

$$\tan° = \frac{a}{9.14}$$

where tangent of 64° = 2.0503 (Table 8-I)

$$\frac{a}{30} = 2.0503$$

$$a = 30 \times 2.0503$$
$$a = 61.5 \text{ ft}$$

$$\frac{a}{9.14} = 2.0503$$

$$a = 9.14 \times 2.0503$$
$$a = 18.74 \text{ m}$$

Sine

8.035   In a right triangle, there are other ratios that may be used instead of the tangent ratio. For example, the ratio of the side opposite, *a*, to the hypotenuse, *c*, is the sine of angle *A*, abbreviated as *sin A*. In Figure 8-19, we know that side *a* = 61.5 ft (18.75 m), the base or adjacent side *b* = 30 ft (9.14 m), and the hypotenuse *c* is 68.43 ft (20.86 m). Assuming that we know only the length of the hypotenuse and the angle of *A* in Figure 8-19, we may calculate the height of the cliff *a* by using Formula 8-4:

United States

$$\sin A = \frac{a}{c}$$

$$\therefore \sin 64° = \frac{a}{68.43}$$

Metric

$$\sin A = \frac{a}{c}$$

$$\therefore \sin 64° = \frac{a}{20.86}$$

where sin of 64° = .8988 (*see* Table 8-I)

$$a = 68.43 \times .8988$$
$$a = 61.5 \text{ ft}$$

$$a = 20.86 \times .8988$$
$$a = 18.75 \text{ m}$$

TABLE 8-I

TABLE OF TRIGONOMETRIC RATIOS

θ	sin θ	cos θ	tan θ	csc θ	sec θ	cot θ
0	.0000	1.0000	.0000		1.0000	
1	.0175	.9998	.0175	57.299	1.0002	57.290
2	.0349	.9994	.0349	28.654	1.0006	28.636
3	.0523	.9986	.0524	19.107	1.0014	19.081
4	.0698	.9976	.0699	14.336	1.0024	14.301
5	.0872	.9962	.0875	11.474	1.0038	11.4301
6	.1045	.9945	.1051	9.5668	1.0055	9.5144
7	.1219	.9925	.1228	8.2055	1.0075	8.1443
8	.1392	.9903	.1405	7.1853	1.0098	7.1154
9	.1564	.9877	.1584	6.3925	1.0125	6.3138
10	.1736	.9848	.1763	5.7588	1.0154	5.6713
11	.1908	.9816	.1944	5.2408	1.0187	5.1446
12	.2079	.9781	.2126	4.8097	1.0223	4.7046
13	.2250	.9744	.2309	4.4454	1.0263	4.3315
14	.2419	.9703	.2493	4.1336	1.0306	4.0108
15	.2588	.9659	.2679	3.8637	1.0353	3.7321
16	.2756	.9613	.2867	3.6280	1.0403	3.4874
17	.2924	.9563	.3057	3.4203	1.0457	3.2709
18	.3090	.9511	.3249	3.2361	1.0515	3.0777
19	.3256	.9455	.3443	3.0716	1.0576	2.9042
20	.3420	.9397	.3640	2.9238	1.0642	2.7475
21	.3584	.9336	.3839	2.7904	1.0711	2.6051
22	.3746	.9272	.4040	2.6695	1.0785	2.4751
23	.3907	.9205	.4245	2.5593	1.0864	2.3559
24	.4067	.9135	.4452	2.4586	1.0946	2.2460
25	.4226	.9063	.4663	2.3662	1.1034	2.1445
26	.4384	.8988	.4877	2.2812	1.1126	2.0503
27	.4540	.8910	.5095	2.2027	1.1223	1.9626
28	.4695	.8829	.5317	2.1301	1.1326	1.8807
29	.4848	.8746	.5543	2.0627	1.1434	1.8041
30	.5000	.8660	.5774	2.0000	1.1547	1.7321
31	.5150	.8572	.6009	1.9416	1.1666	1.6643
32	.5299	.8480	.6249	1.8871	1.1792	1.6003
33	.5446	.8387	.6494	1.8361	1.1924	1.5399
34	.5592	.8290	.6745	1.7883	1.2062	1.4826
35	.5736	.8192	.7002	1.7434	1.2208	1.4281
36	.5878	.8090	.7265	1.7013	1.2361	1.3764
37	.6018	.7986	.7536	1.6616	1.2521	1.3270
38	.6157	.7880	.7813	1.6243	1.2690	1.2799
39	.6293	.7771	.8098	1.5890	1.2868	1.2349
40	.6428	.7660	.8391	1.5557	1.3054	1.1918
41	.6561	.7547	.8693	1.5243	1.3250	1.1504
42	.6691	.7431	.9004	1.4945	1.3456	1.1106
43	.6820	.7314	.9325	1.4663	1.3673	1.0724
44	.6947	.7193	.9657	1.4396	1.3902	1.0355

Reproduced with permission of Gage Educational Publishing, Limited, Agincourt, Ontario.

TABLE 8-I *(Continued)*
TABLE OF TRIGONOMETRIC RATIOS

θ	sin θ	cos θ	tan θ	csc θ	sec θ	cot θ
45	.7071	.7071	1.0000	1.4142	1.4142	1.0000
46	.7193	.6947	1.0355	1.3902	1.4396	.9657
47	.7314	.6820	1.0724	1.3673	1.4663	.9325
48	.7431	.6691	1.1106	1.3456	1.4945	.9004
49	.7547	.6561	1.1504	1.3250	1.5243	.8693
50	.7660	.6428	1.1918	1.3054	1.5557	.8391
51	.7771	.6293	1.2349	1.2868	1.5890	.8098
52	.7880	.6157	1.2799	1.2690	1.6243	.7813
53	.7986	.6018	1.3270	1.2521	1.6616	.7536
54	.8090	.5878	1.3764	1.2361	1.7013	.7265
55	.8192	.5736	1.4281	1.2208	1.7434	.7002
56	.8290	.5592	1.4826	1.2062	1.7883	.6745
57	.8387	.5446	1.5399	1.1924	1.8361	.6494
58	.8480	.5299	1.6003	1.1792	1.8871	.6249
59	.8572	.5150	1.6643	1.1666	1.9416	.6009
60	.8660	.5000	1.7321	1.1547	2.0000	.5774
61	.8746	.4848	1.8041	1.1434	2.0627	.5543
62	.8829	.4695	1.8807	1.1326	2.1301	.5317
63	.8910	.4540	1.9626	1.1223	2.2027	.5095
64	.8988	.4384	2.0503	1.1126	2.2812	.4877
65	.9063	.4226	2.1445	1.1034	2.3662	.4663
66	.9135	.4067	2.2460	1.0946	2.4586	.4452
67	.9205	.3907	2.3559	1.0864	2.5593	.4245
68	.9272	.3746	2.4751	1.0785	2.6695	.4040
69	.9336	.3584	2.6051	1.0711	2.7904	.3839
70	.9397	.3420	2.7475	1.0642	2.9238	.3640
71	.9455	.3256	2.9042	1.0576	3.0716	.3443
72	.9511	.3090	3.0777	1.0515	3.2361	.3249
73	.9563	.2924	3.2709	1.0457	3.4203	.3057
74	.9613	.2756	3.4874	1.0403	3.6280	.2867
75	.9659	.2588	3.7321	1.0353	3.8637	.2679
76	.9703	.2419	4.0108	1.0306	4.1336	.2493
77	.9744	.2250	4.3315	1.0263	4.4454	.2309
78	.9781	.2079	4.7046	1.0223	4.8097	.2126
79	.9816	.1908	5.1446	1.0187	5.2408	.1944
80	.9848	.1736	5.6713	1.0154	5.7588	.1763
81	.9877	.1564	6.3138	1.0125	6.3925	.1584
82	.9903	.1392	7.1154	1.0098	7.1853	.1405
83	.9925	.1219	8.1443	1.0075	8.2055	.1228
84	.9945	.1045	9.5144	1.0055	9.5668	.1051
85	.9962	.0872	11.4301	1.0038	11.474	.0875
86	.9976	.0698	14.301	1.0024	14.336	.0699
87	.9986	.0523	19.081	1.0014	19.107	.0524
88	.9994	.0349	28.636	1.0006	28.654	.0349
89	.9998	.0175	57.290	1.0002	57.299	.0175
90	1.0000	.0000		1.0000		.0000

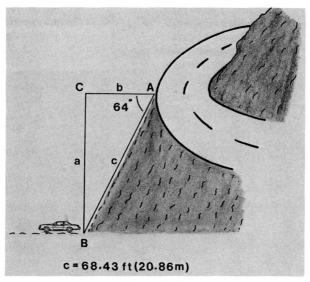

c = 68.43 ft (20.86m)

Figure 8-20

Example

In Figure 8-20, a vehicle left the highway at *A* and rolled down an embankment to *B*. The angle at *A* was 64°. By using a tape, the embankment (hypotenuse of the right triangle), *c*, was measured at 68.43 ft (20.86 m). The height of the embankment, side *a* of the triangle, was 61.5 ft (18.75 m), as calculated in the foregoing example.

Cosine

8.036 If the angle of *A* and the length of the hypotenuse, *c*, are known, the length of the *adjacent* side, *b*, may be calculated. This is the ratio of the adjacent side, *b*, to the hypotenuse, *c*, and is called the *cosine* of the angle *A*, abbreviated as *cos A* (Formula 8-5):

United States	*Metric*
$\cos A = \dfrac{b}{c}$	$\cos A = \dfrac{b}{c}$

Again, using Figure 8-19, we know that angle A = 64°. The length of the hypotenuse is 68.43 ft (20.86 m). We will assume our problem is to determine the length of the adjacent side, *b*.

$$\therefore \cos 64° = \frac{b}{68.43} \qquad\qquad \therefore \cos 64° = \frac{b}{20.86}$$

where cosine of 64° = .4384 (*see* Table 8-I)

$$\frac{b}{68.45} = .4384 \qquad\qquad\qquad \frac{b}{20.86} = .4384$$

$$b = 68.43 \times .4384 \qquad\qquad b = 20.86 \times .4384$$

$$b \doteq 30 \text{ ft} \qquad\qquad\qquad\quad b = 9.14 \text{ m}$$

Congruent Triangles

8.037 Congruent triangles are triangles that are equal in all their corresponding sides and angles.

The positions of vehicles in lakes, rivers and other areas that are difficult to reach may be measured indirectly by using a baseline along a shoreline, for example, and sighting and preparing two congruent triangles.

Example
  a. Lay a baseline *BD* at any convenient length. The end of the baseline, *B*, must be at a right angle (90°) with the vehicle, *A*.
  b. Find the midpoint of the baseline and mark it *C*. The lines from *B* to *C* and *C* to *D* are equal in length.
  c. From *D*, proceed at an angle of 90° (south in this example) to a point where *C* may be sighted in direct line with point *A*. Mark this point *E*.
  d. Measure the distance from point *D* to point *E*. This represents the distance the vehicle is out in the river because in congruent triangles, all sides and angles are equal.

PREPARING A FIELD SKETCH AND SCALE DIAGRAM

8.038 A *field sketch* is a freehand map of an accident scene or site of an accident showing certain features of the accident or road configuration, usually for the purpose of recording measurements.[25]

8.039 Most measurements for a field sketch should be taken from a *reference point* (RP). A *reference point* is a point from which measurements are made to locate spots in an area.[26] A reference point can be any permanent (tangible) object, or a point or points marked on the roadway (intangible). All intangible points should be measured and related to a tangible reference point.

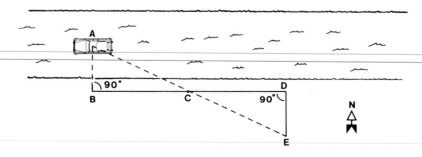

Figure 8-21. Using congruent triangles to measure distance vehicle or other object is from shoreline.

Figure 8-22. Utility pole identification number, *A*, used as a tangible reference point of accident location.

8.040 A *preliminary field sketch* should be made as soon as possible after the investigator arrives at the scene. A preliminary field sketch should record such items as tire prints in snow or mud, blood, water, spatter, light skid marks, and other short-lived evidence. Similarly, it is important to record the positions of bodies, vehicles and other objects or evidence that might be mutilated or moved from their positions before the on-scene investigation is completed. Such evidence should be outlined with yellow lumber crayon so that additional measurements can be made later.

8.041 A field sketch should be prepared by first showing outlines of the roadways and then filling in all things in their relative positions, for example, vehicles, obstructions, bodies, road defects and other objects. Measurements should then be taken and recorded on the field sketch. The person who prepares the field sketch must be the person who reads the measurements from the measuring device and records these measurements on the field sketch.

8.042 The edges of the roadway or extensions of curb lines may be used as baselines. The zero point from which measurements are taken should be related to a permanent or recognizable tangible reference point such as fire hydrant, tree, utility pole, bridge abutment, and so on. In intersections, the intersection corners may be used as permanent reference points. If curb edges are rounded, however, corner extension lines with tempo-

Figure 8-23. Bridge number, *A*, and year of construction, *B*, used as tangible reference points of accident location.

Figure 8-24. Method of tying an intangible reference point, *C*, to two tangible reference points, *A* and *B*, by triangulation.

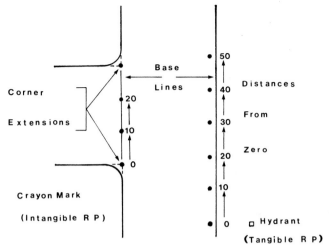

Figure 8-25

rary, intangible reference points may be marked on the roadway and used as reference points (Figs. 8-25 and 8-26).

8.043 A field sketch should be prepared in a form and manner that is comfortable to the investigator. Two methods of preparing a sketch are shown in Figs. 8-27 and 8-28.

8.044 A field sketch must be factual. An investigator must show only what is visible to him at the scene. For example, the point of impact must not be shown unless the investigator actually saw the vehicle collide with something. Evidence that might infer where the point of impact was such as skid marks, gouges, chips and debris should be shown.

8.045 A field sketch is part of an investigator's field notes, recording many of his observations. Once completed, the sketch should not be rewritten for sake of neatness, as this could rule out the admissibility in court of the measurements taken and other information recorded on the sketch. If a mistake is made, do not erase the mistake, but cross it out, write in the correction and initial the correction.

8.046 The symbols shown in Figure 8-29 may be used in making field sketches and scale diagrams.

8.047 A field sketch should include (Fig. 8-30):

a. Outlines of roadways and their names
b. Relative positions of all things of significance
c. Reference points, including both tangible and intangible reference points
d. Direction of north

Figure 8-26. Curb line extensions, *a* and *b*, used to establish an intangible reference point at X.

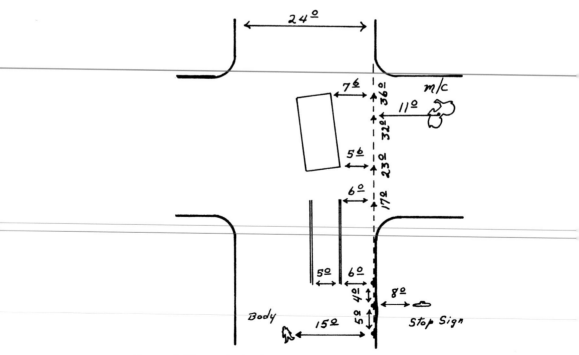

Figure 8-27. Method of recording measurements on a field sketch.

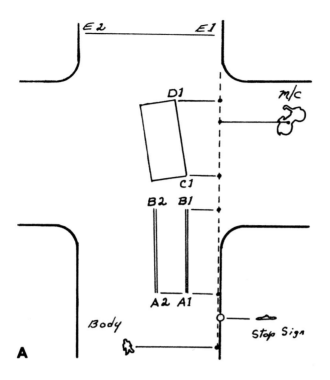

FROM POINT	TO POINT	N	W	S	E	COMMENTS
O	Stop Sign				8º	Red with white letters
O	A1	4º	6º			
A1	A2		5º			
O	B1	17º	6º			
O	C1	23º	5⁶			
O	D1	36º	7⁶			
E1	E2	24º				
O	m/c	32º			11º	Lying on left side
O	Body		15º	5º		Face down

B

Figure 8-28 (A and B). Method of preparing a field sketch using a key to record measurements and give explanatory detail.

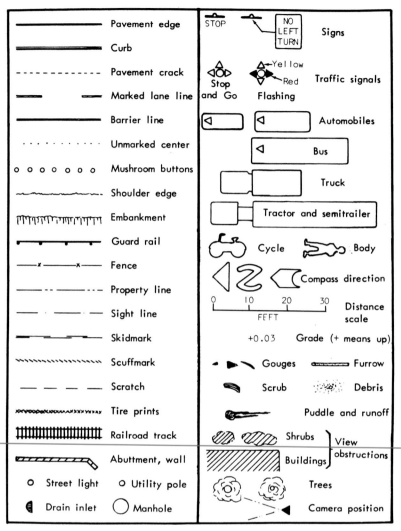

Figure 8-29. Symbols are useful for accident field sketches, diagrams and maps. Reproduced with permission of the Traffic Institute, Northwestern University, Evanston, Illinois.

   e. Roadway marks, e.g., skid marks, gouges, scuffs, blood, etc.

   f. Debris, e.g., dirt, glass, vehicle parts, parts of load, etc.

   g. Identification of things, e.g., vehicle licence number, body, glass, etc.

   h. All measurements, including radii of curves, angles of intersections not at 90°, and grades and superelevations

   i. Locations of traffic-control devices, view obstructions, embankments, roadway dividers, etc.

   j. Distances and directions to well-known landmark, city or town

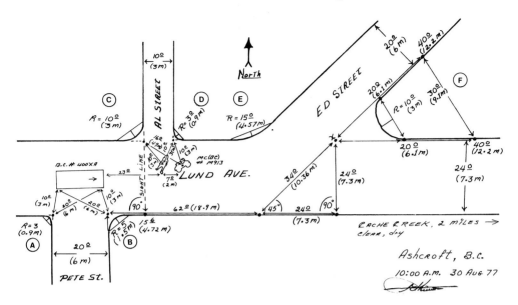

Figure 8-30

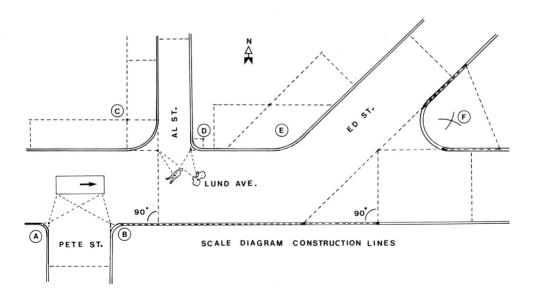

Figure 8-31

   k. Weather, road and light conditions
   l. Names of assistants in taking measurements
  m. Date and time sketch was prepared
  n. Signature of investigator

Construction lines to prepare a scale diagram of the limited field sketch measurements outlined in Figure 8-30 can be found in Figure 8-31. Detailed methods of completing various curves, corners and angles of the field sketch measurements to scale are covered later in this chapter.

Grade

8.048 Grade is the change in elevation per unit distance in a specified direction along the center line of a roadway or the path of a vehicle; grade is the difference in level of two points divided by the level distance between the points. Grade is designated in feet (meters) or rise or fall per foot (meter) of level distance or in rise or fall as a percent of the level distance. Grade is positive (+) if the surface rises in the specified geographic direction and negative (−) if it falls in that direction.[27]

8.049 Figure 8-32 outlines a method of measuring the grade of a roadway using a carpenter's level. The superelevation or grade *across* a roadway may be measured in a similar manner. In this example, if the length, *L*, of the board were 120 in (300 cm) and the rise or fall, *r*, was 12 in (30 cm), the percentage grade, *e*, could be calculated using Formula 8-6:

<table>
<tr><td align="center">United States</td><td align="center">Metric</td></tr>
<tr><td align="center">$e = \dfrac{r}{L} \times \dfrac{100}{1}$</td><td align="center">$e = \dfrac{r}{L} \times \dfrac{100}{1}$</td></tr>
</table>

where e = percentage grade (±)
       r = rise or fall
      L = length or distance

$$e = \frac{12}{120} \times \frac{100}{1} \qquad\qquad e = \frac{30}{300} \times \frac{100}{1}$$

$$e = 10\% \qquad\qquad\qquad\qquad e = 10\%$$

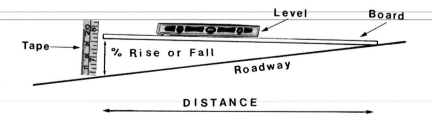

Figure 8-32. Method of measuring the grade or superelevation of a roadway using a carpenter's level.

Triangulation Measuring Method

8.050 *Triangulation* is a method of locating a spot in an area by measurements from two or more reference points (RPs), the locations of which are identified for future reference (compare with coordinates, paragraph 8.056).[28] The purpose in measuring by triangulation is simply to measure triangles that connect movable objects or evidence to permanent reference points (Figs. 8-33 and 8-34).

8.051 Triangulation should be used to locate vehicles, bodies and other objects where there are no definite roadway edges or curbs or in curves, intersections or any other locations where things cannot be easily located from roadway edges.

8.052 It is often necessary, and in many cases desirable, to fix one or more points, for example, on a vehicle, with more than one triangle; many triangles may be formed using the same bases, as indicated in Figures 8-33 and 8-34. By using more than one triangle, it is much easier to plot the positions of vehicles and objects later, whether it be to reposition the objects at the scene or in preparing a scale diagram.

8.053 To fix the positions of small objects or pieces of evidence such as bodies, debris or a motorcycle, measurements should be made to their centers. To fix the positions of objects larger than a body, at least two

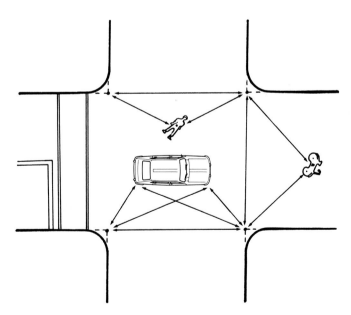

Figure 8-33. Fixing the position of a vehicle by using two triangles attached to two intangible reference points (curb extensions). Also, fixing the positions of smaller objects such as body and motorcycle by triangulation measured to their centers.

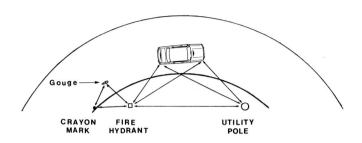

Figure 8-34. Method of using triangulation on a curve by using both tangible and intangible reference points.

points on the object must be fixed by triangulation, as shown in Figures 8-33 and 8-34.

8.054   Triangles that are long and thin are difficult to use to reposition things at the scene or to prepare a scale diagram to the necessary degree of accuracy. If at all possible, this type of triangle should be avoided.

8.055   To prepare a scale diagram of the field measurements shown in Figure 8-35, complete the roadways to their correct measurements. Then, using the compass (Fig. 8-36):

  a. Set the compass point at 20 ft (6 m).
  b. Place the compass pinpoint at point *A* and scribe an arc at *B*.
  c. Set the compass point at 23 ft (7 m).
  d. Place the compass pinpoint at *C* and scribe an arc, *D*, bisecting the first arc, *B*.
  e. The point where the two arcs, *B* and *D*, intersect is the position, to scale, of the body described in the field sketch Figure 8-35.

Coordinate Measuring Method

8.056   *Coordinates* are distances measured at right angles from a baseline to an object or point. When the edge of a roadway is straight or has only a very slight curve, the edge may be used as a baseline. For purposes of location and for future reference, the baseline must be related by measurement to a reference point. The reference or zero point from which measurements are begun should be a point on the baseline or roadway edge either at or related to a permanent recognizable landmark.

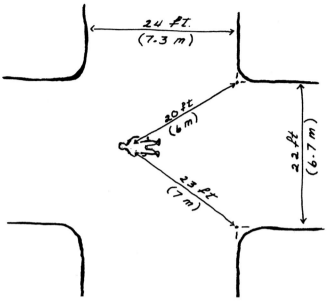

Figure 8-35. Method of using triangulation to fix location of small object in intersection. Measurements in these situations should be made from reference points to center of object.

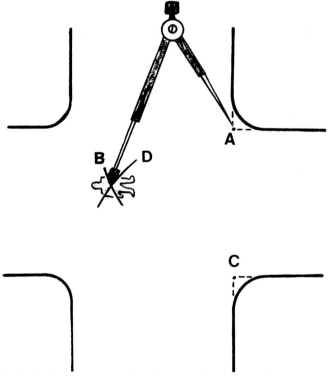

Figure 8-36. Method of preparing scale diagram of field measurements taken in Figure 8-35.

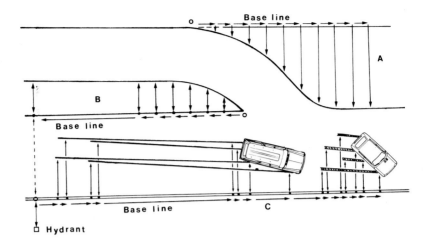

Figure 8-37. Using coordinate method of measuring to fix positions of vehicles, to measure lengths of skid marks and their relationships to vehicles and roadways, and to measure roadways, including irregular curves, corner *A*.

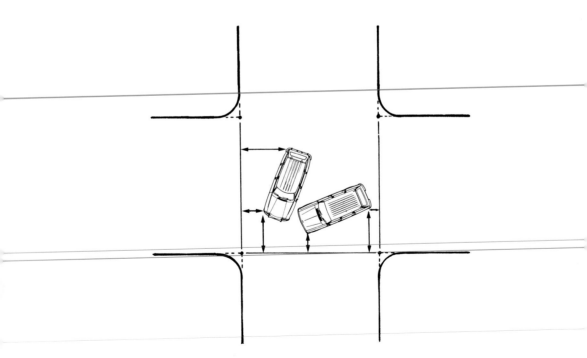

Figure 8-38. Using curb extension lines as intangible reference points and baselines from which to fix positions of vehicles using coordinates.

Curves

8.057   A curve is a part of a circle or an arc. To determine the size or degree of a circle, it is necessary to first calculate the radius of the circle. The radius, *R*, of a curve, may be calculated by using Formula 5-11:

United States

$$R = \frac{C^2}{8M} + \frac{M}{2}$$

Metric

$$R = \frac{C^2}{8M} + \frac{M}{2}$$

where R = radius
   C = chord
   M = middle ordinate

Measuring a Curve

8.058   To measure a curve, locate a point on either side of the curve just before the place where the curve straightens out *(tangent)*. Mark these points *a* and *b*. Measure the distance between *a* and *b* to obtain the chord, *C*, of the circle. Find the middle of the chord by dividing its length by 2, and mark the middle as *c*. To find the length of the middle ordinate, *M*, measure at a 90° angle from *c* to the outside of the curve or arc to *d*. This distance is the length of the middle ordinate.

Example

In Figure 8-39, we assume the chord, *C*, is 24 ft (7.32 m) and the middle ordinate, *M*, is 4 ft (1.22 m). The radius is (Formula 5-11):

United States

$$R = \frac{24^2}{8 \times 4} + \frac{4}{2}$$

$$R = \frac{576}{32} + \frac{4}{2}$$

$$R = 18 + 2$$

$$R = 20 \text{ ft}$$

Metric

$$R = \frac{7.32^2}{8 \times 1.22} + \frac{1.22}{2}$$

$$R = \frac{53.58}{9.76} + \frac{1.22}{2}$$

$$R = 5.49 + 0.61$$

$$R = 6.1 \text{ m}$$

Irregular Curves

8.059   Curves that are not compatible with measurements described above and reconstruction using Formula 5-11 may be measured by using a baseline and coordinates as outlined in Figure 8-37 areas *A* and *B*.

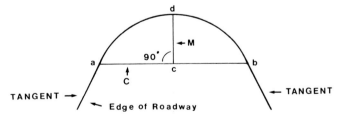

Figure 8-39. Parts of a curve.

Figure 8-40. Method of making field measurements of a curve.

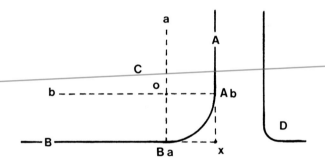

LUND AVE.

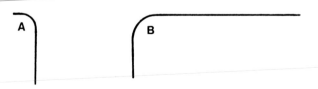

Figure 8-41

8.060 When the radius of a curve is known, the curve may be placed on a scale diagram. In corner *C* of the field sketch Fig. 8-30, for example, the radius is 10 ft (3 m). This curve may be plotted on a scale diagram in the following manner (Fig. 8-41):

a. Draw in street edges. Show the streets where the curve is to be completed as intersecting at a right angle (point *X*).
b. Draw construction lines *a* and *b* 10 ft (3 m) (the length of the radius) inside and parallel to curb lines *A* and *B*. Where lines *a* and *b* intersect, mark point *o*.
c. Set compass at 10 ft (3 m) on the scale being used. Place compass pinpoint at *o* and scribe an arc from *Ab* to *Ba* to complete the curve.

This same procedure may be followed to reconstruct curves on obtuse angles as found at corners *A, B, D* and *E* of Figure 8-30.

8.061 A curve on an acute angle such as that at corner *F* of the field sketch Figure 8-30 may be drawn to scale in the same manner as described above for corner *C*. However, there is an additional method of plotting the curve when the radius is known. In the case of the curve at corner *F*, the radius is 10 ft (3 m) (Fig. 8-42). To reconstruct this curve to scale:

a. Draw in road edges as lines *A* and *B* at required angle so that they meet at an apex point *X*.
b. From point *X*, mark in points *a* and *b* along lines *A* and *B* where the curve begins. In the case of corner *F*, this distance is 20 ft (6.1 m). Beyond these points, the roadway edges are straight and are considered tangents of the curve.
c. Set the compass at 10 ft (3 m) at the scale being used.

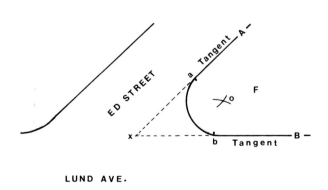

Figure 8-42

   d. Place the compass pinpoint at points *a* and *b* and scribe arcs so that they intersect at point *o*.

   e. Place the compass pinpoint at point *o* and scribe an arc from point *a* to point *b*. This completes the curve.

Large Curves

8.062 A different method of obtaining measurements to calculate the radius of a curve must be employed for large highway curves. In these cases, it is necessary that a chord of sufficient length be measured to allow for a middle ordinate long enough to compensate for any irregularities in the edge of the roadway.

The radius of any part of a roadway may be found by measuring a chord and middle ordinate as outlined in Figure 8-44. Often it is difficult or impossible to measure a chord and middle ordinate for the desired area. In this situation, the radius of the desired area may be measured indirectly. Where it might be necessary to determine the radius for the path of travel of a vehicle at location *D* in Figure 8-44, it would be possible to calculate the radius of the curve at roadway edge *C* and add the distance of half the roadway (*a* to *b*) to that radius to obtain the radius of the area *D*.

Example

   If the radius for *C* were calculated at 100 ft (30.5 m), the radius of *D* would be 100 + 6 = 106 ft (30.5 + 1.8 = 32.3 m). Similarly, if the radius

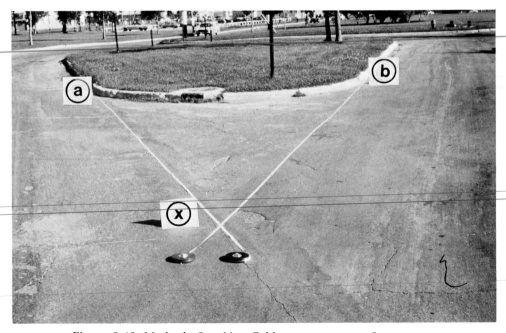

Figure 8-43. Method of making field measurements of a curve.

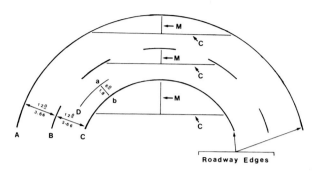

Figure 8-44

of A were calculated at 124 ft (37.8 m), the radius of D may be found by subtracting 18 ft (5.49 m) or 106 ft (32.3 m).

Angles at Intersections

8.063 When a street intersects another street at an angle other than 90°, special field measurements are required in order to plot the intersection on a scale diagram. Again using the intersection at corner F in Figure 8-30 as an example, field measurements and the field sketch should include the following additional measurements (Fig. 8-45):

a. Measure back from the apex X for a convenient distance to c and d.
b. Measure the distance from c to d. This completes the triangle and fixes the angle of the intersecting street.
c. Sight along tangent A to the roadway edge of Lund Avenue to establish point e. Measure along the roadway edge to establish point f which when measured to point X at an angle of 90°, completes the right triangle.
d. Measure from the reference point at Pete Street along Lund Avenue to e. This measurement fixes the position of Ed Street at the intersection with Lund Avenue.

8.064 To plot on a scale diagram the angle at which Ed Street intersects Lund Avenue using the measurements from the field sketch Figure 8-30 (Fig. 8-45):

a. Measure the distance from the reference point at Pete Street to point e, mark it, and then measure on to point f. Measure from f at 90° to point X. Mark a line from x to e to complete a triangle. This establishes x in relation to the RP.
b. The angle of tangent B to point X is already known, since it is the north edge of Lund Avenue.
c. From point e, follow along the hypotenuse of the triangle to X and

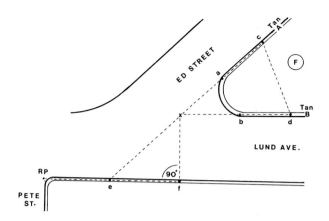

Figure 8-45

draw a line on to *a* and *c* of tangent *A*, using the known distances from
X.

d. Similarly, draw a line from X to *b* and *d* along tangent *B*.

e. As a check of your work, measure the distance from *c* to *d*, which
should be the same as shown on the field sketch.

8.065   To plot an offset street on a scale diagram using Al Street and the
measurements found in the field sketch Figure 8-30 as an example (Fig.
8-46):

a. Draw in Lund Avenue and Pete Street to scale.

b. Measure eastward from the RP at Pete Street to point *a*, which is in
direct line with the west edge of Al Street.

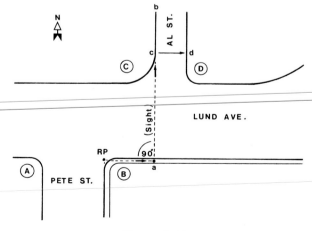

Figure 8-46

c. Draw a line, *b,* at 90° northward from point *a* to desired length to form the west edge of Al Street.
d. Plot the width of Al Street, *c* to *d,* and draw another line parallel to line *b* to form the east edge of Al Street.
e. Complete edges of Al Street with permanent lines, construct corners *C* and *D* to scale and erase unnecessary construction lines.

REFERENCES

1. National Safety Council: *Accident Facts* (Stock No. 021.57). National Safety Council, Chicago, 1977.
2. National Safety Council: *Manual on Classification of Motor Vehicle Traffic Accidents,* 3rd ed. (ANSI D16.1). National Safety Council, Chicago, 1970.
3. Baker, J. Stannard: *Traffic Accident Investigation Manual.* Traffic Institute, Northwestern University, Evanston, Illinois, 1975, p. 318.
4. Baker, J. Stannard: *Traffic Accident Investigation Manual.* Traffic Institute, Northwestern University, Evanston, Illinois, 1975, p. 318.
5. Baker, J. Stannard: *Traffic Accident Investigation Manual.* Traffic Institute, Northwestern University, Evanston, Illinois, 1975, p. 319.
6. Baker, J. Stannard: *Traffic Accident Investigation Manual.* Traffic Institute, Northwestern University, Evanston, Illinois, 1975, p. 318.
7. National Safety Council: *Manual on Classification of Motor Vehicle Traffic Accidents,* 3rd ed. (ANSI D16.1). National Safety Council, Chicago, 1970.
8. Evans, Henry K.: *Traffic Engineering Handbook.* Institute of Traffic Engineers, New Haven, Connecticut, 1950, p. 92.
9. Evans, Henry K.: *Traffic Engineering Handbook.* Institute of Traffic Engineers, New Haven, Connecticut, 1950, p. 89.
10. Evans, Henry K.: *Traffic Engineering Handbook.* Institute of Traffic Engineers, New Haven, Connecticut, 1950, p. 89.
11. Goldenson, R. M.: *The Encyclopedia of Human Behaviour.* Doubleday & Company, Inc., New York, 1970, p. 291.
12. Goldenson, R. M.: *The Encyclopedia of Human Behaviour.* Doubleday & Company, Inc., New York, 1970, p. 1099.
13. Evans, Henry K.: *Traffic Engineering Handbook.* Institute of Traffic Engineers, New Haven, Connecticut, 1950, p. 81.
14. Evans, Henry K.: *Traffic Engineering Handbook.* Institute of Traffic Engineers, New Haven, Connecticut, 1950, p. 88.
15. Goldenson, R. M.: *The Encyclopedia of Human Behaviour.* Doubleday & Company, Inc., New York, 1970, p. 186.
16. Baker, J. Stannard: *Traffic Accident Investigator's Manual for Police.* Traffic Institute, Northwestern University, Evanston, Illinois, 1971, p. 215.
17. Baker, J. Stannard: *Traffic Accident Investigation Manual.* Traffic Institute, Northwestern University, Evanston, Illinois, 1975, pp. 208-209.
18. Collins, J. C. and Morris, J. L.: *Highway Collision Analysis.* Charles C Thomas, Springfield, Illinois, 1974, p. 215.
19. Baker, J. Stannard: *Traffic Accident Investigation Manual.* Traffic Institute, Northwestern University, Evanston, Illinois, 1975, p. 319.
20. Canada Safety Council: *Effectiveness of Studded Tires.* Canada Safety Council, Ottawa, Ontario, 1970.
21. Collins, J. C. and Morris, J. L.: *Highway Collision Analysis.* Charles C Thomas, Springfield, Illinois, 1974, p. 116.

22. Collins, J. C. and Morris, J. L.: *Highway Collision Analysis.* Charles C Thomas, Springfield, Illinois, 1974, p. 115.
23. *Tires.* Moneysaver Book Division of Optima Publishing, Inc., Canoga Park, California, 1973, p. 35.
24. Baker, J. Stannard: *Traffic Accident Investigation Manual.* Traffic Institute, Northwestern University, Evanston, Illinois, 1975, pp. 146.
25. Baker, J. Stannard: *Traffic Accident Investigation Manual.* Traffic Institute, Northwestern University, Evanston, Illinois, 1975, p. 316.
26. Baker, J. Stannard: *Traffic Accident Investigation Manual.* Traffic Institute, Northwestern University, Evanston, Illinois, 1975, p. 319.
27. Baker, J. Stannard: *Traffic Accident Investigation Manual.* Traffic Institute, Northwestern University, Evanston, Illinois, 1975, pp. 316-317.
28. Baker, J. Stannard: *Traffic Accident Investigation Manual.* Traffic Institute, Northwestern University, Evanston, Illinois, 1975, p. 321.

BIBLIOGRAPHY

Allbert, B. J.: *Tires and Hydroplaning*. Society of Automotive Engineers, Inc., New York, 1968.

Baker, J. Stannard: *Traffic Accident Investigator's Manual For Police*. Traffic Institute, Northwestern University, Evanston, Illinois, 1971.

Baker, J. Stannard: *Traffic Accident Investigation Manual*. Traffic Institute, Northwestern University, Illinois, 1975.

British Columbia: *The British Columbia Air Brake Manual* (J00203). Motor Vehicle Branch, Province of British Columbia, Canada.

British Columbia Research: *Motor Vehicle Accident Investigation Reports* (Various). British Columbia Research, Vancouver, Canada.

Bryant, D.: *Physics*. Teach Yourself Books, St. Paul's House, London, 1973.

Canada Safety Council: *Effectiveness of Studded Tires*. Canada Safety Council, Ottawa, Ontario, Canada, 1970.

Canadian Institute of Science and Technology: *Technical Mathematics and Traffic Engineering Reports* (Various). Canadian Institute of Science and Technology, Toronto, Ontario, Canada.

Canadian Standards Association: *Canadian Metric Practice Guide* (CAN3-Z234.1-76). Canadian Standards Association, Ottawa, Ontario, Canada, 1976.

Carlisle, Jud B.: *Speed and Acceleration Problems in Motor Vehicle Accidents*. Jud B. Carlisle, Austin, Texas, 1964.

Collins, J. C. and Morris, J. L.: *Highway Collision Analysis*. Charles C Thomas, Publisher, Springfield, Illinois, 1974.

Consumer Reports: *Tire Construction*. Published by Consumer Union of the United States, Inc., Mt. Vernon, New York, Oct. 1973, p. 605.

Evans, Henry K.: *Traffic Engineering Handbook*. Institute of Traffic Engineers, New Haven, Connecticut, 1950.

Freeman, I. M.: *Physics Made Simple*. Doubleday & Co., Inc., New York, 1965.

Goldenson, R. M.: *The Encyclopedia of Human Behaviour*. Doubleday & Co., Inc., New York, 1970.

Institute of Traffic Engineers: *Transportation and Traffic Engineering Handbook*. Prentice-Hall, Inc., Englewood Cliffs, New Jersey, 1976.

Krech, D., Crutchfield, R. S. and Livson, N.: *Elements of Psychology*. Alfred A. Knopf, Inc., Publisher, New York, 1969.

Metropolitan Police Driver Training School: *Metropolitan Police Traffic Accident Investigation Formulae*. Metropolitan Police Driver Training School, London, 1970.

National Safety Council: *Manual on Classification of Motor Vehicle Traffic Accidents*, 3rd ed. (ANSI D16.1). National Safety Council, Chicago, 1970.

National Safety Council: *Accident Facts* (Stock No. 021.57). National Safety Council, Chicago, 1977.

National Transportation Safety Board: *Highway Accident Reports* (Various). National Transportation Safety Board, Washington, D.C.

Peach, J.: *Metrication*. Teach Yourself Books, St. Paul's House, London, 1974.

Petersen Publishing Company: *Petersen's Basic Chassis, Suspension and Brakes*, 3rd ed. Petersen Publishing Company, Los Angeles, 1974.

Pitcher, E. M.: *Table of Formulas Useful in Accident Reconstruction*. Cornell Aeronautical Laboratory, Inc., Buffalo, 1971.

Schimizzi, Ned V.: *Mastering the Metric System*. New American Library, New York, 1975.

Tires. Moneysaver Book Division of Optima Publishing, Inc., Canoga Park, California, 1973.

INDEX

speedometer accuracy checklist, 5-11
squares and square roots, 1-V
Take off and fall speed, 5.096
Tangent, 8.034
Temperature effect on coefficient of friction,
5.023
Template, traffic, 8.011
Tests, skid — see *coefficient of friction* speedometer, 5.009
Therefore symbol, 1.024
Thrust, 4.013
Time
abbreviation, 1.024
calculations — see *formula* and *speed estimates*
Tire, 2.107, 2.110
action in sideslip, 4.035
air loss, 2.116, 2.117, 3.024
bias-belted, 2.112, 2.114, 2.115
bias-ply, 2.111, 2.114, 2.115
contact with road, 2.114
damage, 2.115-2.118
fragments on road, 2.120
inspection, 2.107, 2.110
marking for removal, 2.122
mixing effect, 2.114
mud grip tread, 2.121
overinflated
mark, 4.039
wear, 2.119
pressure, air, 2.119, 5.039
radial, 2.113-2.115
recap, 2.120
removal for inspection, 2.122
roadway marks, 2.116
slip angle, 2.114
underinflated, 2.119, 3.024
winter grip tread, 2.121
Tire mark, 4.016, 4.018
acceleration, 4.021, 4.022
blow-out, 4.026, 3.024
flat, 4.025, 4.052
furrow, 4.028
matching to
tire, 4.017, 4.019
vehicle, 4.012
measurements, 5.040
rotating and sideslipping, 4.029
rotating wheel, 4.028, 4.029
rut, 4.028
scrub, 4.037, 4.054
striation, 4.023, 4.024, 4.027
studded tire, 4.027
tire print, 4.020
trench, 4.028
underinflated, 4.025, 4.052
wet surface, 4.043
yaw, 4.024, 4.053, 5.060, 5.061-5.063

See also *skid marks*
Tow truck
requirements, 2.001
skid marks, 4.018
Tracking, vehicle, 3.021
Traffic accident — see *accident*
Traffic accident reports — see Figs. 2-50, 2-51,
2-52
Traffic control
at accident scene, 2.011
lights, 2.023
Traffic safety programs, 1.005
Traffic unit, definition, 1.003
Trafficway — see *highway*
Trailer
unloaded tire marks, 4.048
towed speed estimate, 5.038
Trails, water, 4.058
Trench, 4.028
Triangle, definition, 8.026
Triangulation, 8.050
Trip events, 1.007
True area, 1.008
Tunnel vision, 2.037

U

Underbody debris, 4.056, 6.002
See also *debris*
Underinflated tire
mark, 4.052
skid mark, 4.025
wear, 2.119
Under influence of alcohol or drug — see *driver*
United States measurement system, 1.019
See also *measurements*

V

Vaults, speed from, 5.097
See also *formula* and *speed estimates*
Vector
definition, 3.005
quantity, 3.005
Vehicle
definition — see traffic unit *number one* or *first*
symbol, 1.024
See also *damage, vehicle inspection, vehicle
mechanical inspection, Accident Investigation
Guide and Evaluation, Accident Investigation
Guide and Report* and *Mechanical Inspection
Guide and Evaluation*
Vehicle dynamics and the effects of
cross-wind, 3.022
defective brakes, 3.023, 5.053, 5.055
inertia, 3.001, 5.034
momentum, 3.008, 5.099
motion energy, 5.034
rotation of vehicle, 3.019, 4.024